PSI-LORDS®

FRED VAN LENTE

RENATO GUEDES

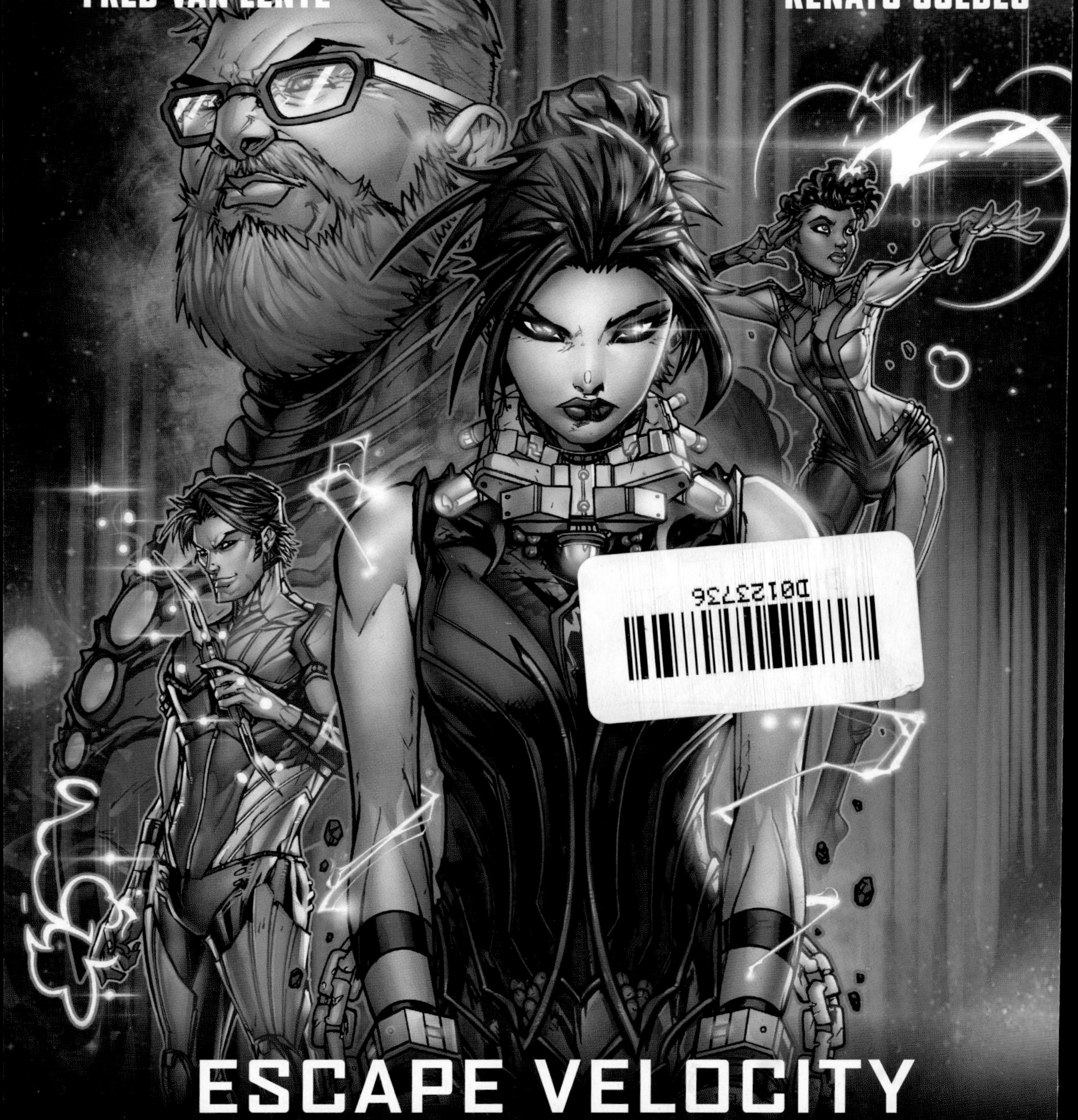

ESCAPE VELOCITY

Who are the cosmic beings known only as the Psi-Lords? And how will they change the course of the Valiant Universe?

Find out here in the complete collection of the galaxy-bending adventure from *New York Times* bestselling writer Fred Van Lente (IVAR, TIMEWALKER; GENERATION ZERO) and stunning artist Renato Guedes (SHADOWMAN)!

Collecting PSI-LORDS #1-8.

TRADE PAPERBACK
ISBN: 978-1-68215-352-9

VALIANT

IVERSE STARTING AT $9.99

HORROR & MYSTERY

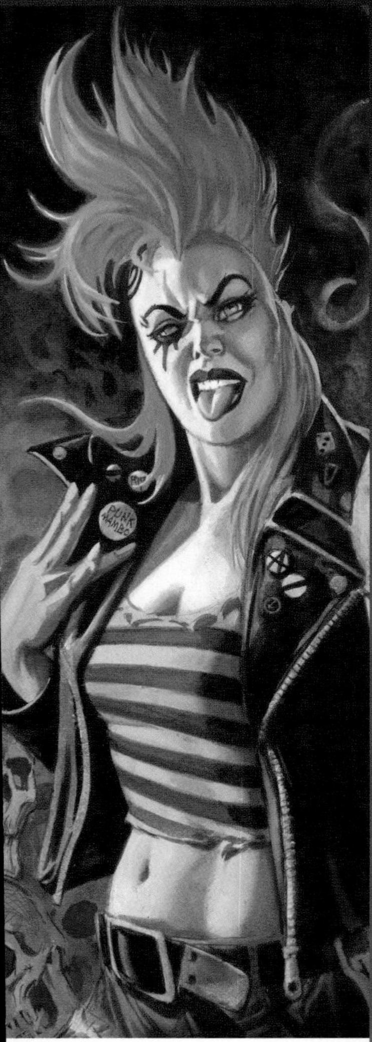

BRITANNIA
ISBN: 978-1-68215-185-3
DOCTOR MIRAGE
ISBN: 978-1-68215-346-8
PUNK MAMBO
ISBN: 978-1-68215-330-7
RAPTURE
ISBN: 978-1-68215-225-6
SHADOWMAN (2018) VOL. 1: FEAR OF THE DARK
ISBN: 978-1-68215-239-3

SCIENCE FICTION & FANTASY

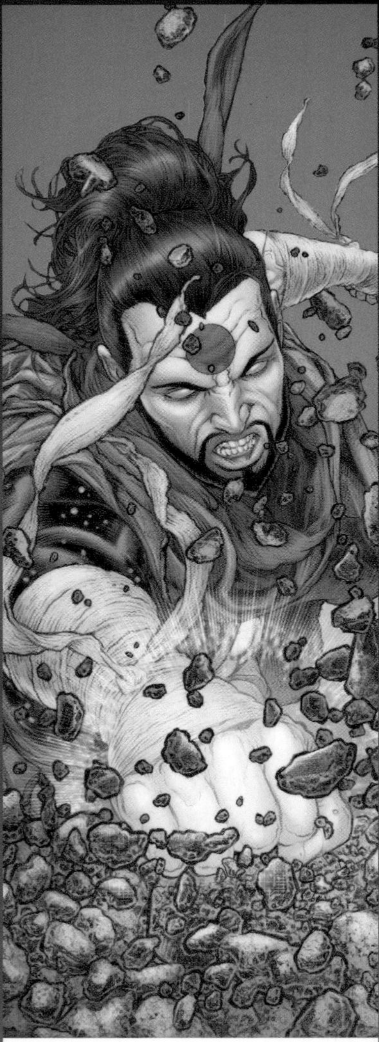

DIVINITY
ISBN: 978-1-939346-76-6
THE FORGOTTEN QUEEN
ISBN: 978-1-68215-324-6
IMPERIUM VOL. 1: COLLECTING MONSTERS
ISBN: 978-1-939346-75-9
IVAR, TIMEWALKER VOL. 1: MAKING HISTORY
ISBN: 978-1-939346-63-6
RAI BOOK ONE
ISBN: 978-1-682153-60-4
WAR MOTHER
ISBN: 978-1-68215-237-9

TEEN ADVENTURE

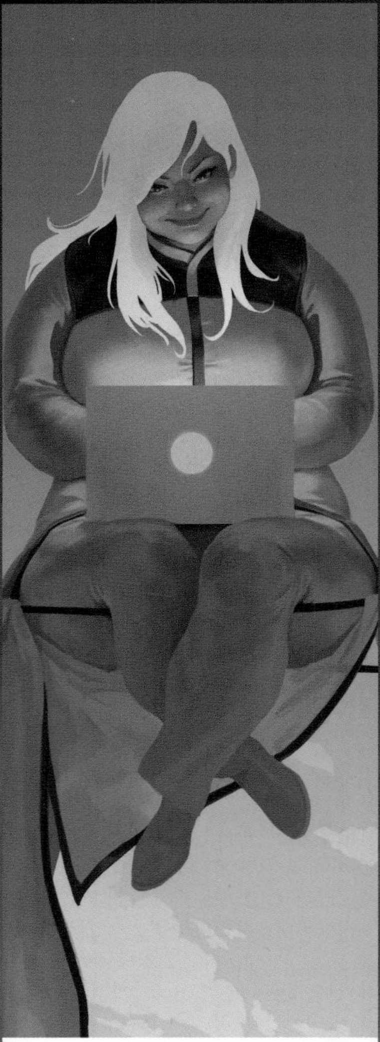

DOCTOR TOMORROW TP
ISBN: 978-1-68215-370-3
FAITH VOL. 1: HOLLYWOOD AND VINE
ISBN: 978-1-68215-121-1
GENERATION ZERO VOL. 1: WE ARE THE FUTURE
ISBN: 978-1-68215-175-4
HARBINGER RENEGADE VOL. 1: THE JUDGMENT OF SOLOMON
ISBN: 978-1-68215-169-3
LIVEWIRE VOL. 1: FUGITIVE
ISBN: 978-1-68215-301-7
SECRET WEAPONS
ISBN: 978-1-68215-229-4

Discover the entire Valiant Universe of titles at VALIANTENTERTAINMENT.COM/ALL-SERIES/

EXPLORE THE VALIANT U

ACTION & ADVENTURE

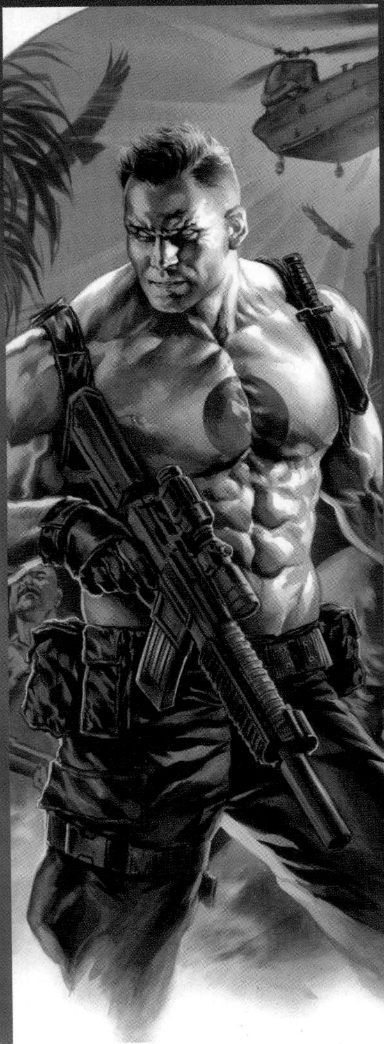

BLOODSHOT BOOK ONE
ISBN: 978-1-68215-255-3
NINJA-K VOL. 1: THE NINJA FILES
ISBN: 978-1-68215-259-1
SAVAGE
ISBN: 978-1-68215-189-1
WRATH OF THE ETERNAL WARRIOR VOL. 1: RISEN
ISBN: 978-1-68215-123-5
X-O MANOWAR (2017) VOL. 1: SOLDIER
ISBN: 978-1-68215-205-8

BLOCKBUSTER ADVENTURE

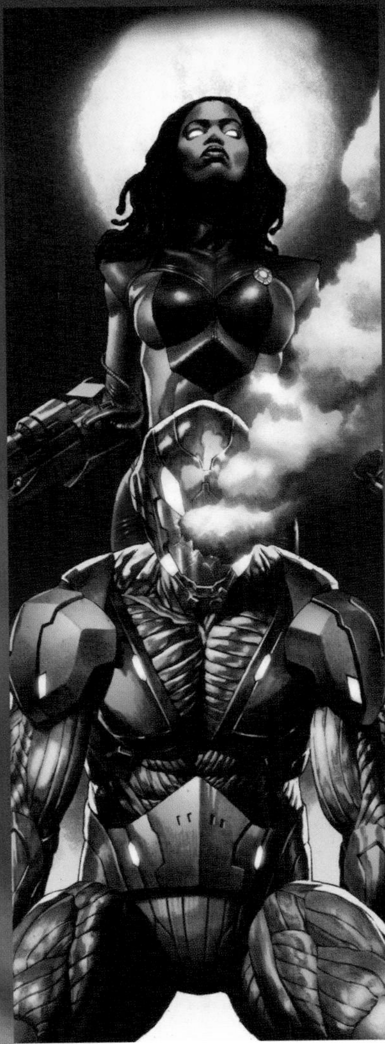

4001 A.D.
ISBN: 978-1-68215-143-3
ARMOR HUNTERS
ISBN: 978-1-939346-45-2
BOOK OF DEATH
ISBN: 978-1-939346-97-1
FALLEN WORLD
ISBN: 978-1-68215-331-4
HARBINGER WARS
ISBN: 978-1-939346-09-4
HARBINGER WARS 2
ISBN: 978-1-68215-289-8
INCURSION
ISBN: 978-1-68215-303-1
THE VALIANT
ISBN: 978-1-939346-60-5

COMEDY

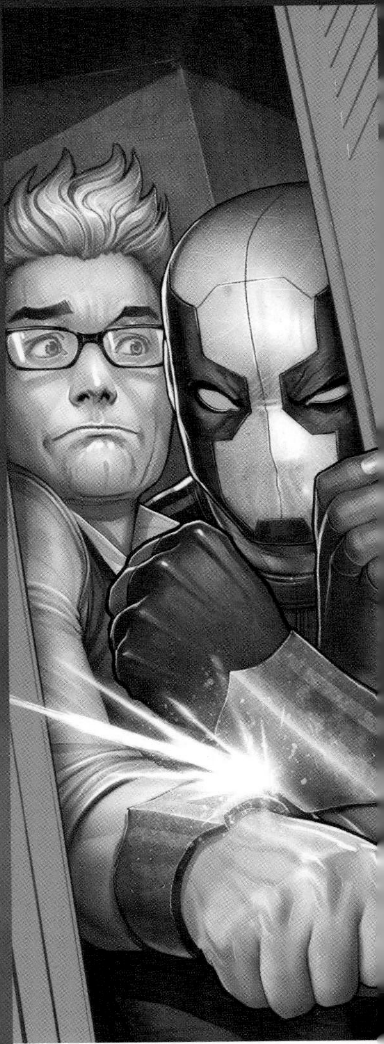

A&A: THE ADVENTURES OF ARCHER & ARMSTRONG VOL. 1: IN THE BAG
ISBN: 978-1-68215-149-5
THE DELINQUENTS
ISBN: 978-1-939346-51-3
QUANTUM AND WOODY! (2020): EARTH'S LAST CHOICE
ISBN: 978-1-68215-362-8

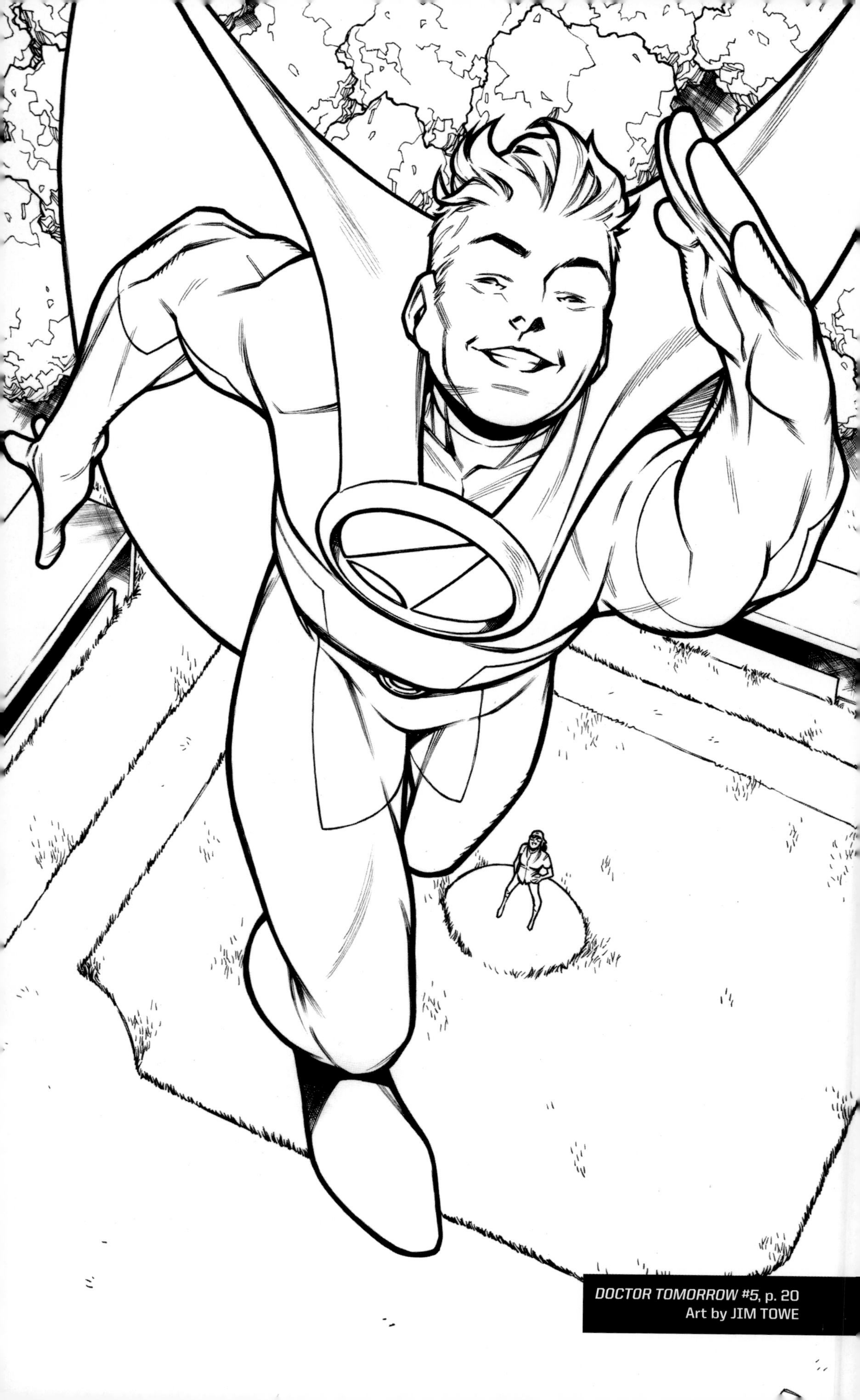

DOCTOR TOMORROW #5, p. 20
Art by JIM TOWE

DOCTOR TOMORROW #4, p. 3 and 4
Art by JIM TOWE

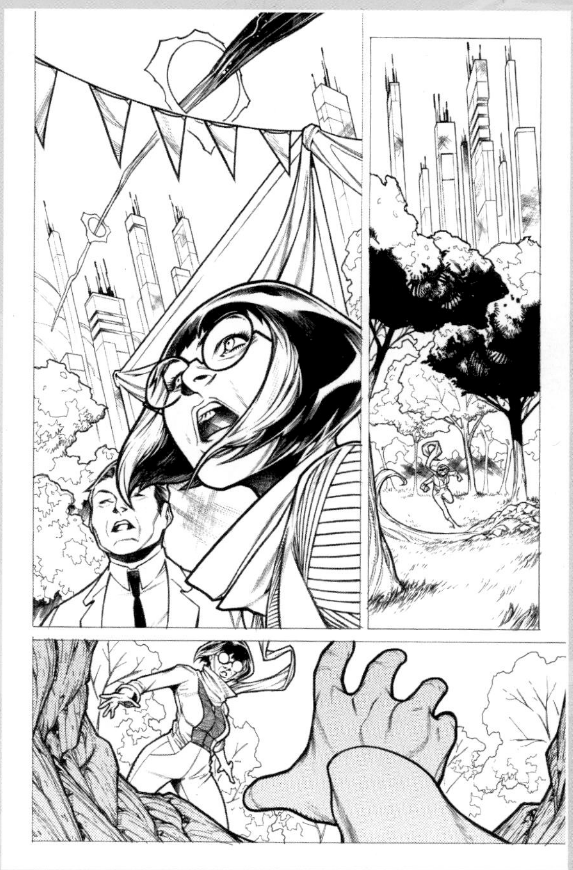

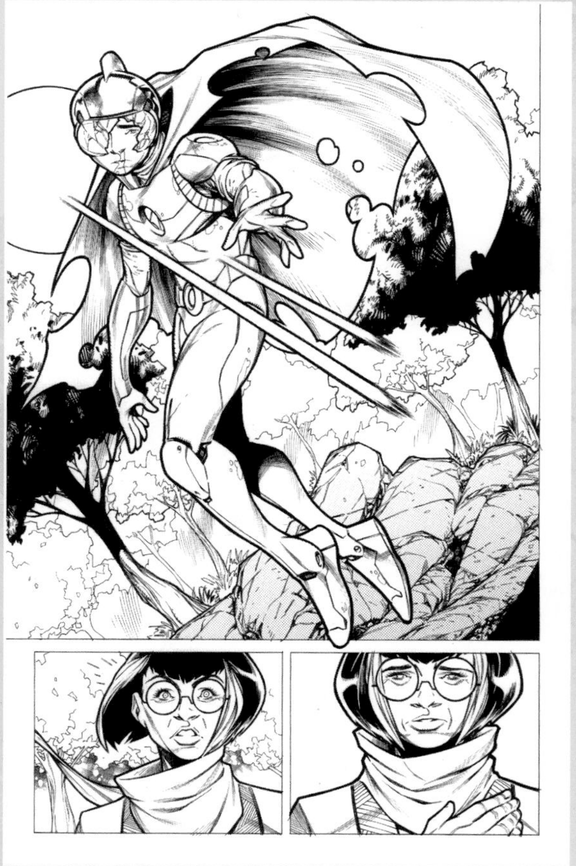

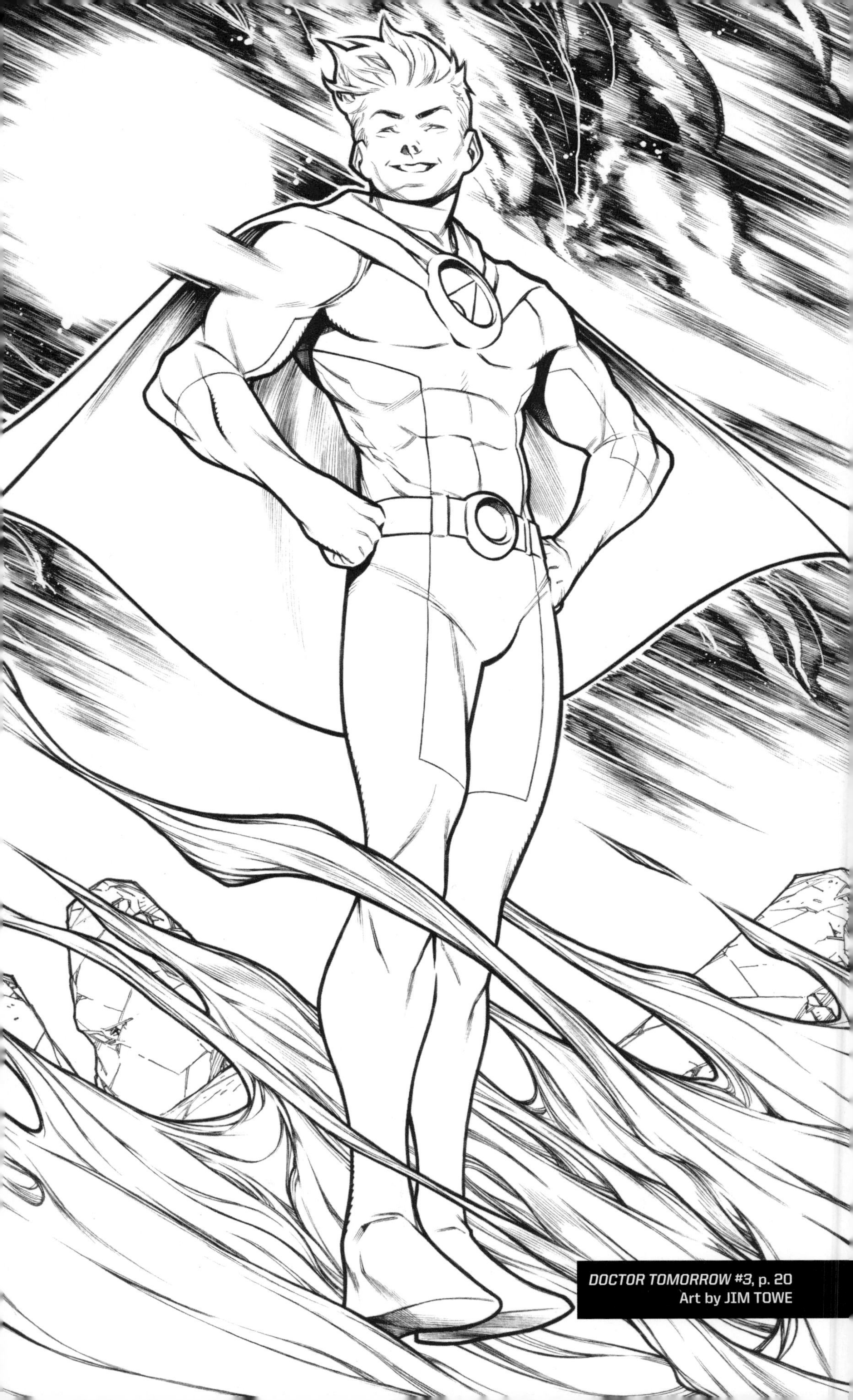

DOCTOR TOMORROW #3, p. 20
Art by JIM TOWE

DOCTOR TOMORROW #2, p. 2 and 3
Art by JIM TOWE

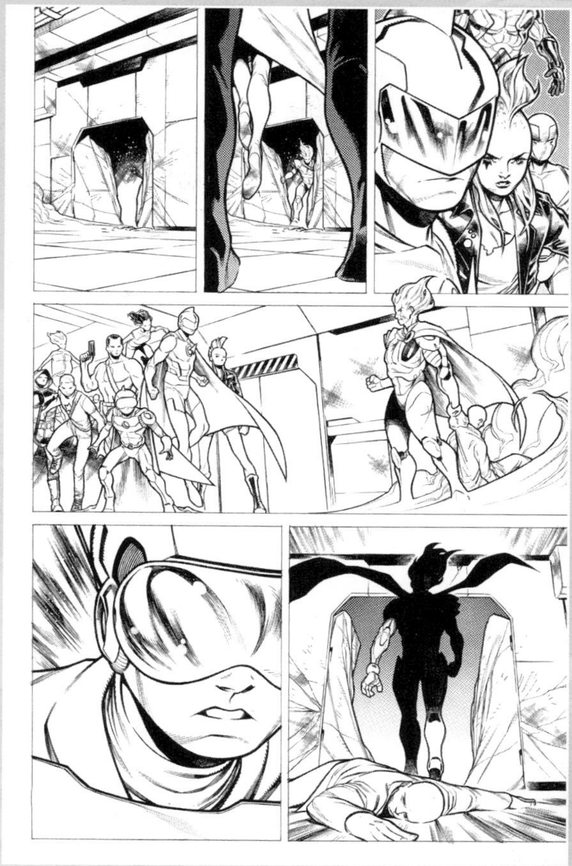

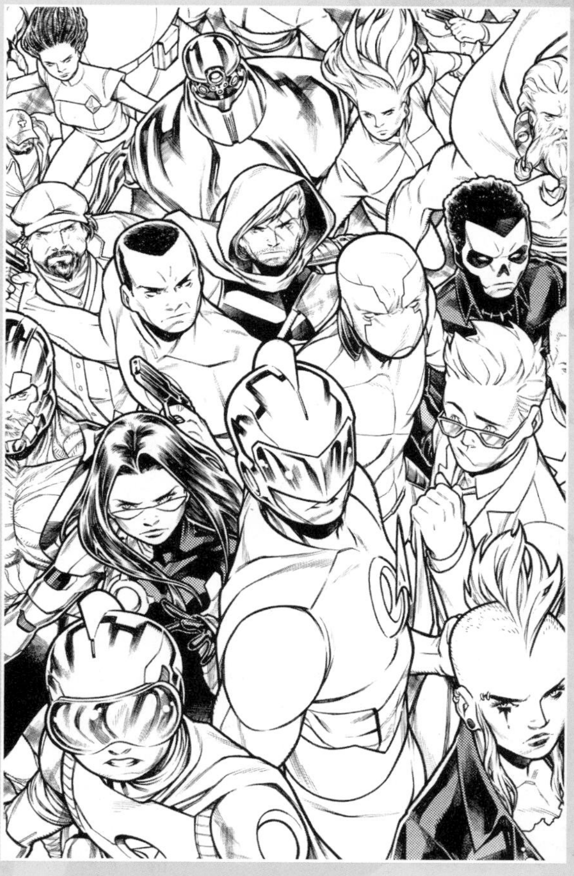

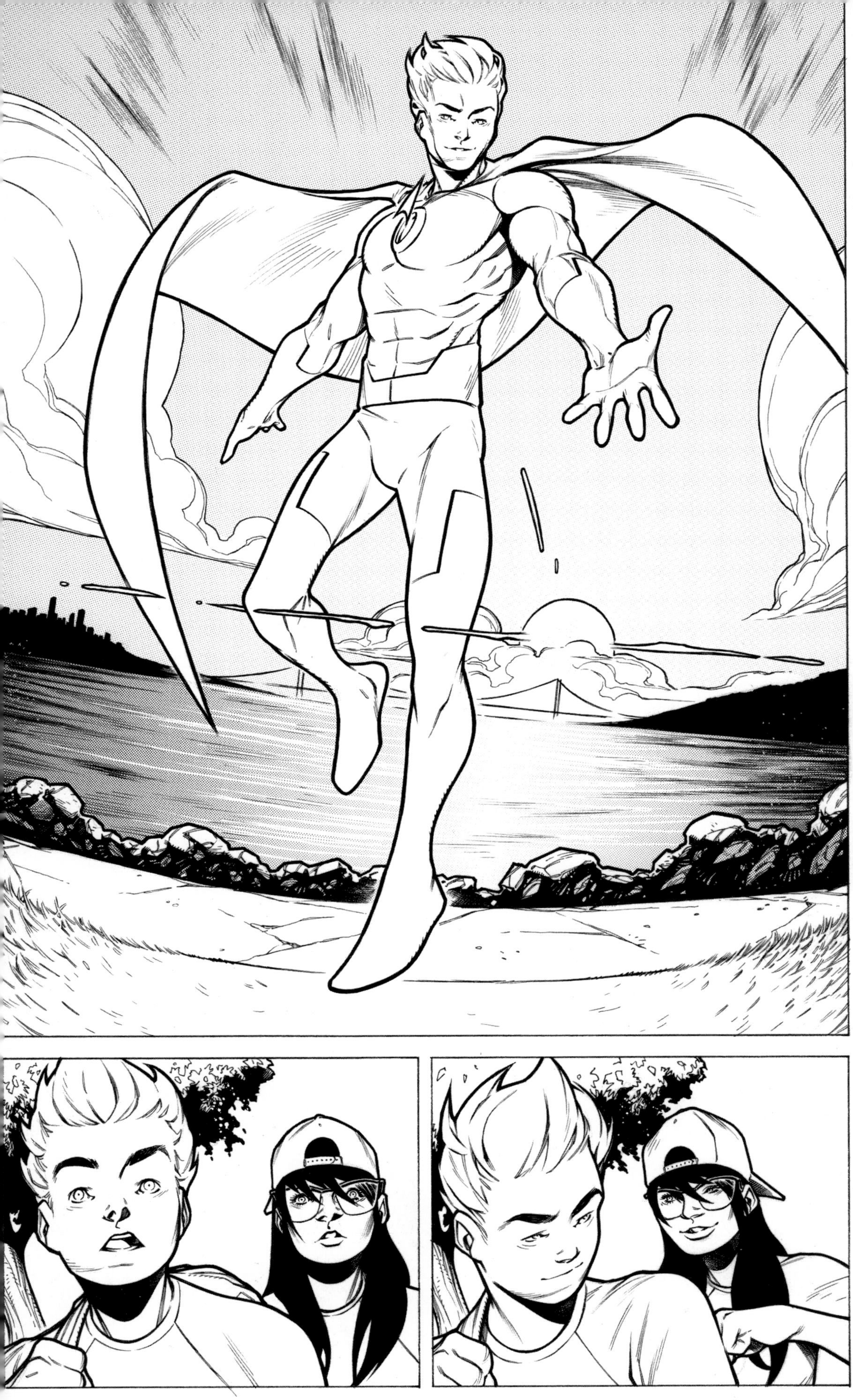

DOCTOR TOMORROW #1, p. 2, 13, and (facing) 14
Art by JIM TOWE

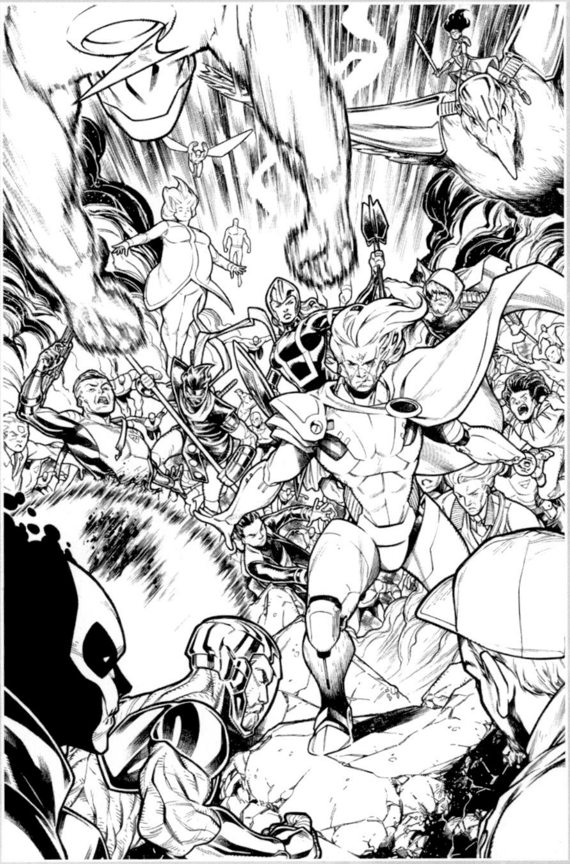

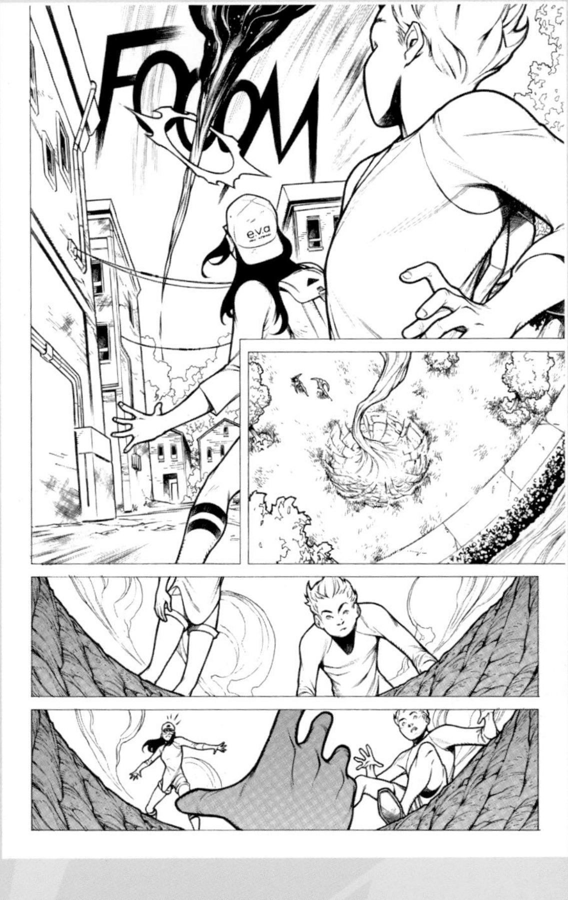
FOOOM
e.v.a

Character designs by JIM TOWE

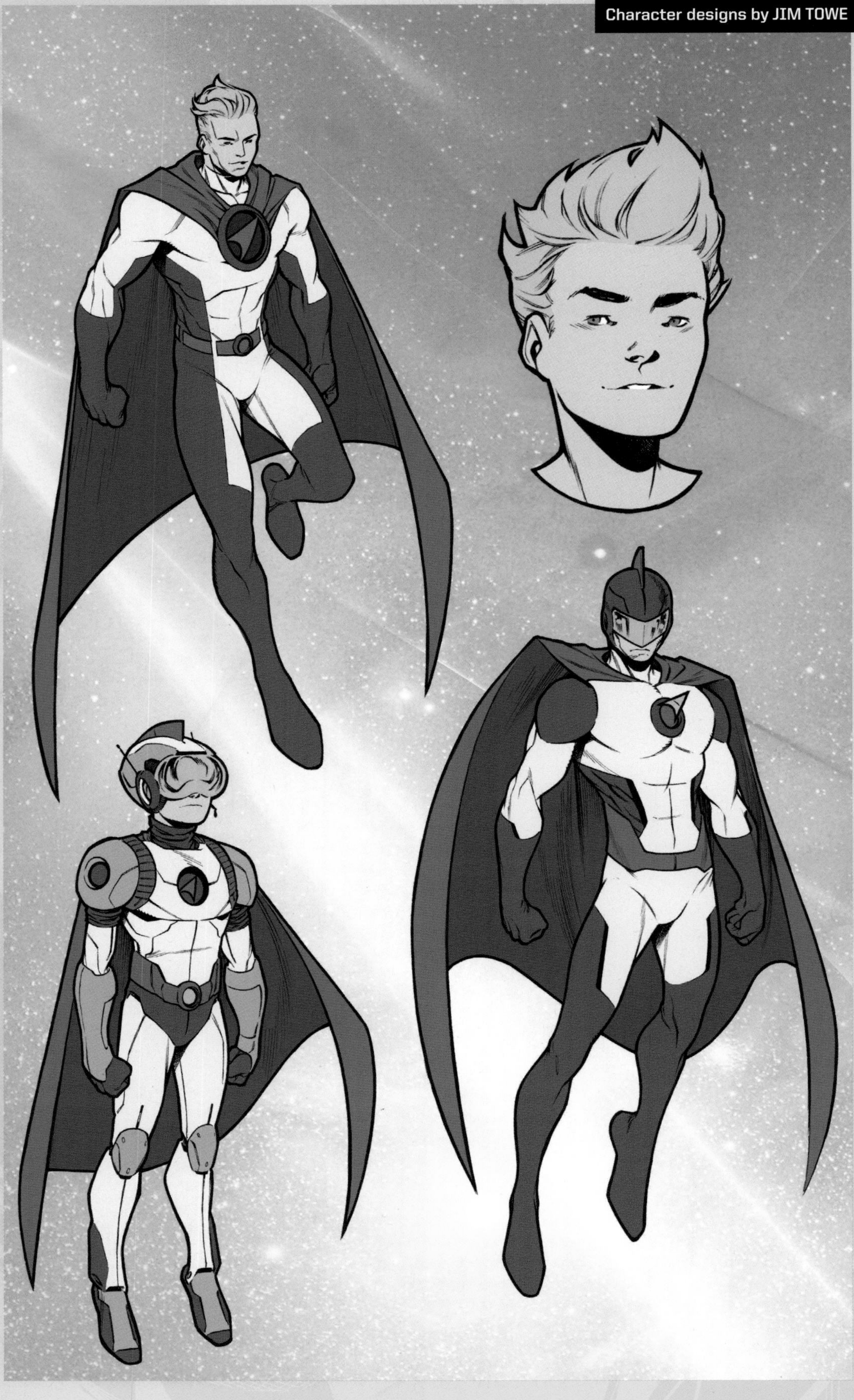

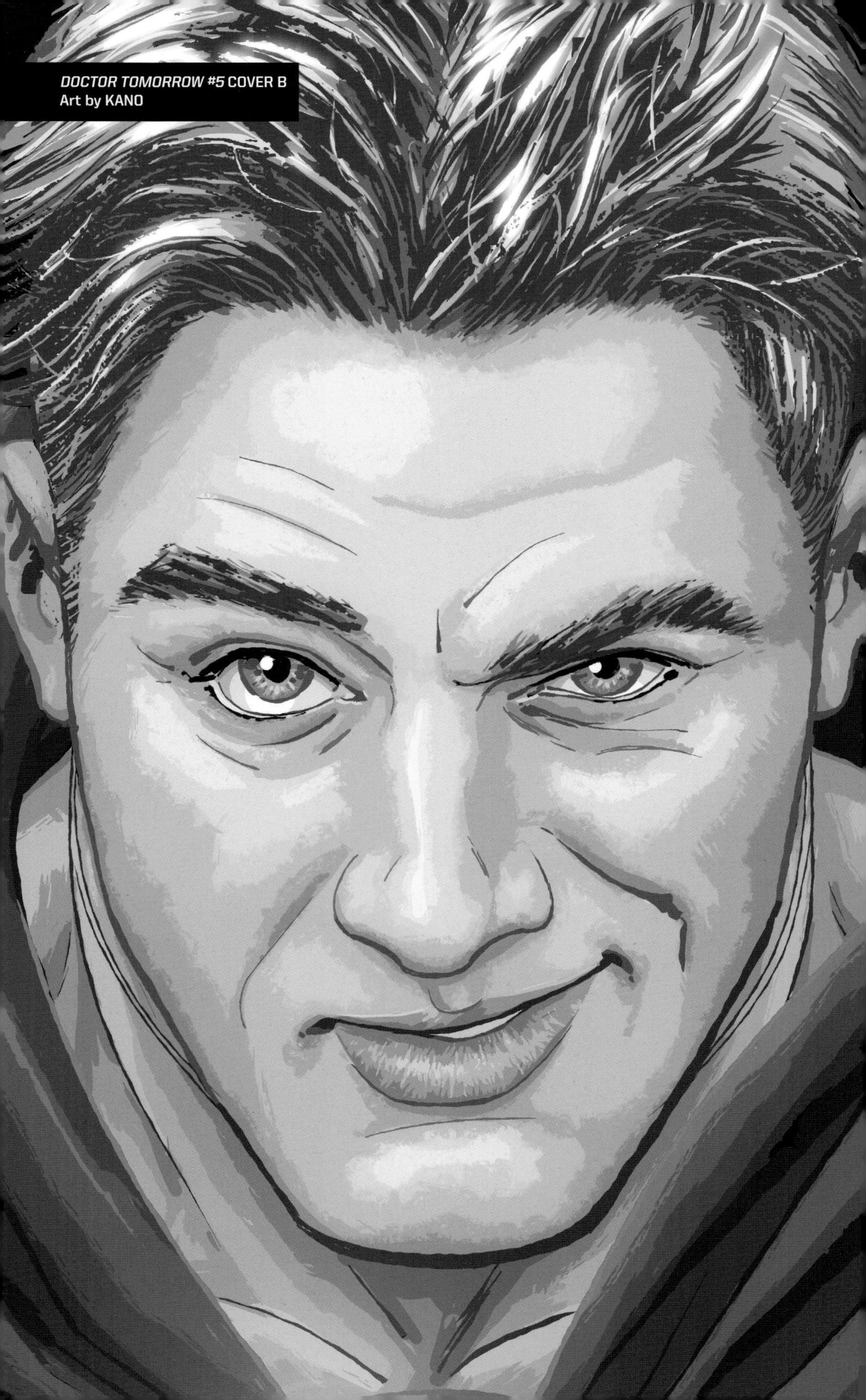

DOCTOR TOMORROW #5 COVER B
Art by KANO

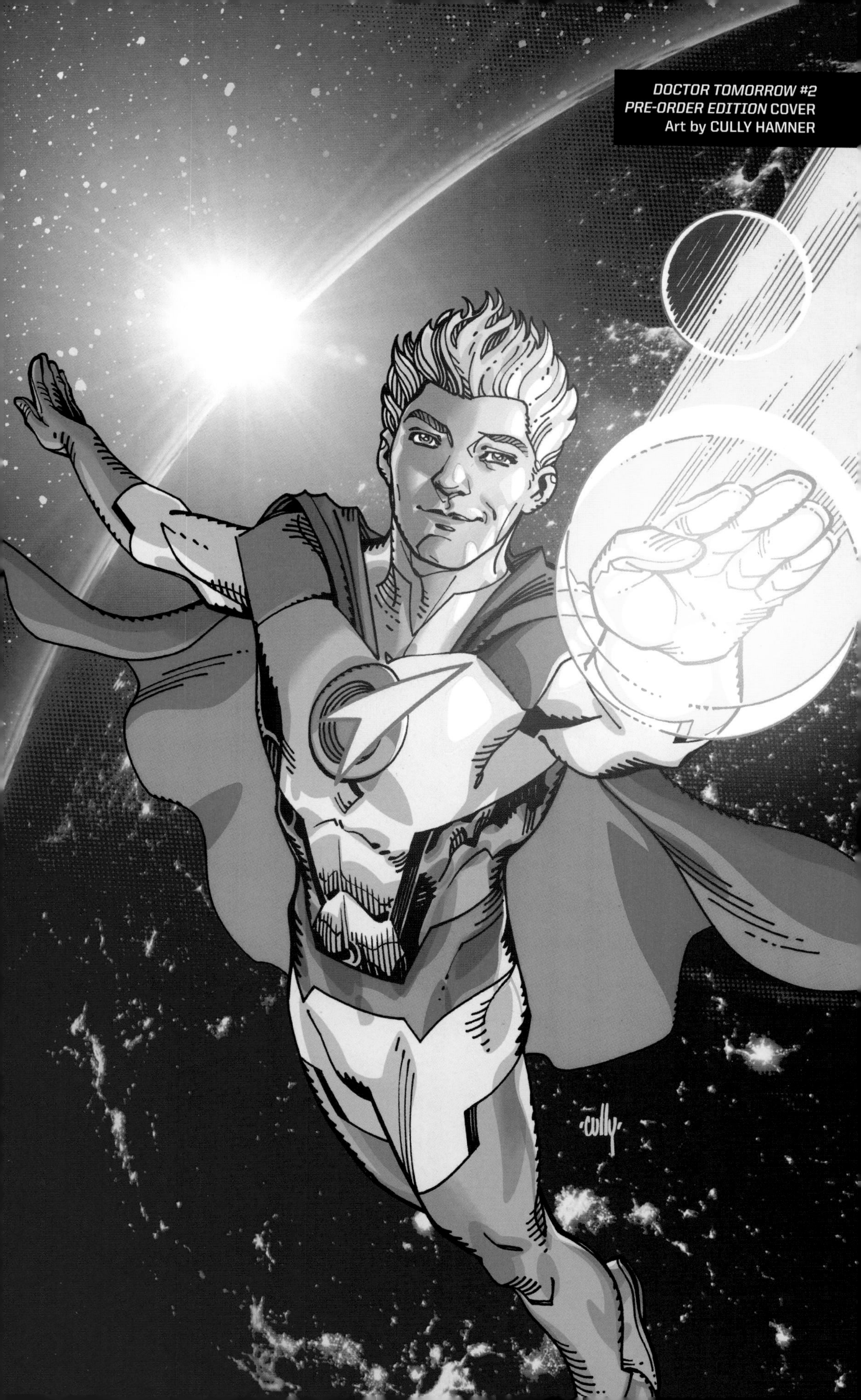
cully

DOCTOR TOMORROW #2
PRE-ORDER EDITION COVER
Art by CULLY HAMNER

DOCTOR TOMORROW #1 COVER C
Art by RAÚL ALLÉN

DOCTOR TOMORROW #3
PRE-ORDER EDITION COVER
Art by HANNAH TEMPLER

GALLERY

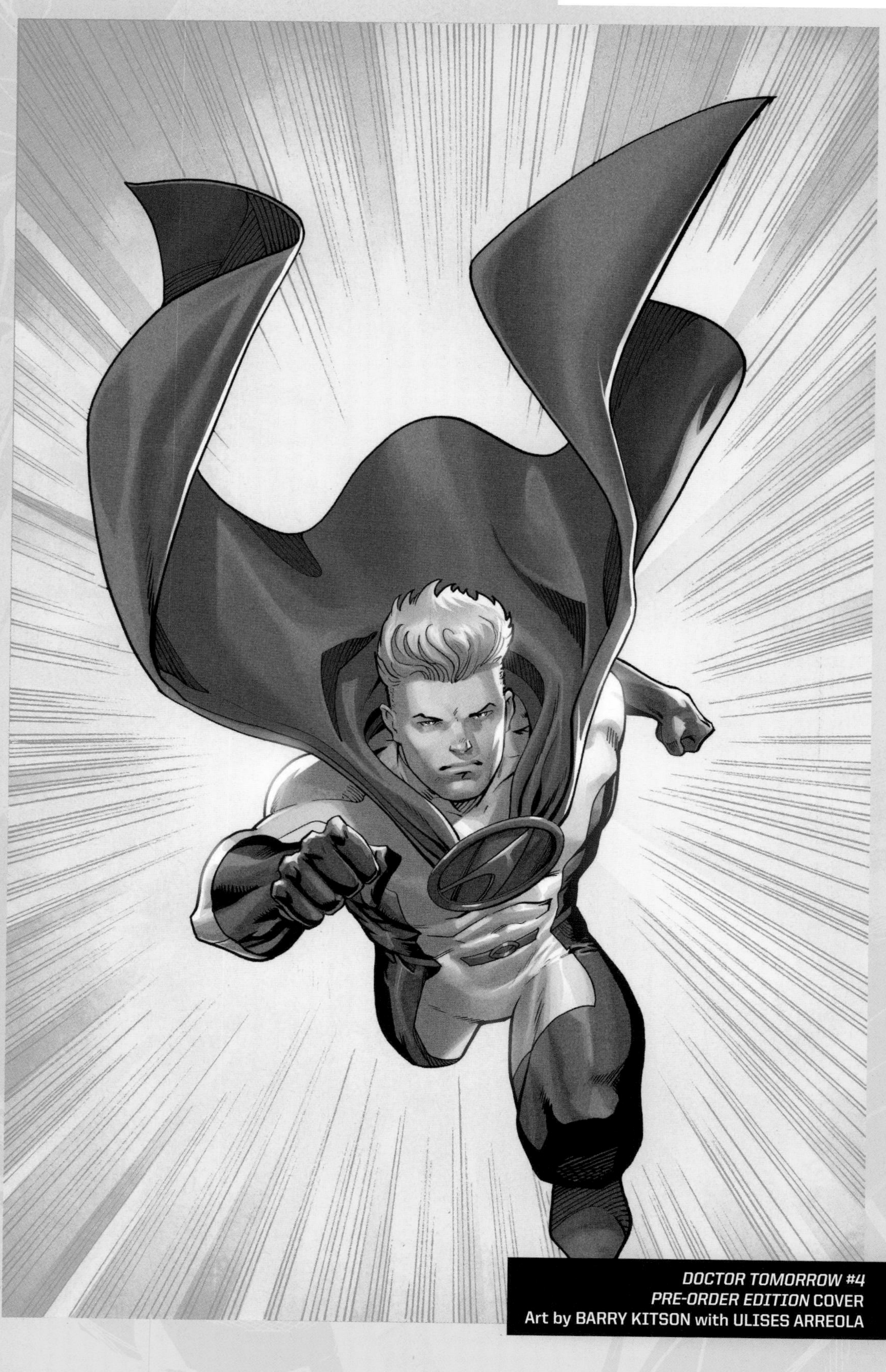

DOCTOR TOMORROW #4
PRE-ORDER EDITION COVER
Art by BARRY KITSON with ULISES ARREOLA

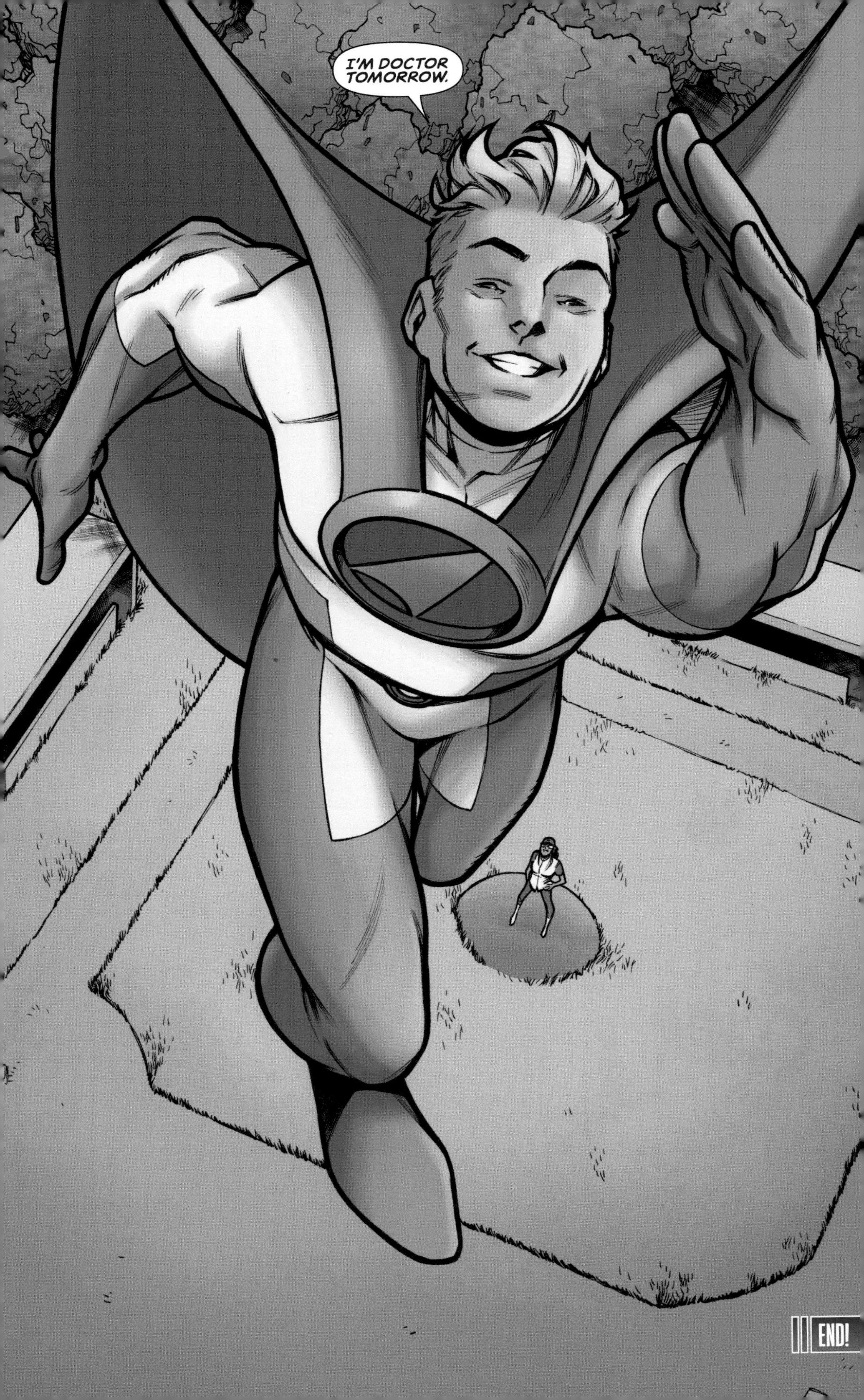
I'M DOCTOR TOMORROW.
END!

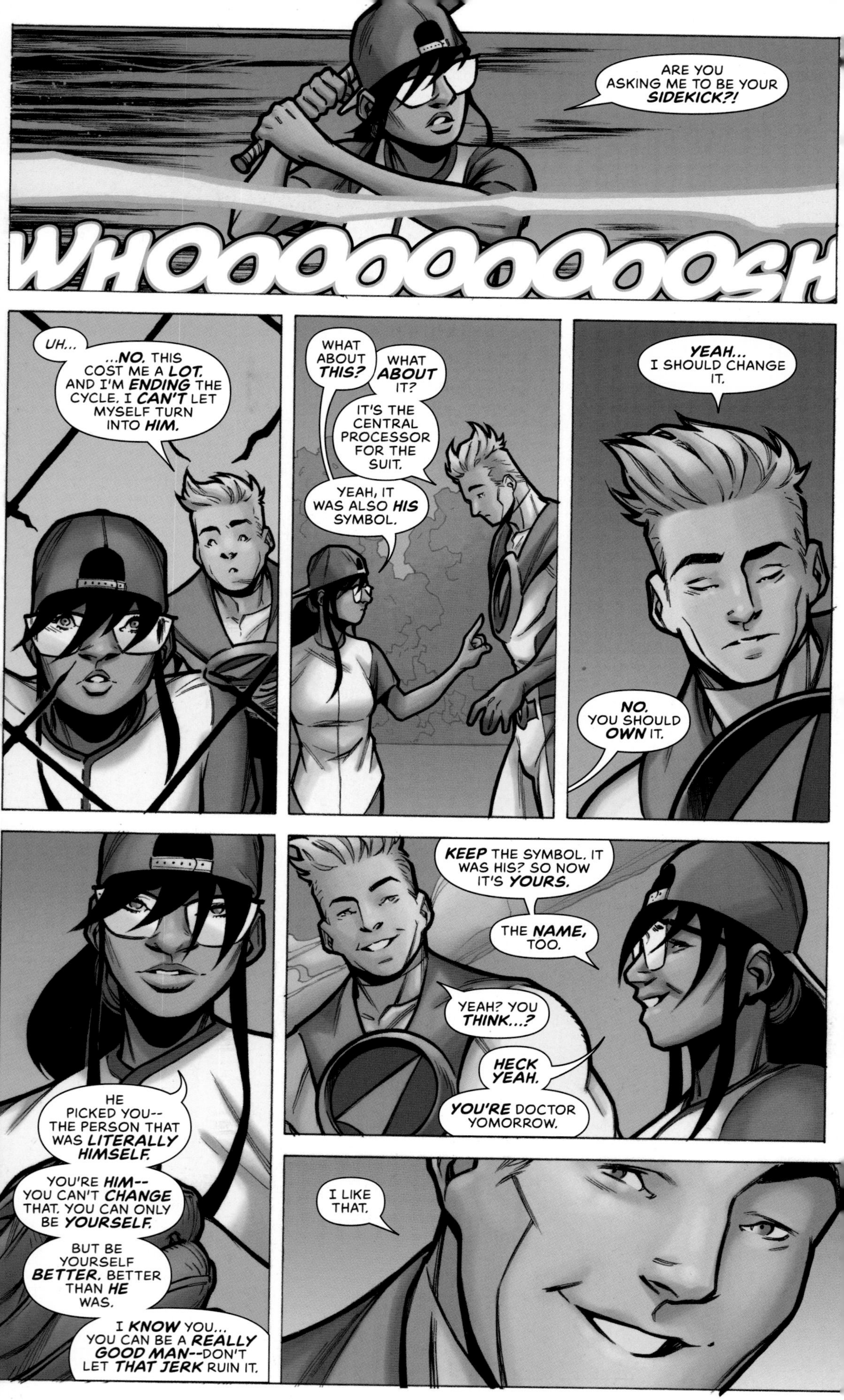
ARE YOU ASKING ME TO BE YOUR SIDEKICK?!
WHOOOOOOOOOSH
UH...
...NO. THIS COST ME A LOT. AND I'M ENDING THE CYCLE. I CAN'T LET MYSELF TURN INTO HIM.
WHAT ABOUT THIS?
WHAT ABOUT IT?
IT'S THE CENTRAL PROCESSOR FOR THE SUIT.
YEAH, IT WAS ALSO HIS SYMBOL.
YEAH... I SHOULD CHANGE IT.
NO. YOU SHOULD OWN IT.
HE PICKED YOU-- THE PERSON THAT WAS LITERALLY HIMSELF.
YOU'RE HIM-- YOU CAN'T CHANGE THAT. YOU CAN ONLY BE YOURSELF.
BUT BE YOURSELF BETTER. BETTER THAN HE WAS.
I KNOW YOU... YOU CAN BE A REALLY GOOD MAN--DON'T LET THAT JERK RUIN IT.
KEEP THE SYMBOL. IT WAS HIS? SO NOW IT'S YOURS.
THE NAME, TOO.
YEAH? YOU THINK...?
HECK YEAH.
YOU'RE DOCTOR YOMORROW.
I LIKE THAT.

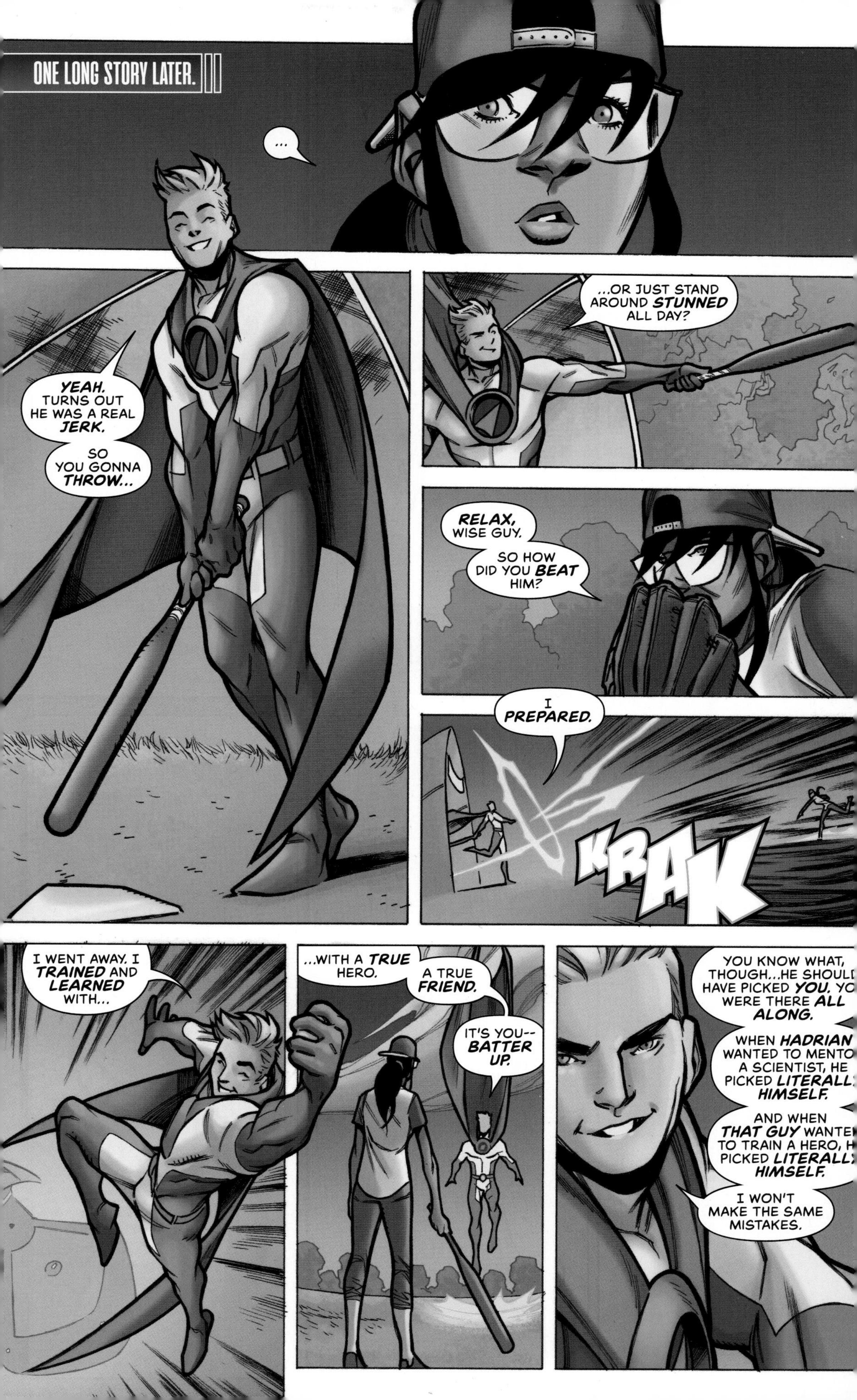
ONE LONG STORY LATER.
...
YEAH. TURNS OUT HE WAS A REAL JERK.
SO YOU GONNA THROW...
...OR JUST STAND AROUND STUNNED ALL DAY?
RELAX, WISE GUY.
SO HOW DID YOU BEAT HIM?
I PREPARED.
KRAK
I WENT AWAY. I TRAINED AND LEARNED WITH...
...WITH A TRUE HERO.
A TRUE FRIEND.
IT'S YOU-- BATTER UP.
YOU KNOW WHAT, THOUGH...HE SHOUL HAVE PICKED YOU. YO WERE THERE ALL ALONG.
WHEN HADRIAN WANTED TO MENTO A SCIENTIST, HE PICKED LITERALL HIMSELF.
AND WHEN THAT GUY WANTE TO TRAIN A HERO, H PICKED LITERALL HIMSELF.
I WON'T MAKE THE SAME MISTAKES.

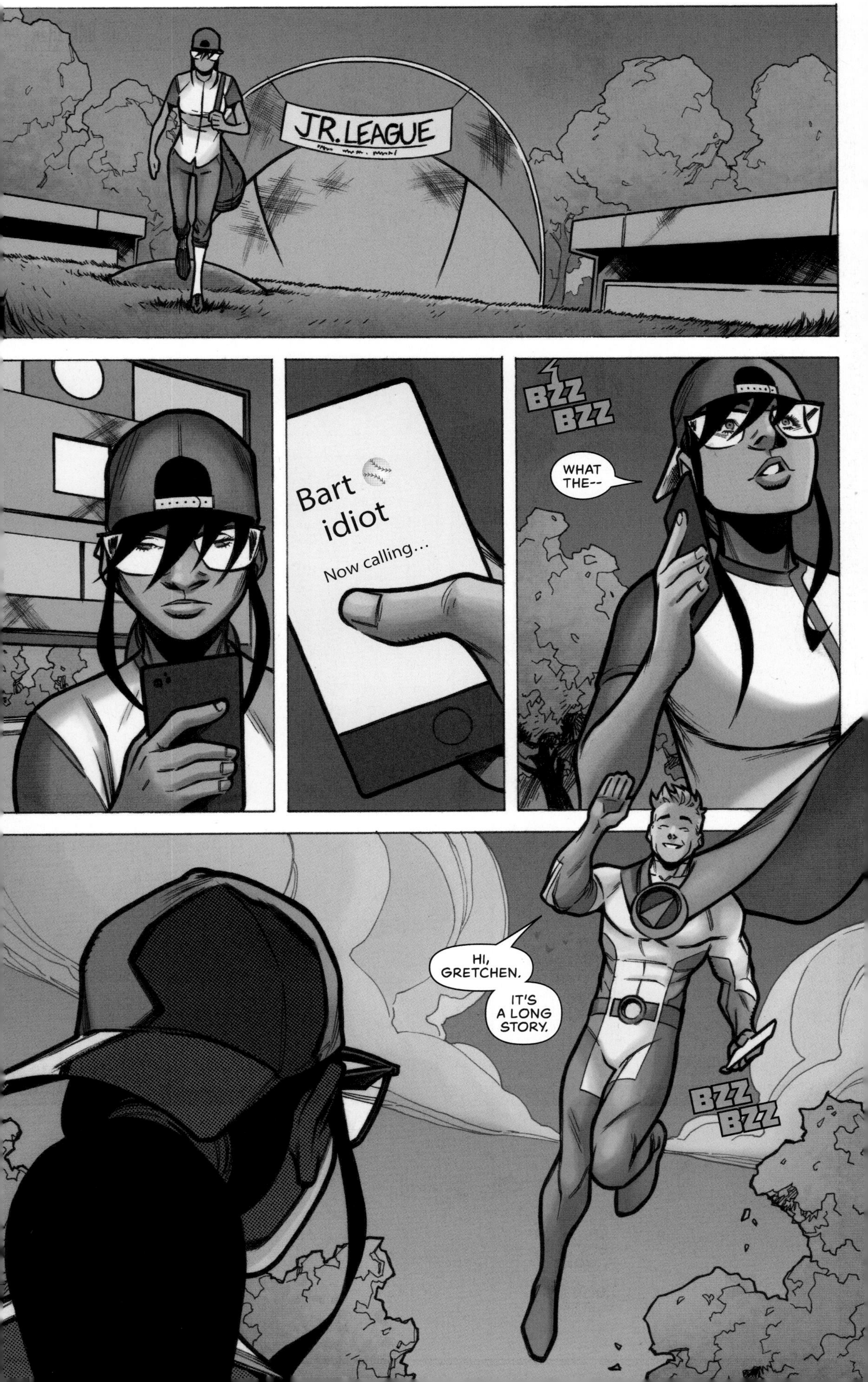
JR. LEAGUE
Bart idiot
Now calling...
BZZ BZZ
WHAT THE--
HI, GRETCHEN.
IT'S A LONG STORY.
BZZ BZZ

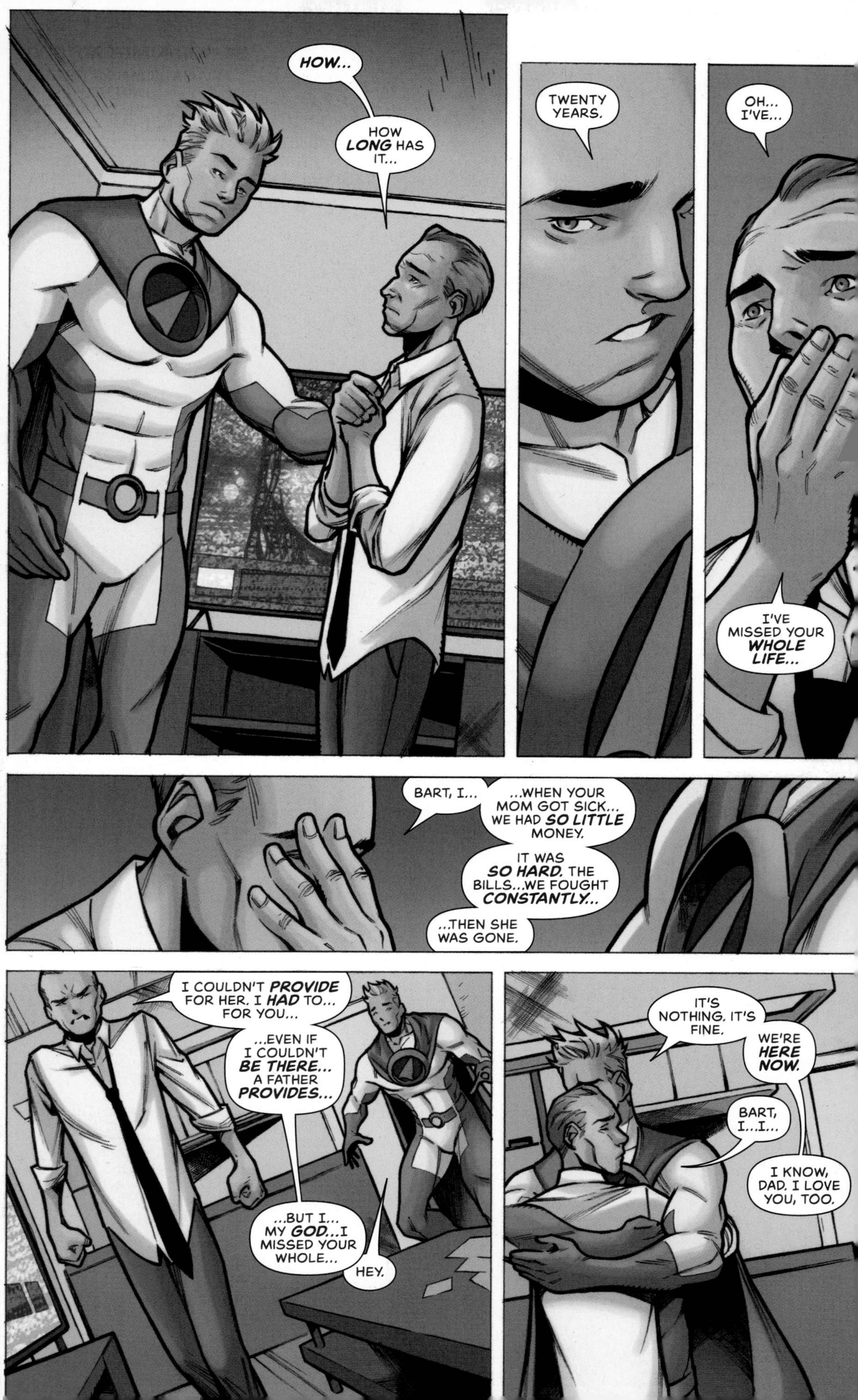
HOW...
HOW LONG HAS IT...
TWENTY YEARS.
OH... I'VE...
I'VE MISSED YOUR WHOLE LIFE...
BART, I...
...WHEN YOUR MOM GOT SICK... WE HAD SO LITTLE MONEY.
IT WAS SO HARD. THE BILLS...WE FOUGHT CONSTANTLY...
...THEN SHE WAS GONE.
I COULDN'T PROVIDE FOR HER. I HAD TO... FOR YOU...
...EVEN IF I COULDN'T BE THERE... A FATHER PROVIDES...
...BUT I... MY GOD...I MISSED YOUR WHOLE...
HEY.
IT'S NOTHING. IT'S FINE.
WE'RE HERE NOW.
BART, I...I...
I KNOW, DAD. I LOVE YOU, TOO.

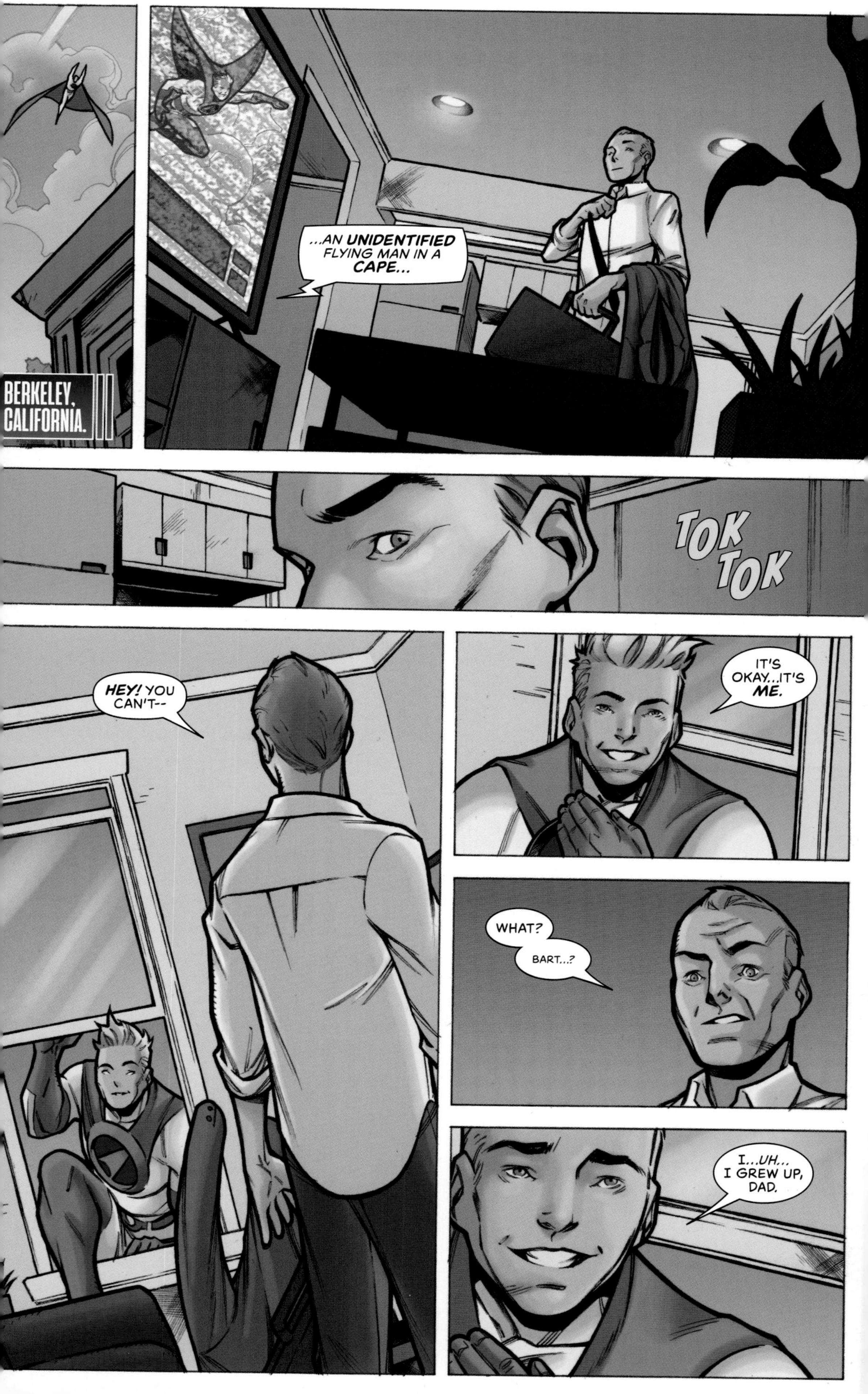
BERKELEY, CALIFORNIA.
...AN UNIDENTIFIED FLYING MAN IN A CAPE...
TOK TOK
HEY! YOU CAN'T--
IT'S OKAY...IT'S ME.
WHAT?
BART...?
I...UH... I GREW UP, DAD.

CAPSHAW! I'M DONE WITH HIM.
GREAT. HEY, WHAT'S YOUR NA--
DOCTOR SETHI!
DOCTOR SETHI...CAN WE TALK A SEC?
SURE, DOCTOR... UH...WAS IT SIMMS?
YEAH, BUT CALL ME BART.
DOCTOR SETHI...NEELA... I TRUST YOU.
YOU'VE SHOWN ME THAT.
HERE.
MY SUIT IS THE SOLE SOURCE OF MY POWER.
AND THAT'S A FULL COPY OF THE SCHEMATICS.
YOU KNOW...IN CASE I...
...IN CASE YOU NEED TO...
GOT IT.
IN CASE OF TOTAL UNIVERSAL DESTRUCTION, BREAK SUIT.
WAIT.
ARE YOU THE ONE THAT FUTURE HISTORY WARNED ME ABOUT?!
I DOUBT IT!
BUT WHAT A GREAT CLIFFHANGER, HUH?!

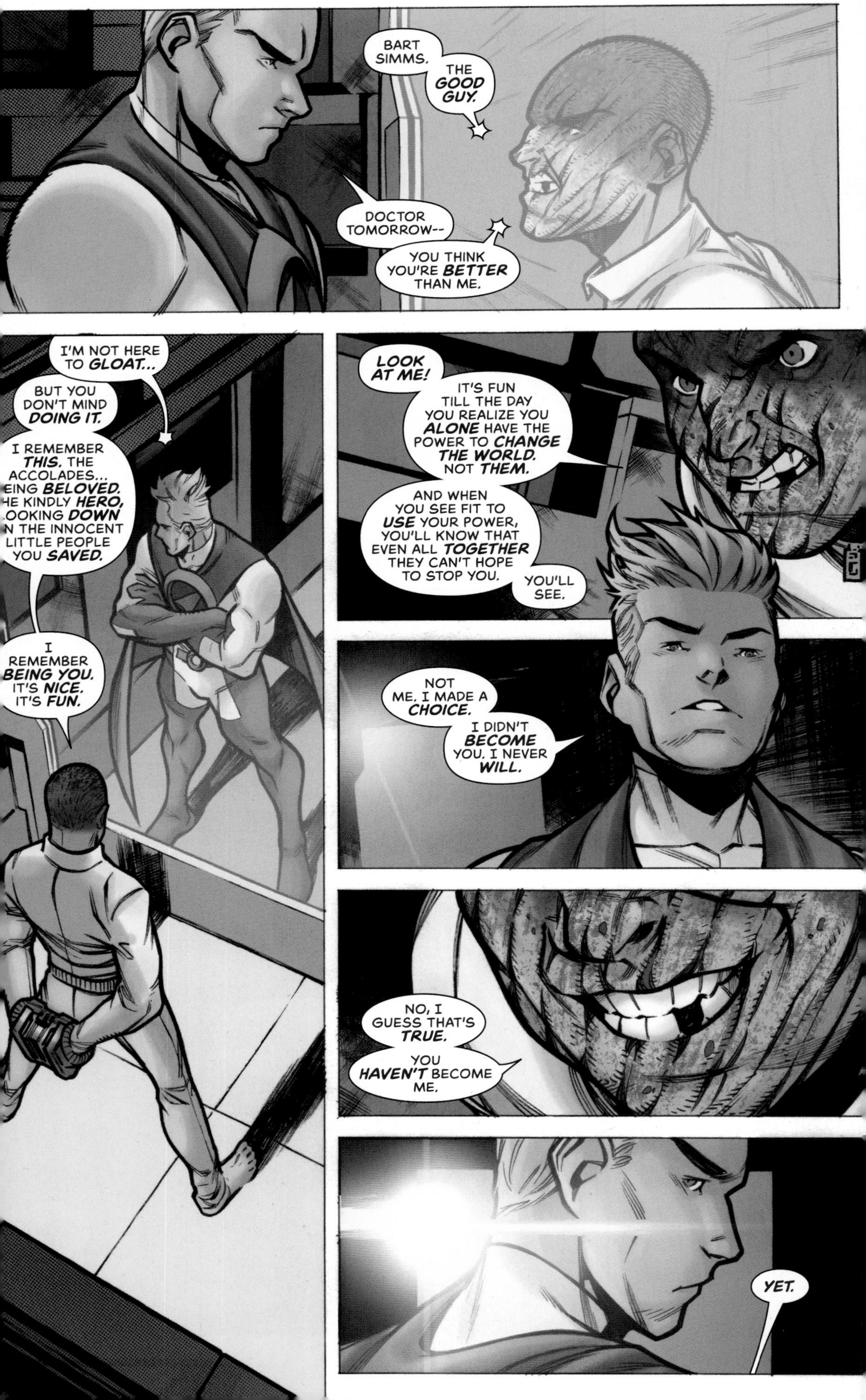
BART SIMMS.
THE GOOD GUY.
DOCTOR TOMORROW--
YOU THINK YOU'RE BETTER THAN ME.
I'M NOT HERE TO GLOAT...
BUT YOU DON'T MIND DOING IT.
I REMEMBER THIS. THE ACCOLADES... EING BELOVED. HE KINDLY HERO, OOKING DOWN N THE INNOCENT LITTLE PEOPLE YOU SAVED.
I REMEMBER BEING YOU. IT'S NICE. IT'S FUN.
LOOK AT ME!
IT'S FUN TILL THE DAY YOU REALIZE YOU ALONE HAVE THE POWER TO CHANGE THE WORLD. NOT THEM.
AND WHEN YOU SEE FIT TO USE YOUR POWER, YOU'LL KNOW THAT EVEN ALL TOGETHER THEY CAN'T HOPE TO STOP YOU.
YOU'LL SEE.
NOT ME. I MADE A CHOICE.
I DIDN'T BECOME YOU. I NEVER WILL.
NO, I GUESS THAT'S TRUE.
YOU HAVEN'T BECOME ME.
YET.

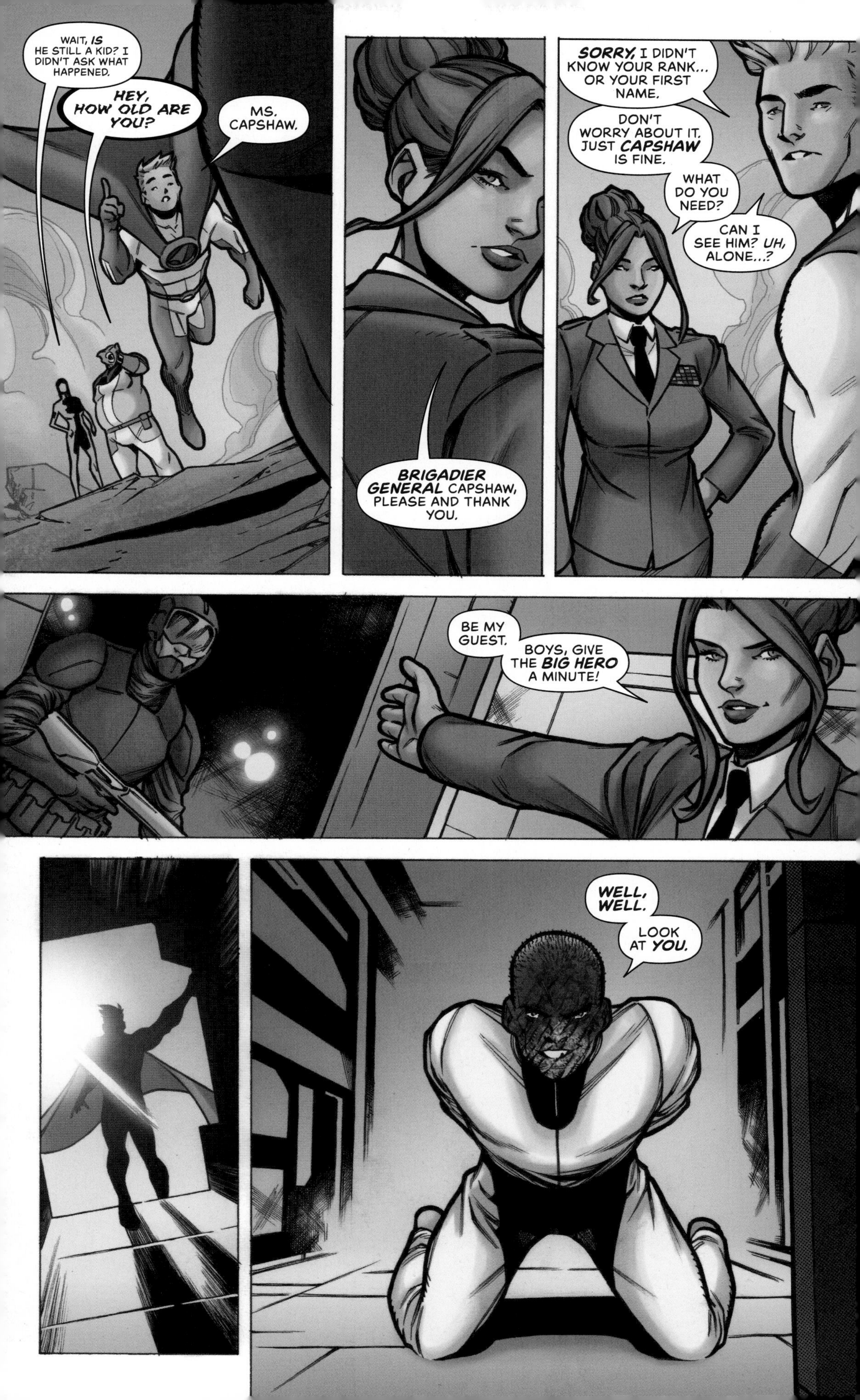
WAIT, IS HE STILL A KID? I DIDN'T ASK WHAT HAPPENED.
HEY, HOW OLD ARE YOU?
MS. CAPSHAW.
BRIGADIER GENERAL CAPSHAW, PLEASE AND THANK YOU.
SORRY, I DIDN'T KNOW YOUR RANK... OR YOUR FIRST NAME.
DON'T WORRY ABOUT IT. JUST CAPSHAW IS FINE.
WHAT DO YOU NEED?
CAN I SEE HIM? UH, ALONE...?
BE MY GUEST.
BOYS, GIVE THE BIG HERO A MINUTE!
WELL, WELL.
LOOK AT YOU.

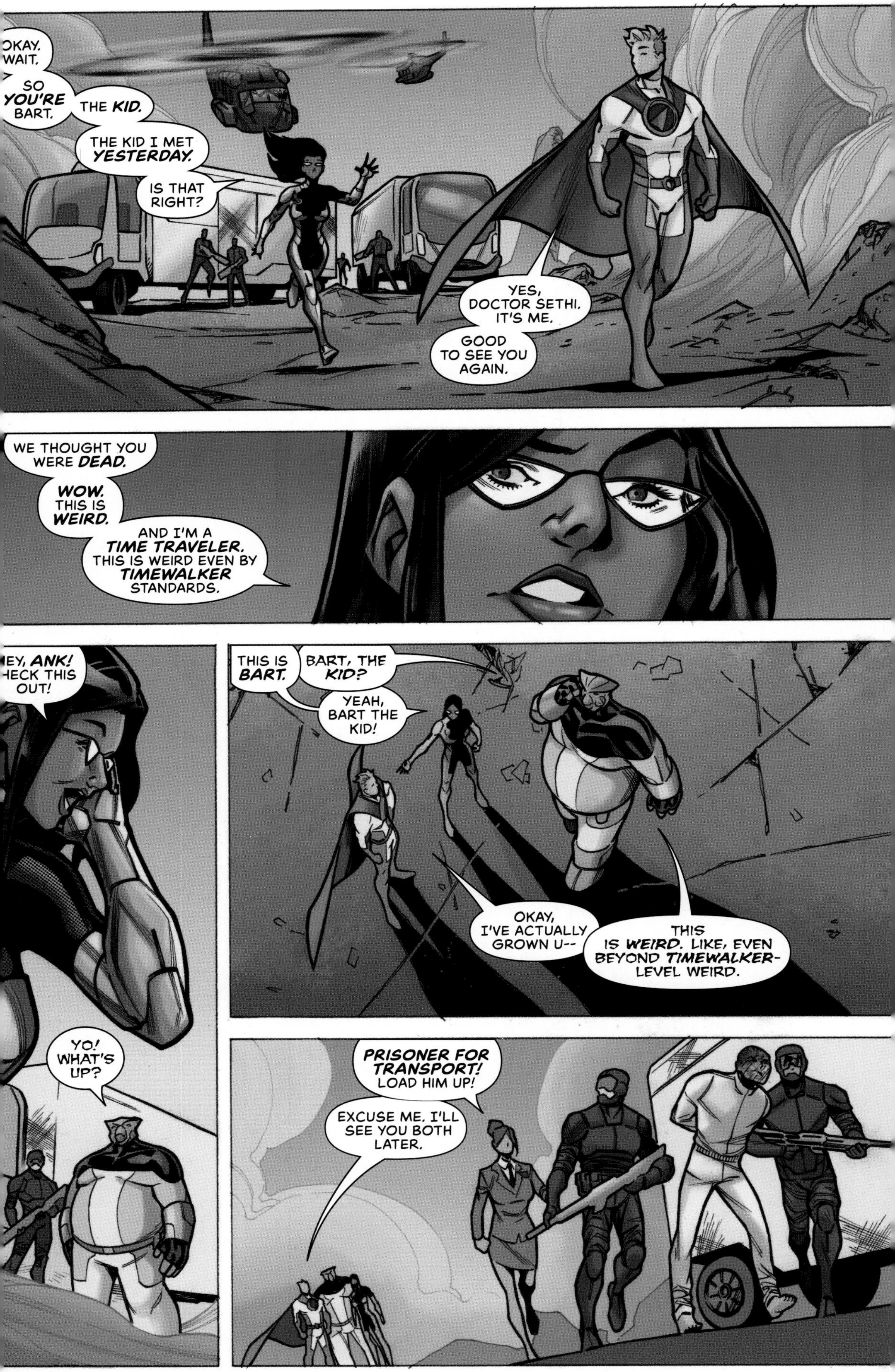

OKAY. WAIT.
SO YOU'RE BART.
THE KID.
THE KID I MET YESTERDAY.
IS THAT RIGHT?
YES, DOCTOR SETHI. IT'S ME.
GOOD TO SEE YOU AGAIN.
WE THOUGHT YOU WERE DEAD.
WOW. THIS IS WEIRD.
AND I'M A TIME TRAVELER. THIS IS WEIRD EVEN BY TIMEWALKER STANDARDS.
EY, ANK! HECK THIS OUT!
YO! WHAT'S UP?
THIS IS BART.
BART, THE KID?
YEAH, BART THE KID!
OKAY, I'VE ACTUALLY GROWN U--
THIS IS WEIRD. LIKE, EVEN BEYOND TIMEWALKER-LEVEL WEIRD.
PRISONER FOR TRANSPORT! LOAD HIM UP!
EXCUSE ME. I'LL SEE YOU BOTH LATER.

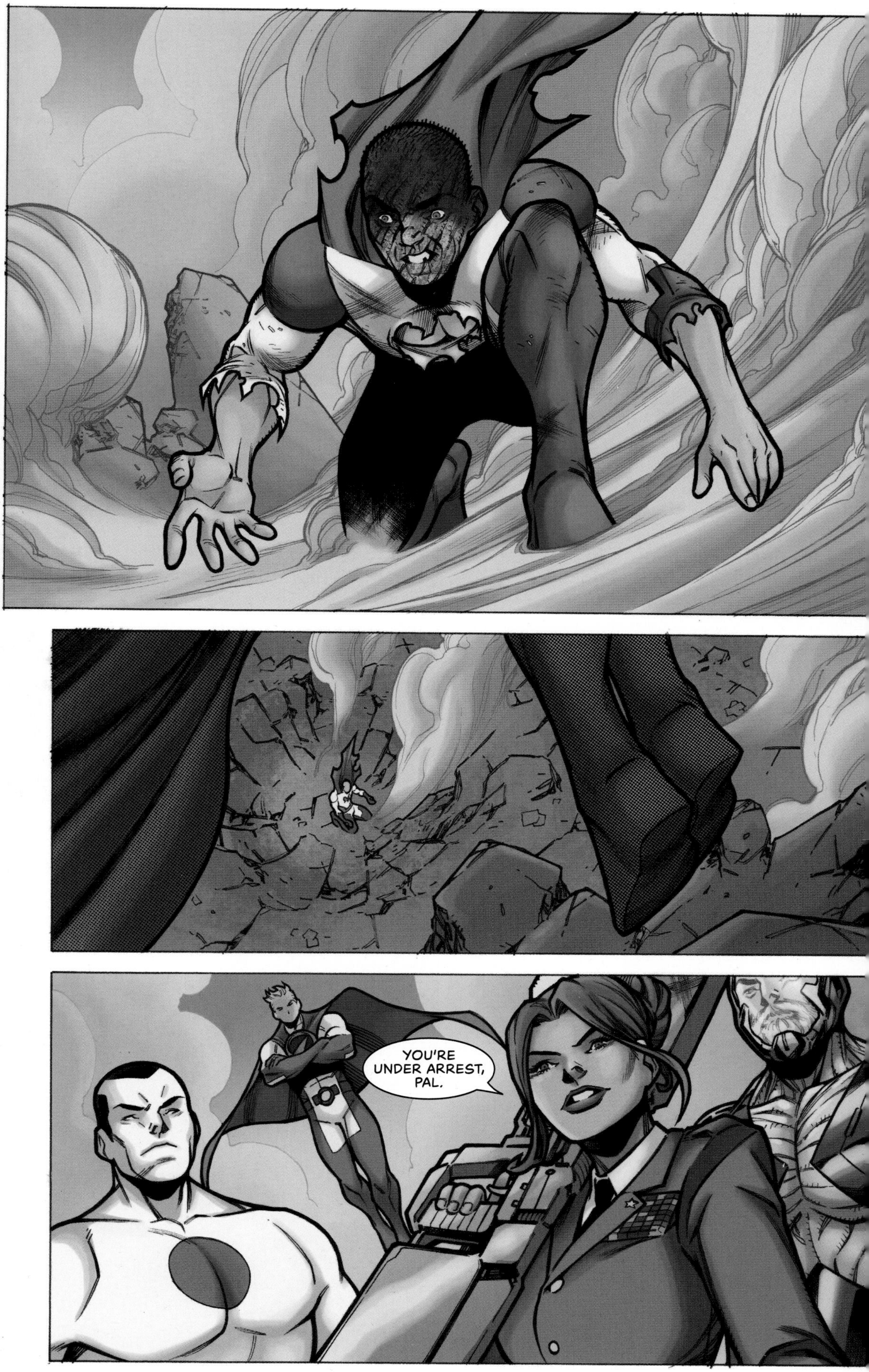
YOU'RE UNDER ARREST, PAL.

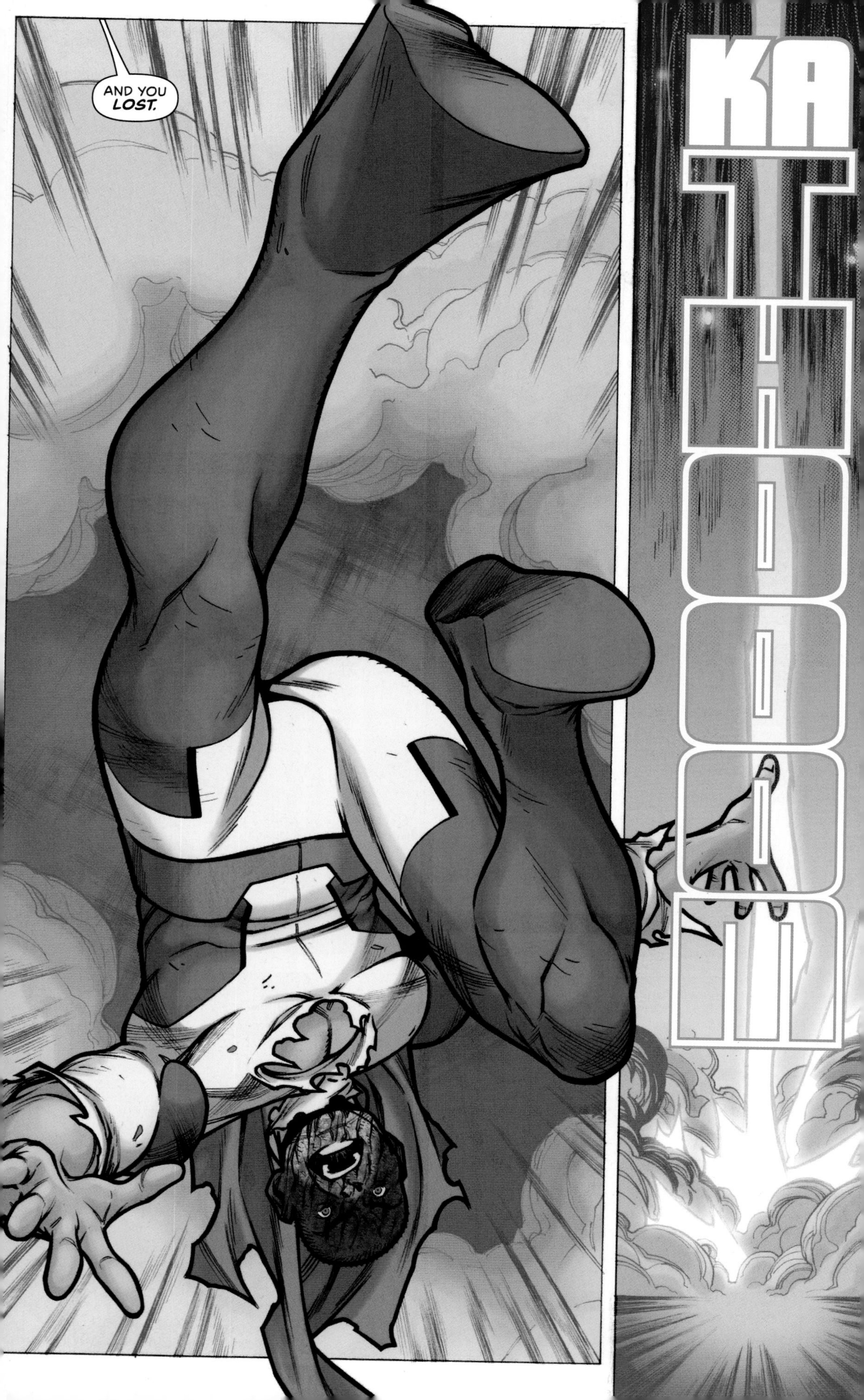
AND YOU LOST.
KATHOOOM

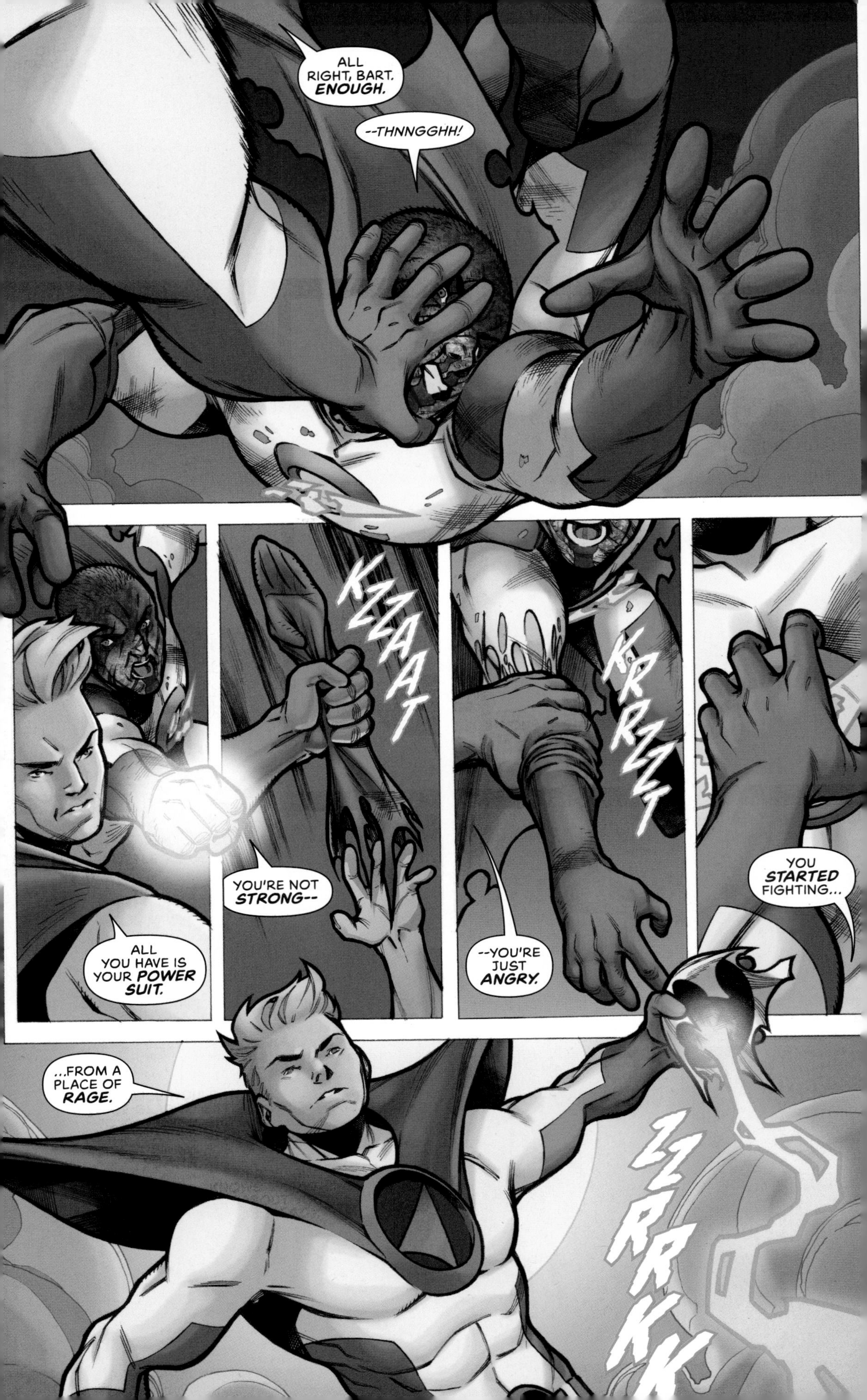
ALL RIGHT, BART. ENOUGH.
--THNNGGHH!
KZZAAAT
YOU'RE NOT STRONG--
ALL YOU HAVE IS YOUR POWER SUIT.
KRRZZZT
--YOU'RE JUST ANGRY.
YOU STARTED FIGHTING...
...FROM A PLACE OF RAGE.
ZZRRKK

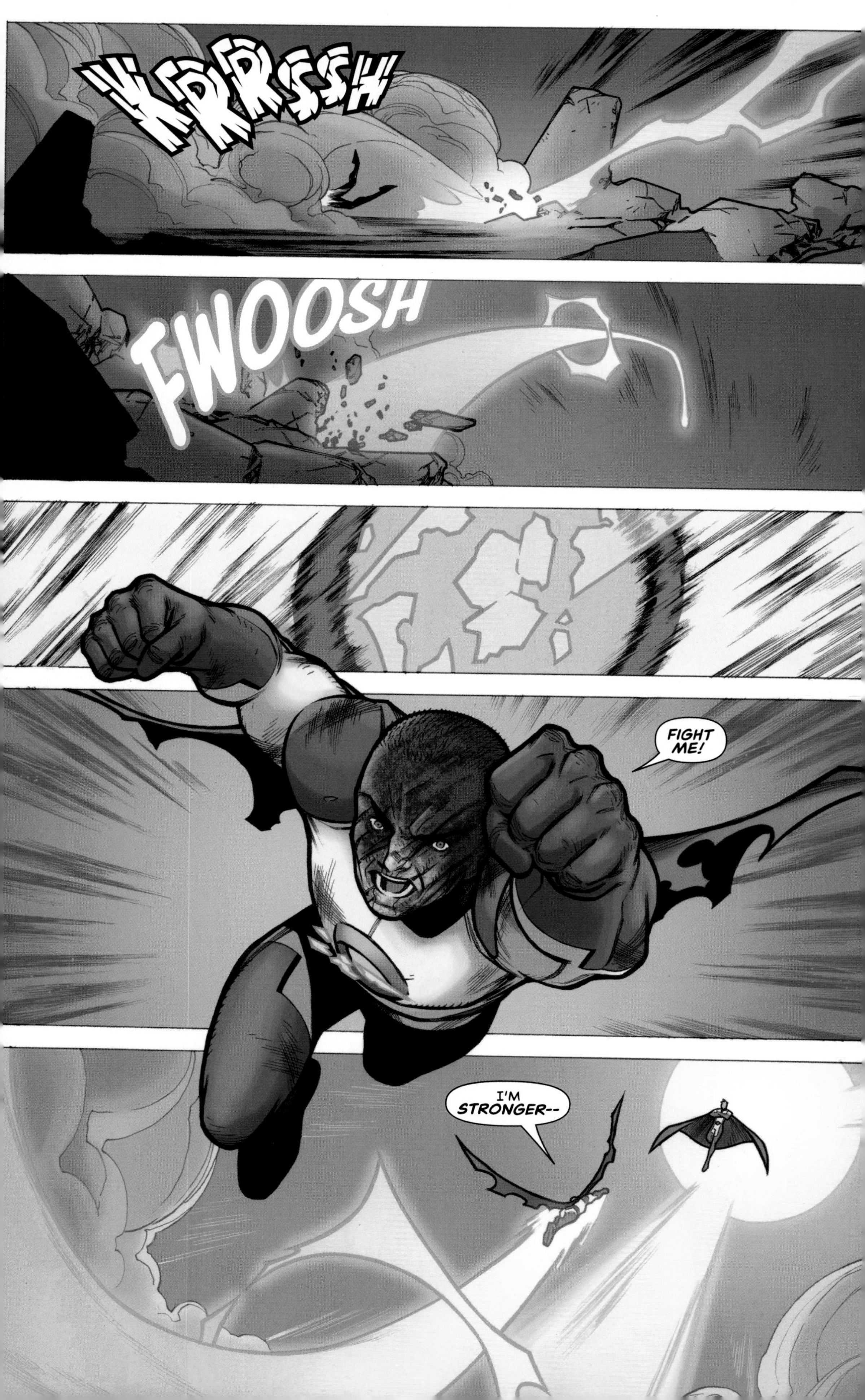
KRRSSH
FWOOSH
FIGHT ME!
I'M STRONGER--

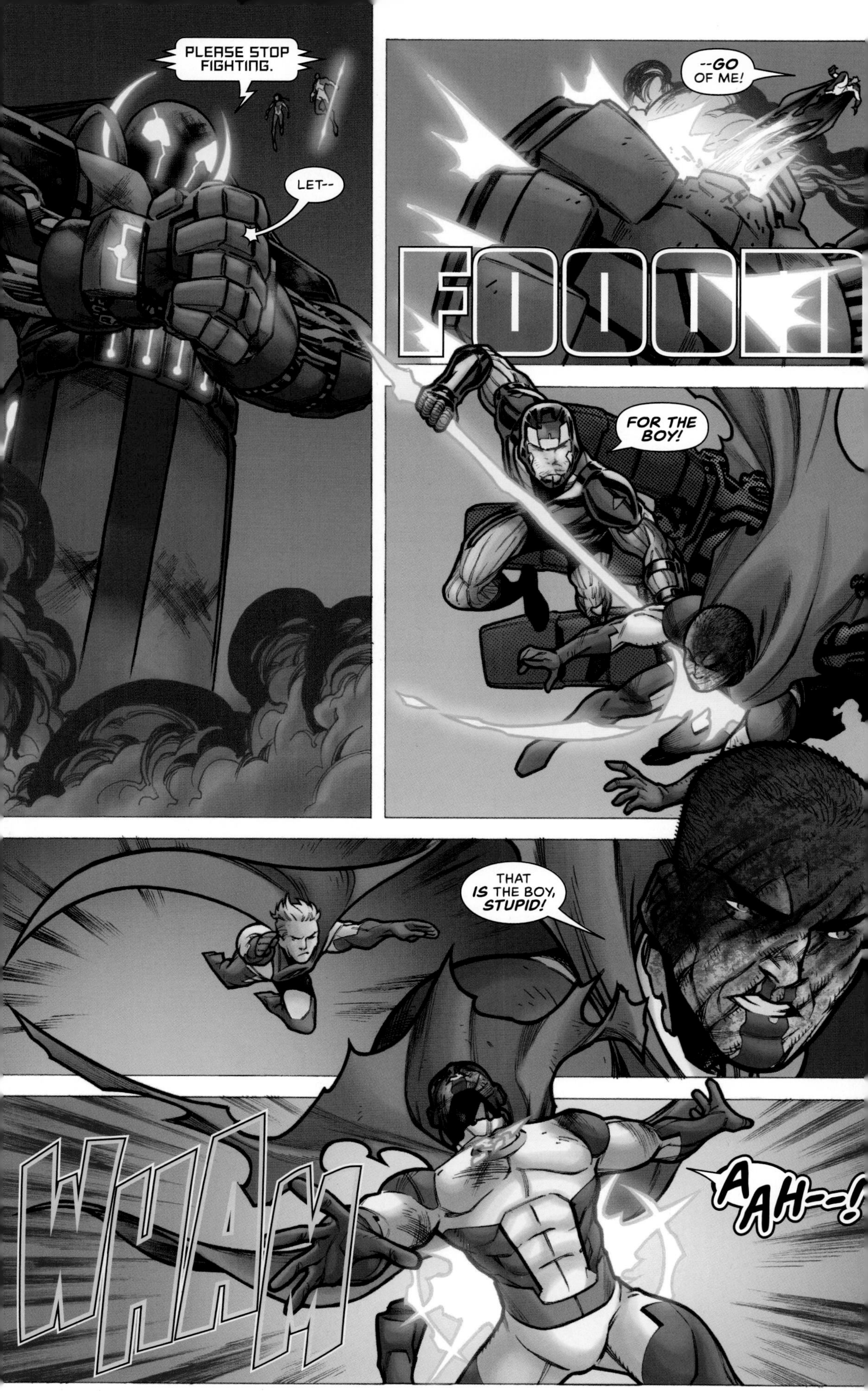
PLEASE STOP FIGHTING.
LET--
--GO OF ME!
FOOOM
FOR THE BOY!
THAT IS THE BOY, STUPID!
WHAM
AAH--!

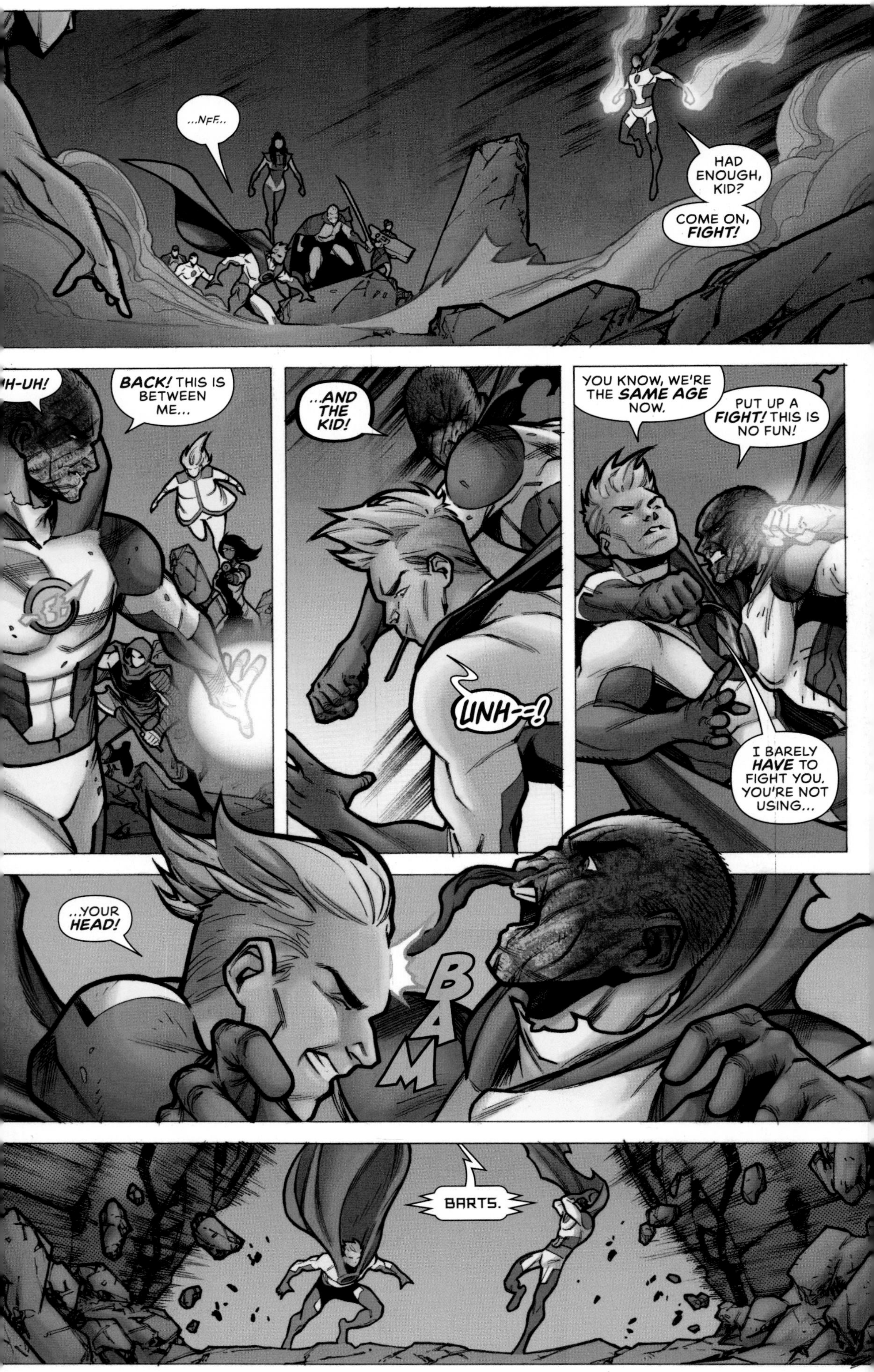
...NFF...
HAD ENOUGH, KID?
COME ON, FIGHT!
H-UH!
BACK! THIS IS BETWEEN ME...
...AND THE KID!
UNH--!
YOU KNOW, WE'RE THE SAME AGE NOW.
PUT UP A FIGHT! THIS IS NO FUN!
I BARELY HAVE TO FIGHT YOU. YOU'RE NOT USING...
...YOUR HEAD!
BAM
BARTS.

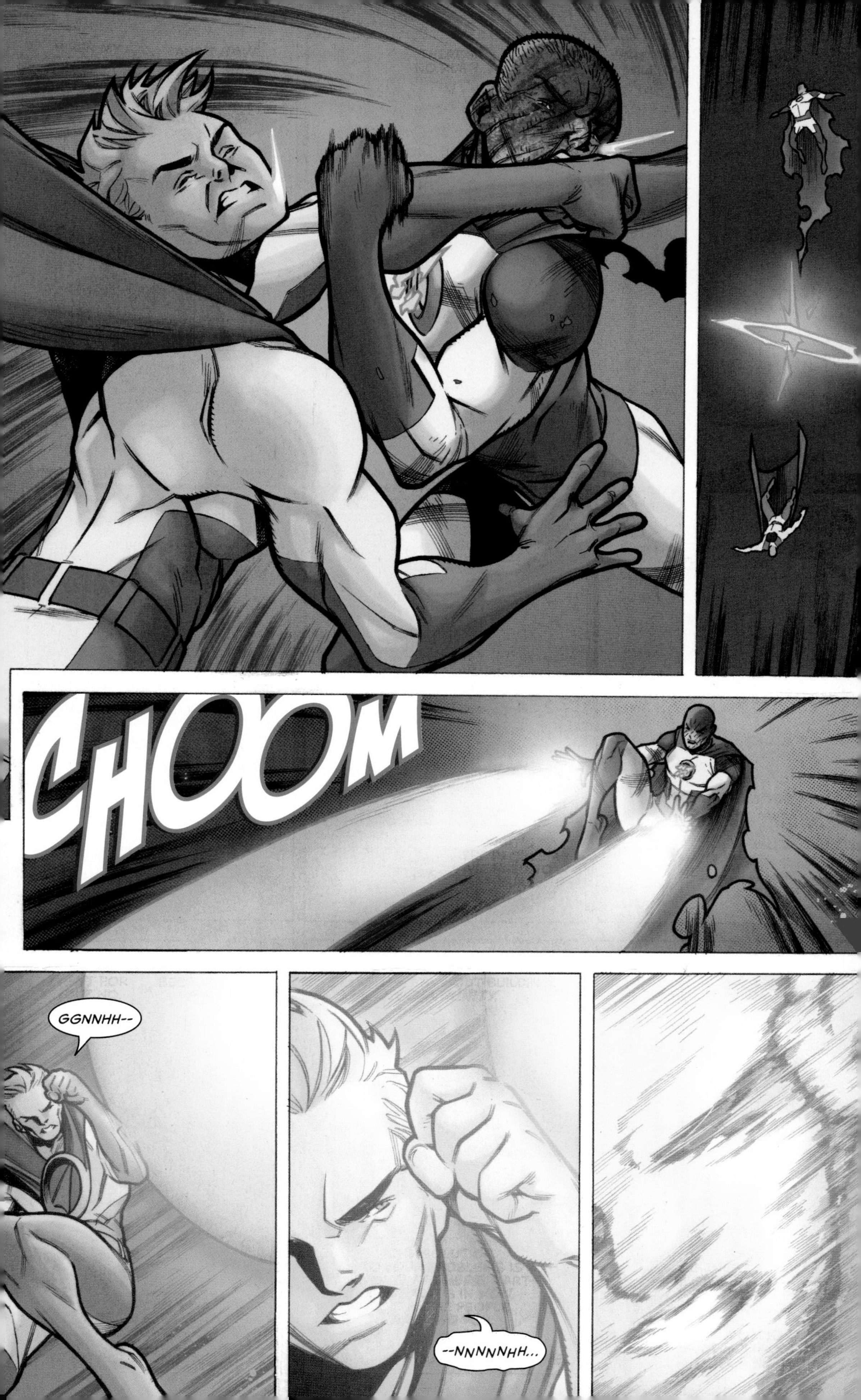
CHOOM
GGNNHH--
--NNNNNHH...

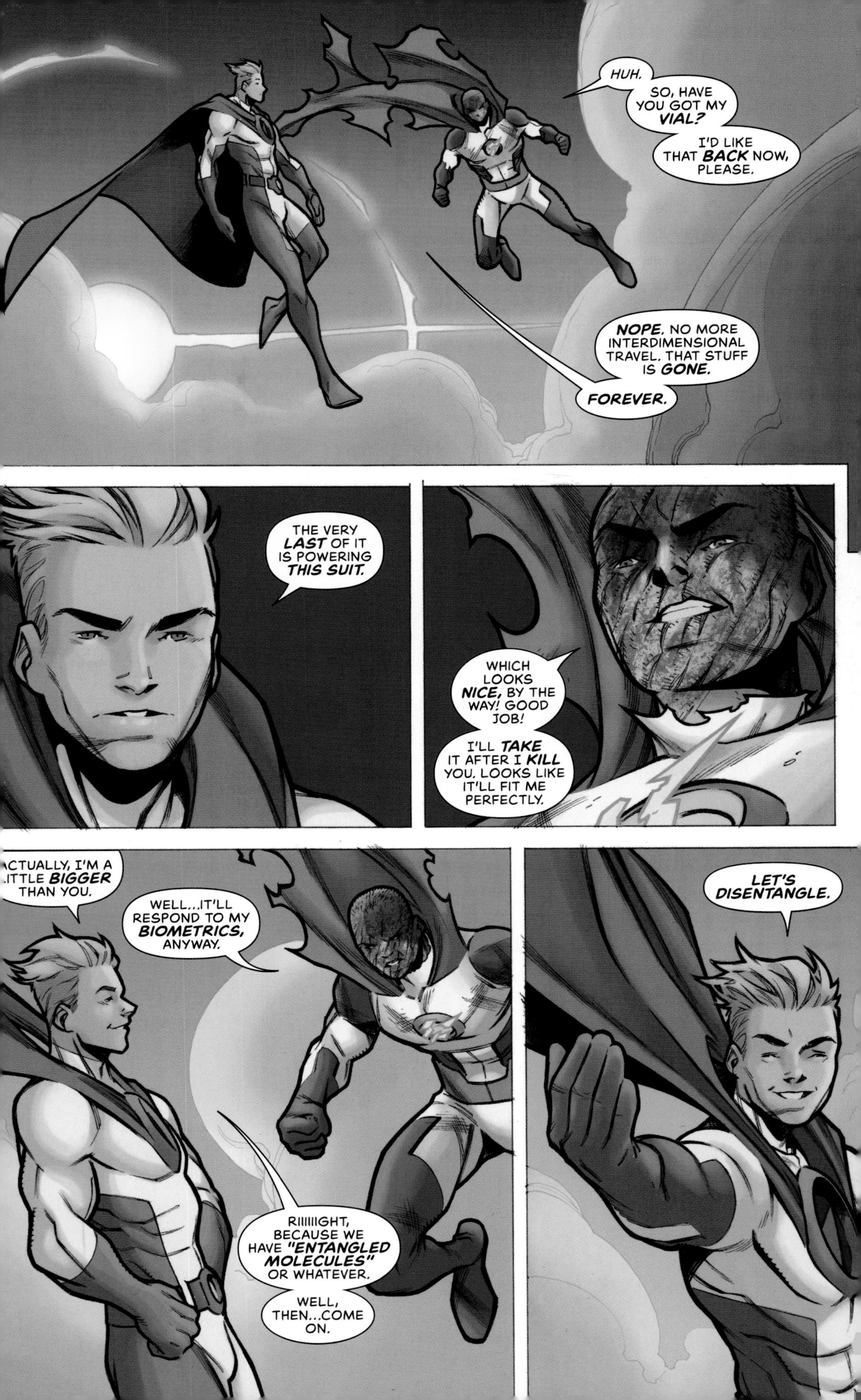
HUH.
SO, HAVE YOU GOT MY VIAL?
I'D LIKE THAT BACK NOW, PLEASE.
NOPE. NO MORE INTERDIMENSIONAL TRAVEL. THAT STUFF IS GONE.
FOREVER.
THE VERY LAST OF IT IS POWERING THIS SUIT.
WHICH LOOKS NICE, BY THE WAY! GOOD JOB!
I'LL TAKE IT AFTER I KILL YOU. LOOKS LIKE IT'LL FIT ME PERFECTLY.
CTUALLY, I'M A ITTLE BIGGER THAN YOU.
WELL...IT'LL RESPOND TO MY BIOMETRICS, ANYWAY.
RIIIIIGHT, BECAUSE WE HAVE "ENTANGLED MOLECULES" OR WHATEVER.
WELL, THEN...COME ON.
LET'S DISENTANGLE.

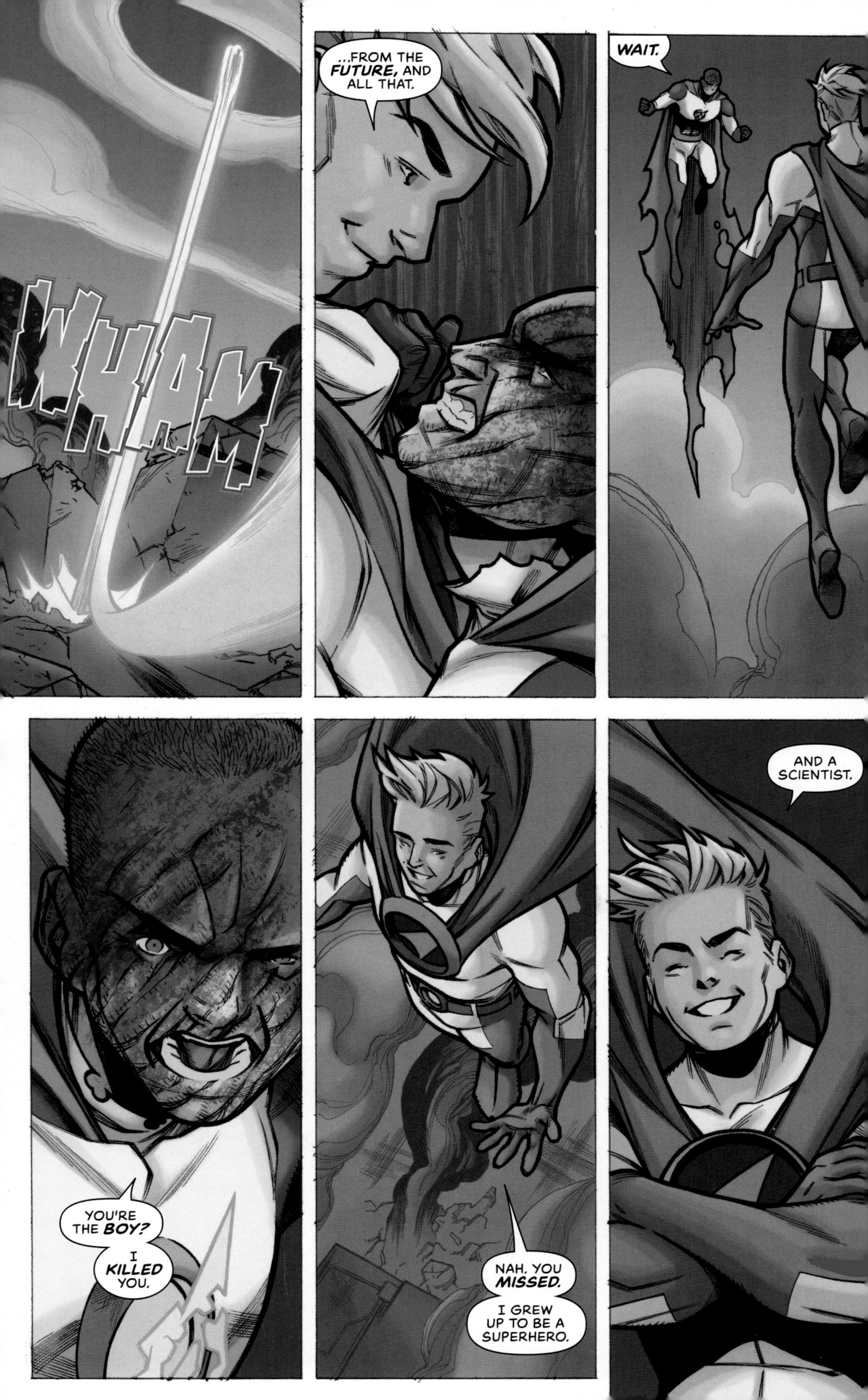
WHAM
...FROM THE FUTURE, AND ALL THAT.
WAIT.
YOU'RE THE BOY?
I KILLED YOU.
NAH. YOU MISSED.
I GREW UP TO BE A SUPERHERO.
AND A SCIENTIST.

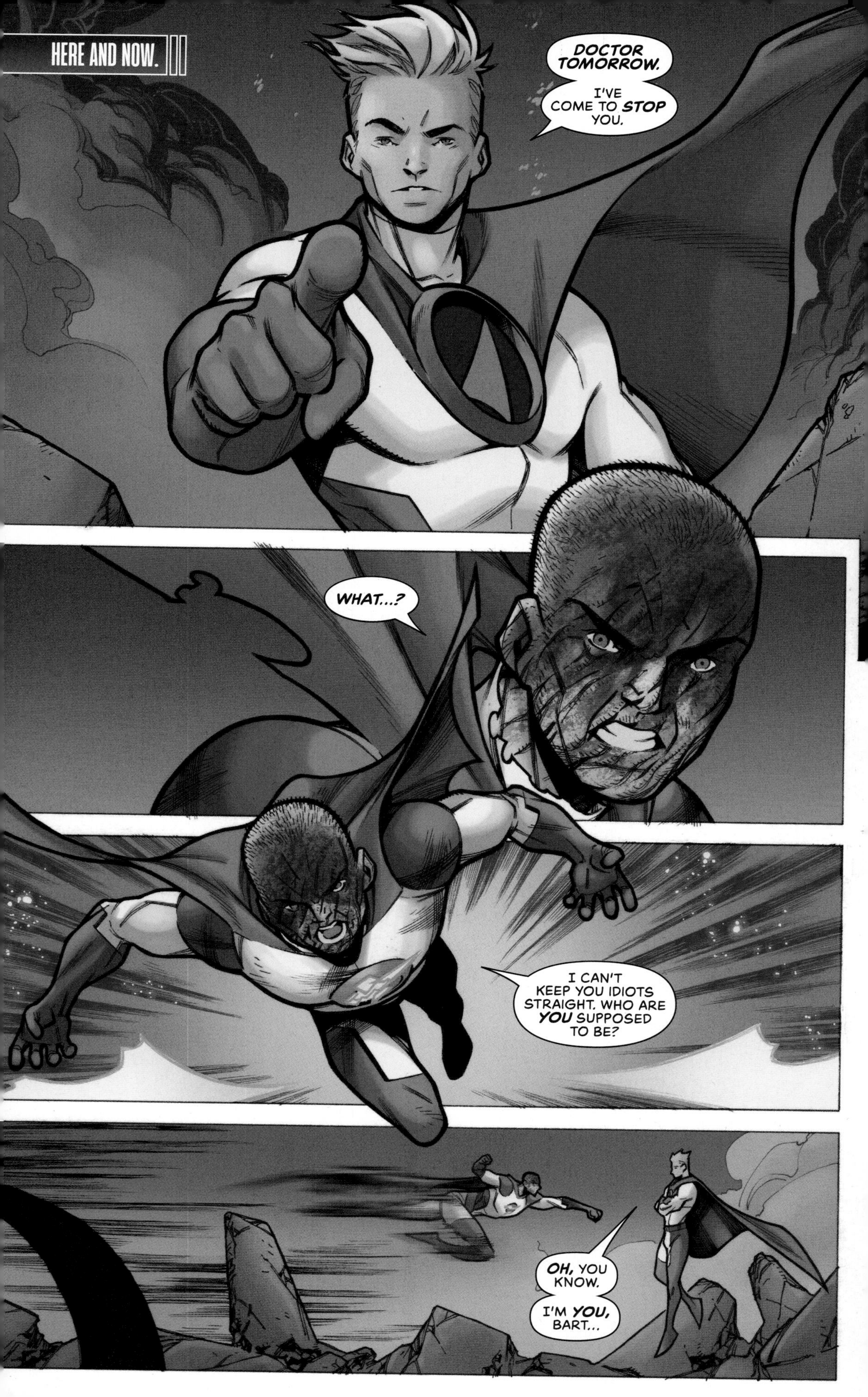
HERE AND NOW.
DOCTOR TOMORROW.
I'VE COME TO STOP YOU.
WHAT...?
I CAN'T KEEP YOU IDIOTS STRAIGHT. WHO ARE YOU SUPPOSED TO BE?
OH, YOU KNOW.
I'M YOU, BART...

DOCTOR TOMORROW #5

WRITER: ALEJANDRO ARBONA
ARTIST: JIM TOWE
COLORIST: KELLY FITZPATRICK
LETTERER: CLAYTON COWLES
COVER ARTISTS: CLAYTON HENRY and ULISES ARREOLA
ASSISTANT EDITOR: DREW BAUMGARTNER
SENIOR EDITORIAL DIRECTOR: ROBERT MEYERS

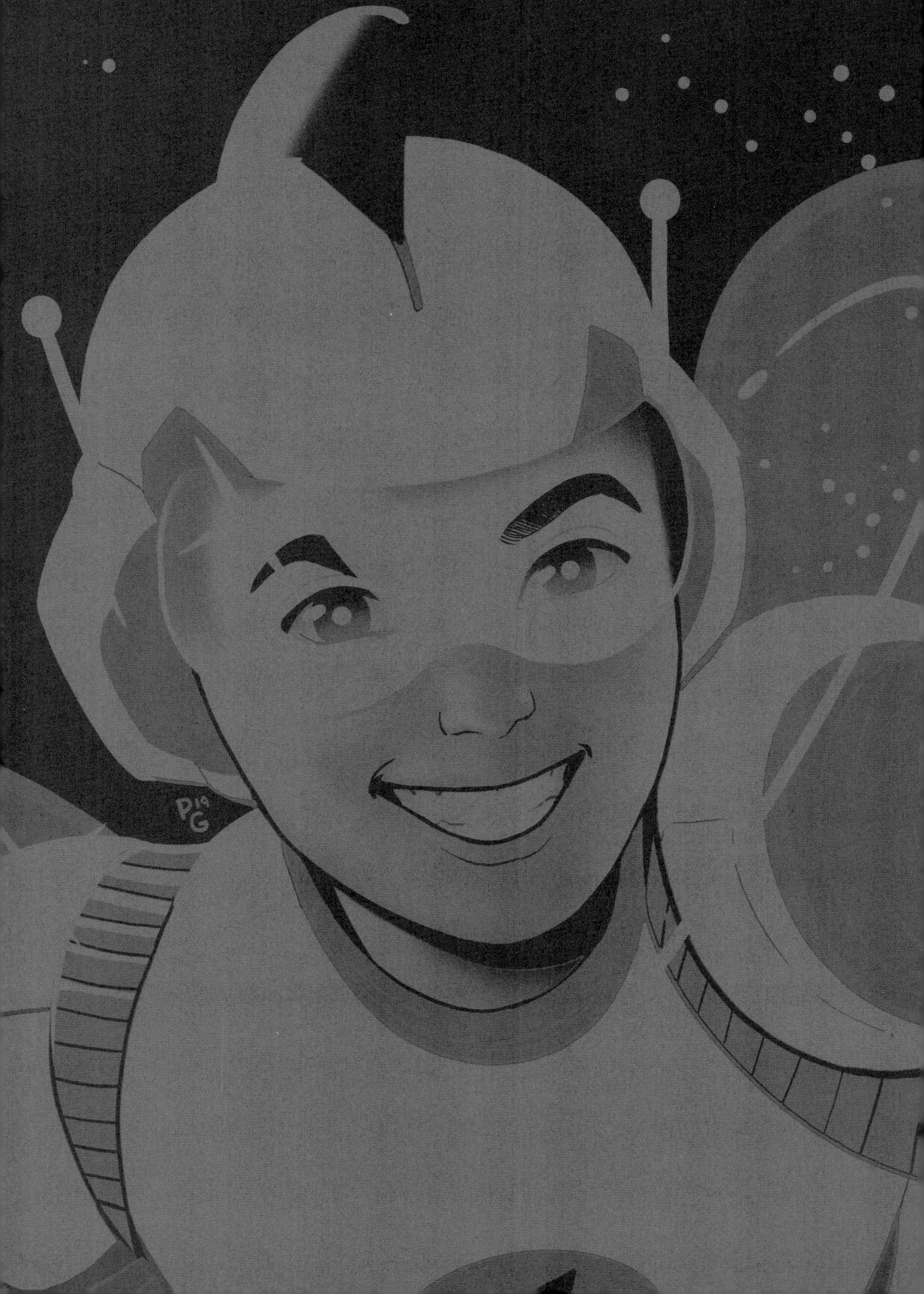

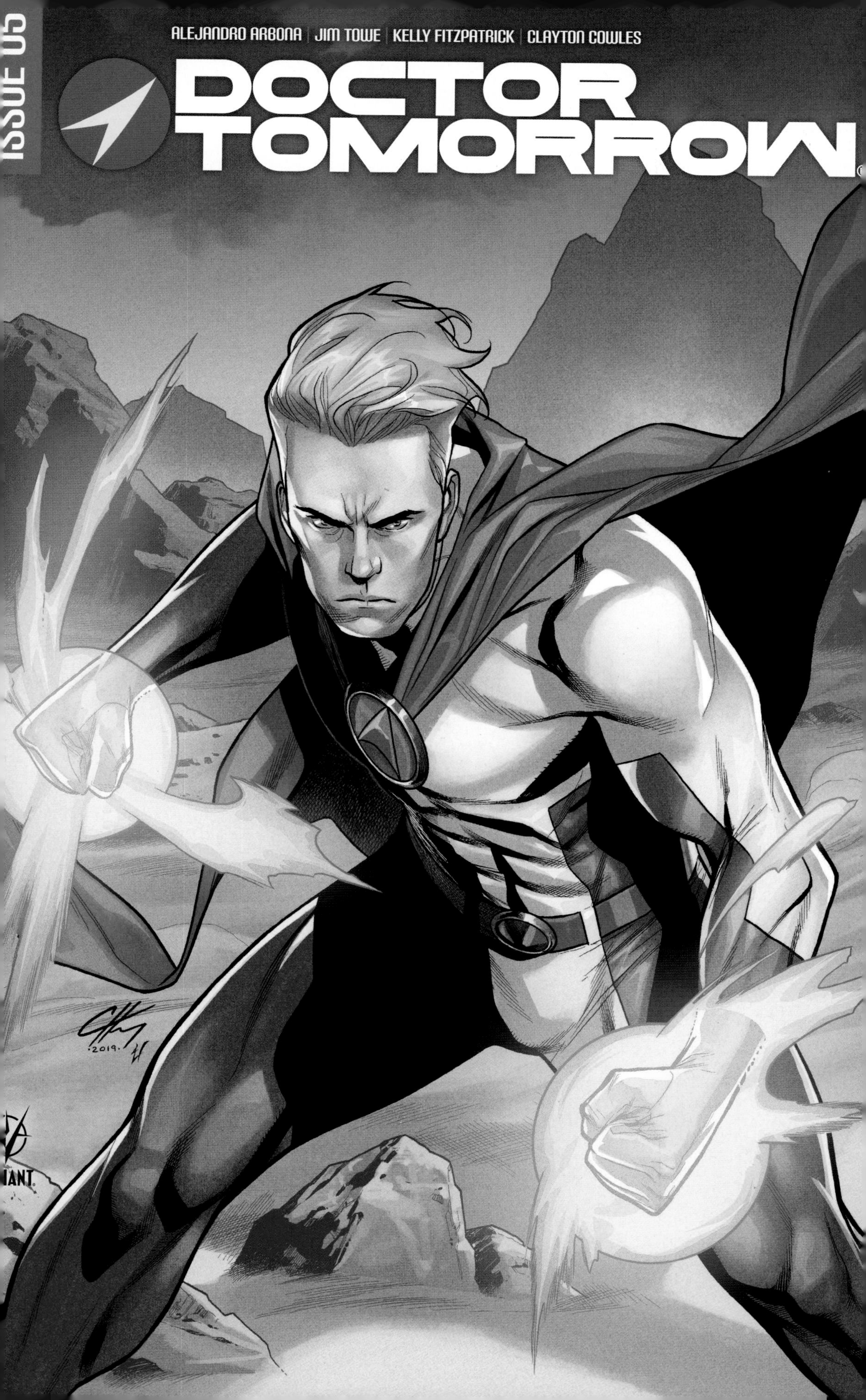
ISSUE 05
ALEJANDRO ARBONA | JIM TOWE | KELLY FITZPATRICK | CLAYTON COWLES
DOCTOR TOMORROW

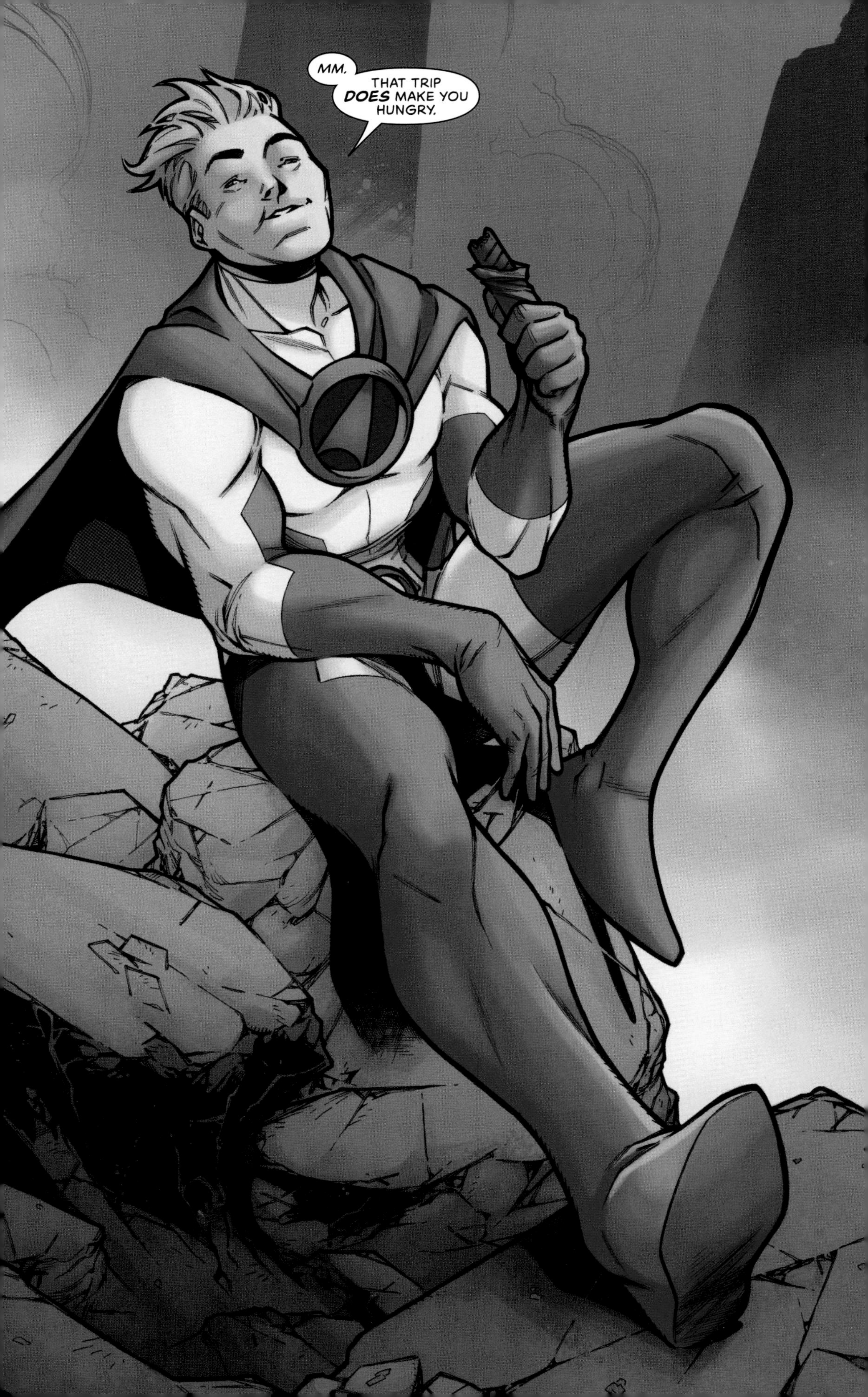
MM,
THAT TRIP **DOES** MAKE YOU HUNGRY.

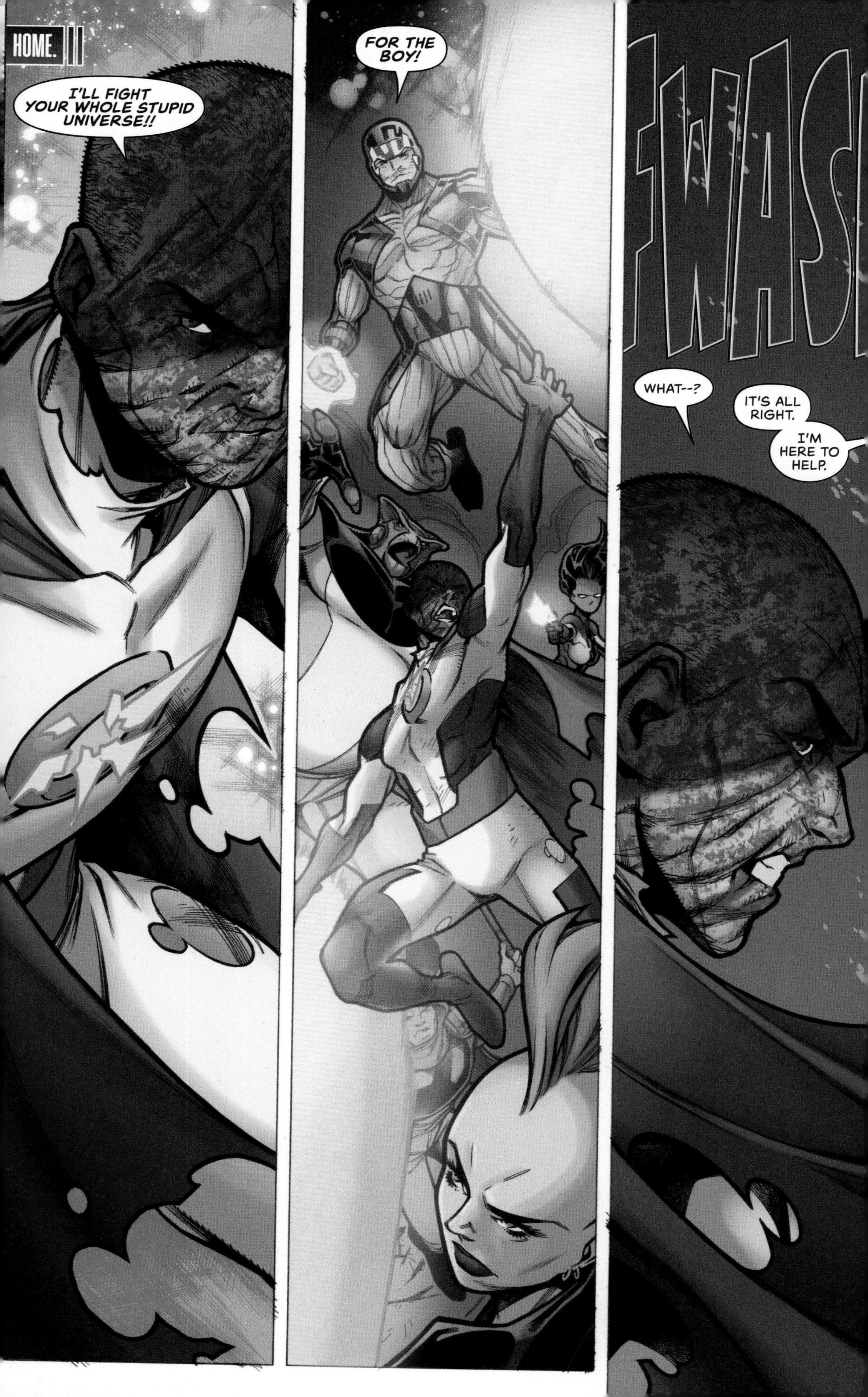
HOME.
I'LL FIGHT YOUR WHOLE STUPID UNIVERSE!!
FOR THE BOY!
FWAS
WHAT--?
IT'S ALL RIGHT.
I'M HERE TO HELP.

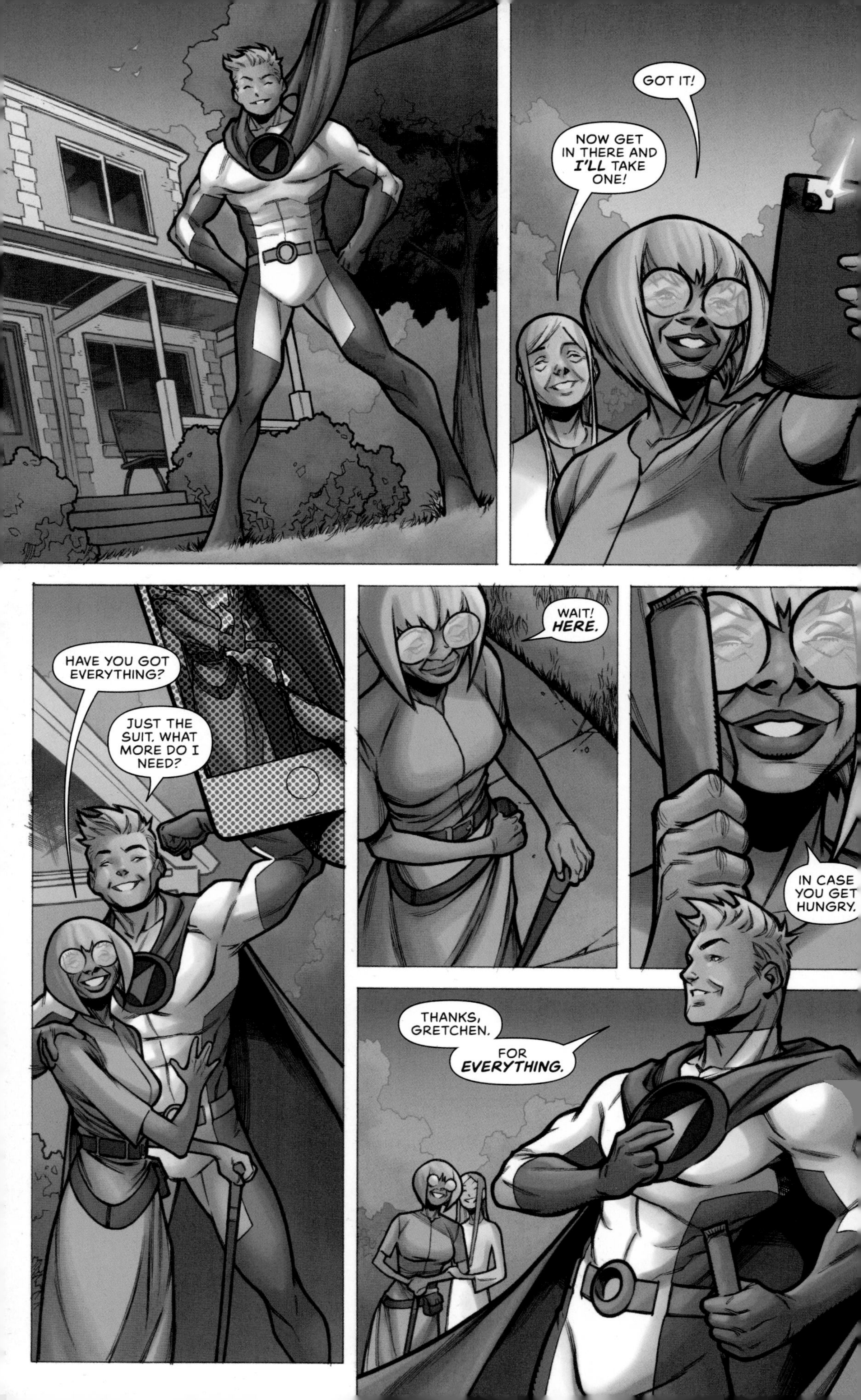
NOW GET IN THERE AND *I'LL* TAKE ONE!
GOT IT!
HAVE YOU GOT EVERYTHING?
JUST THE SUIT. WHAT MORE DO I NEED?
WAIT! *HERE.*
IN CASE YOU GET HUNGRY.
THANKS, GRETCHEN.
FOR *EVERYTHING.*

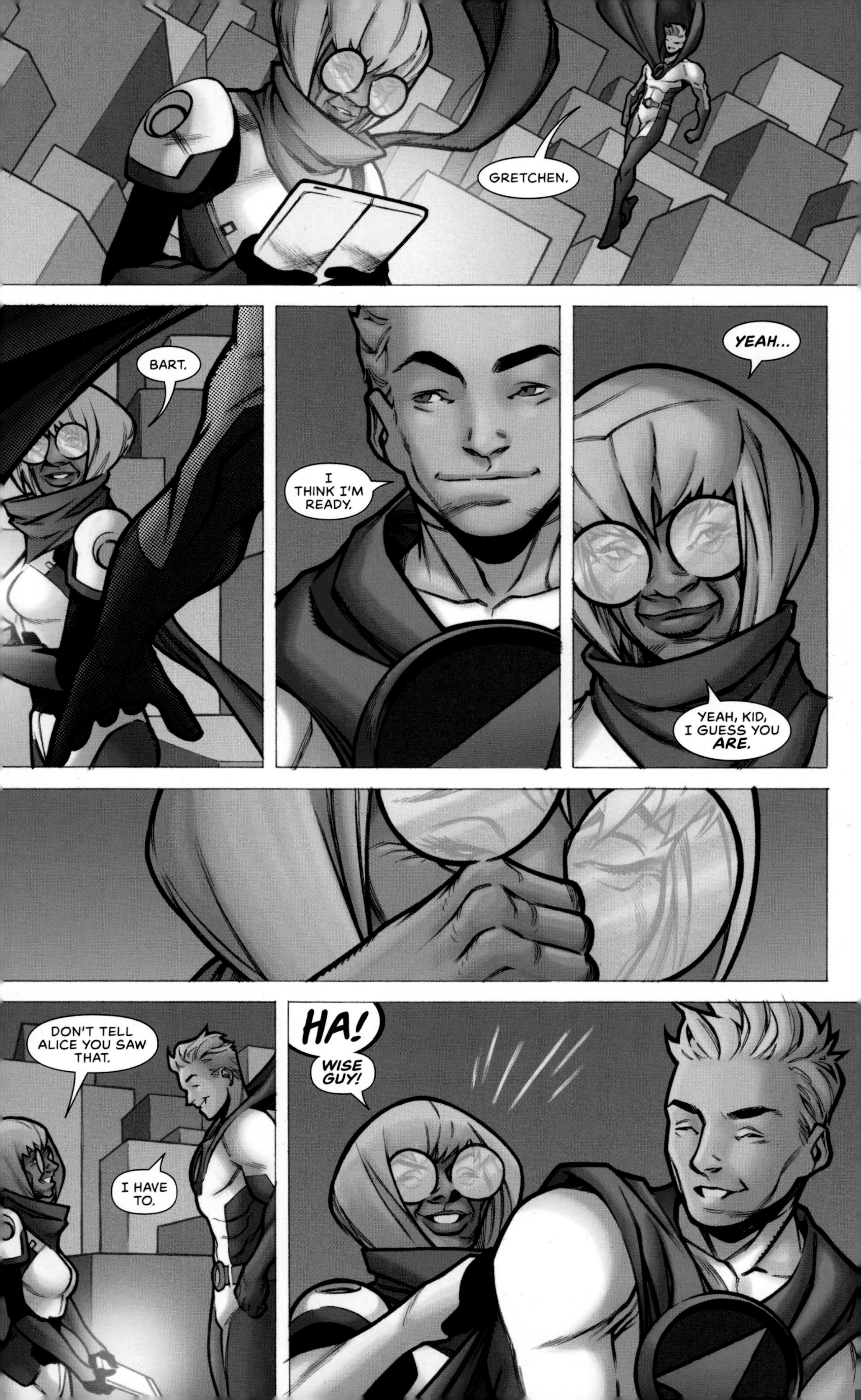
GRETCHEN.
BART.
I THINK I'M READY.
YEAH...
YEAH, KID, I GUESS YOU **ARE.**
DON'T TELL ALICE YOU SAW THAT.
I HAVE TO.
HA!
WISE GUY!

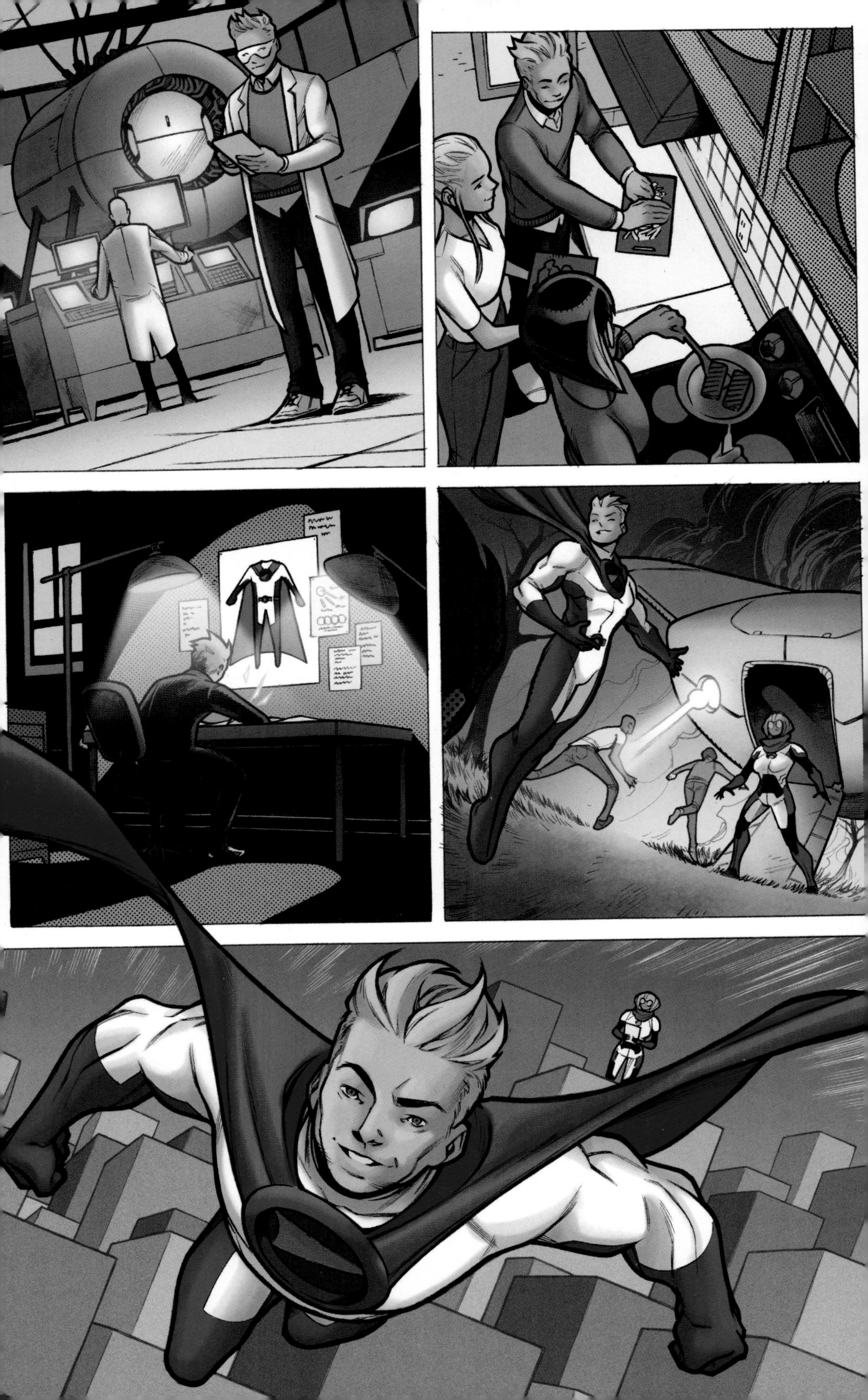

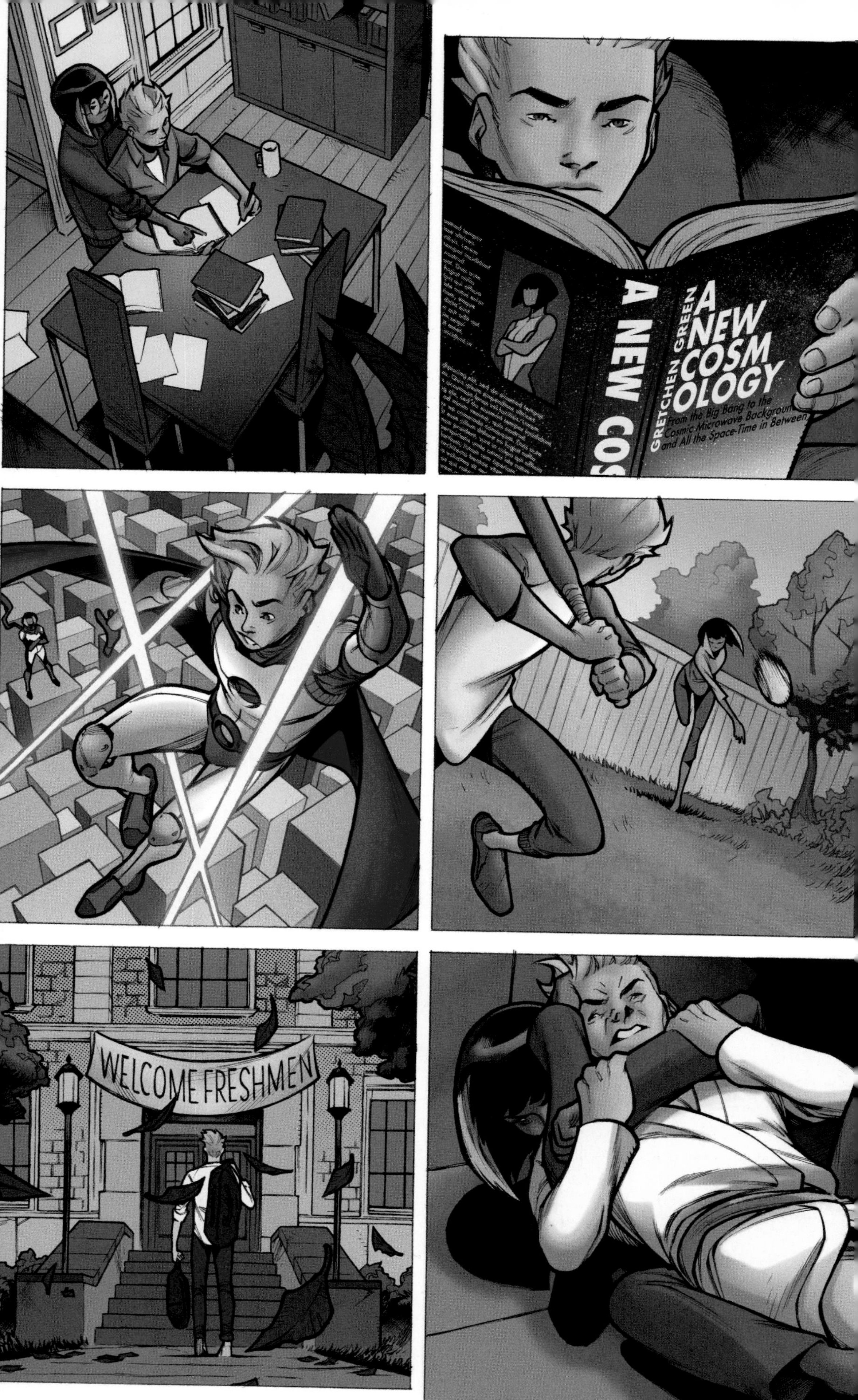
GRETCHEN GREEN
A NEW COSMOLOGY
From the Big Bang to the Cosmic Microwave Backgroun
and All the Space-Time in Between
A NEW COS
WELCOME FRESHMEN

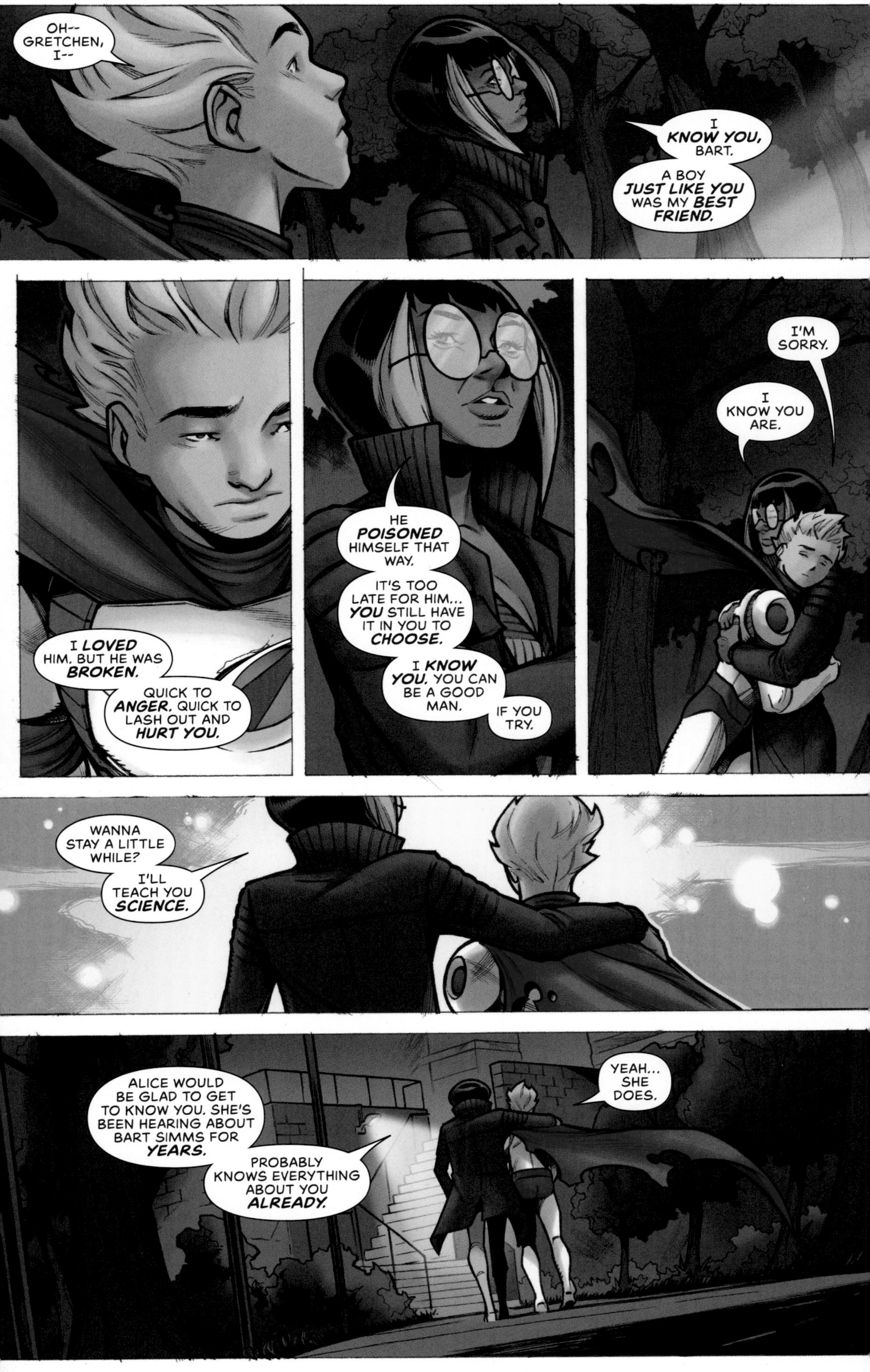
OH-- GRETCHEN, I--
I KNOW YOU, BART.
A BOY JUST LIKE YOU WAS MY BEST FRIEND.
I LOVED HIM. BUT HE WAS BROKEN.
QUICK TO ANGER. QUICK TO LASH OUT AND HURT YOU.
HE POISONED HIMSELF THAT WAY.
IT'S TOO LATE FOR HIM... YOU STILL HAVE IT IN YOU TO CHOOSE.
I KNOW YOU. YOU CAN BE A GOOD MAN.
IF YOU TRY.
I'M SORRY.
I KNOW YOU ARE.
WANNA STAY A LITTLE WHILE?
I'LL TEACH YOU SCIENCE.
ALICE WOULD BE GLAD TO GET TO KNOW YOU. SHE'S BEEN HEARING ABOUT BART SIMMS FOR YEARS.
PROBABLY KNOWS EVERYTHING ABOUT YOU ALREADY.
YEAH... SHE DOES.

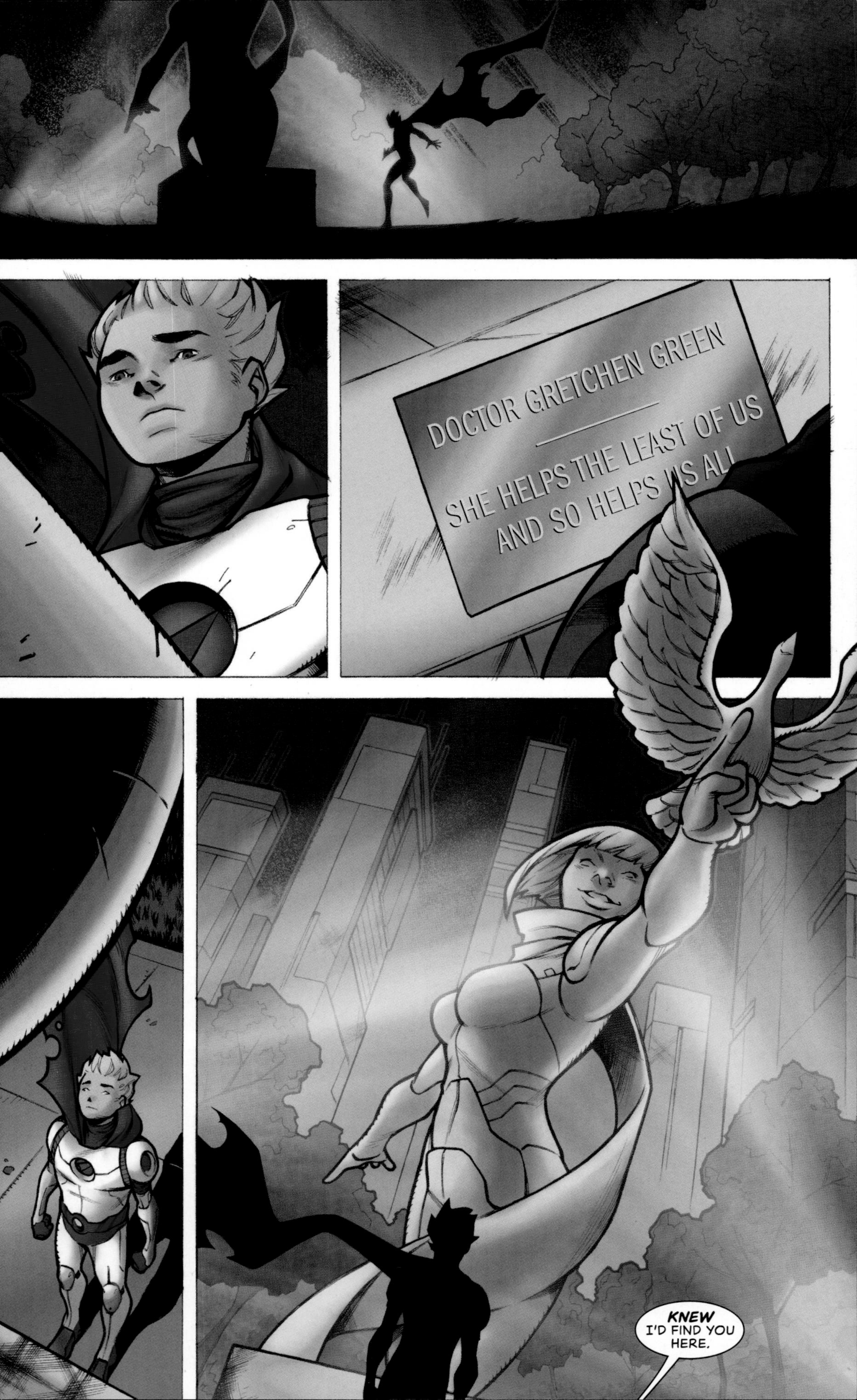
DOCTOR GRETCHEN GREEN
SHE HELPS THE LEAST OF US AND SO HELPS US ALL
KNEW I'D FIND YOU HERE.

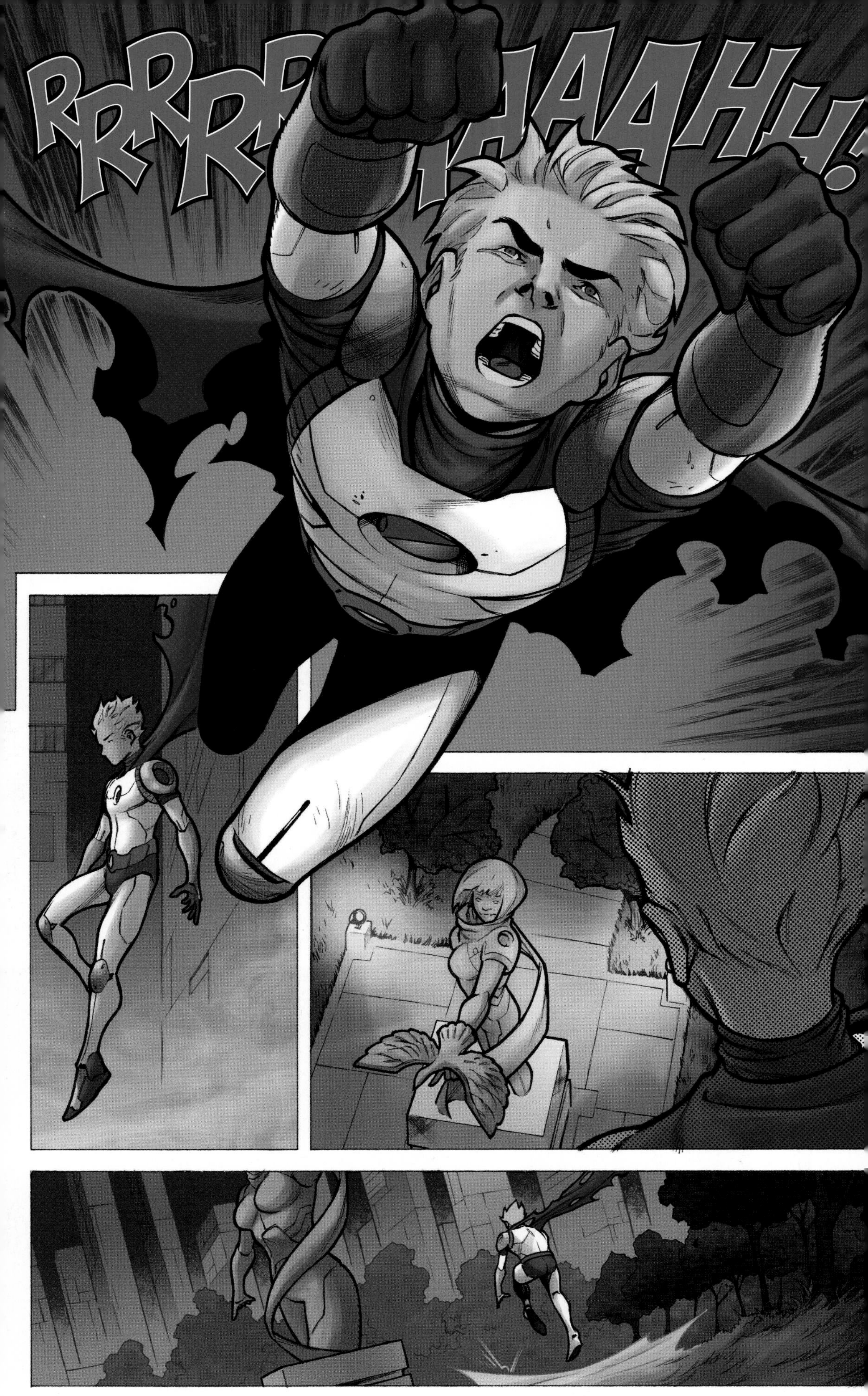
RRRRR AAAAHH!

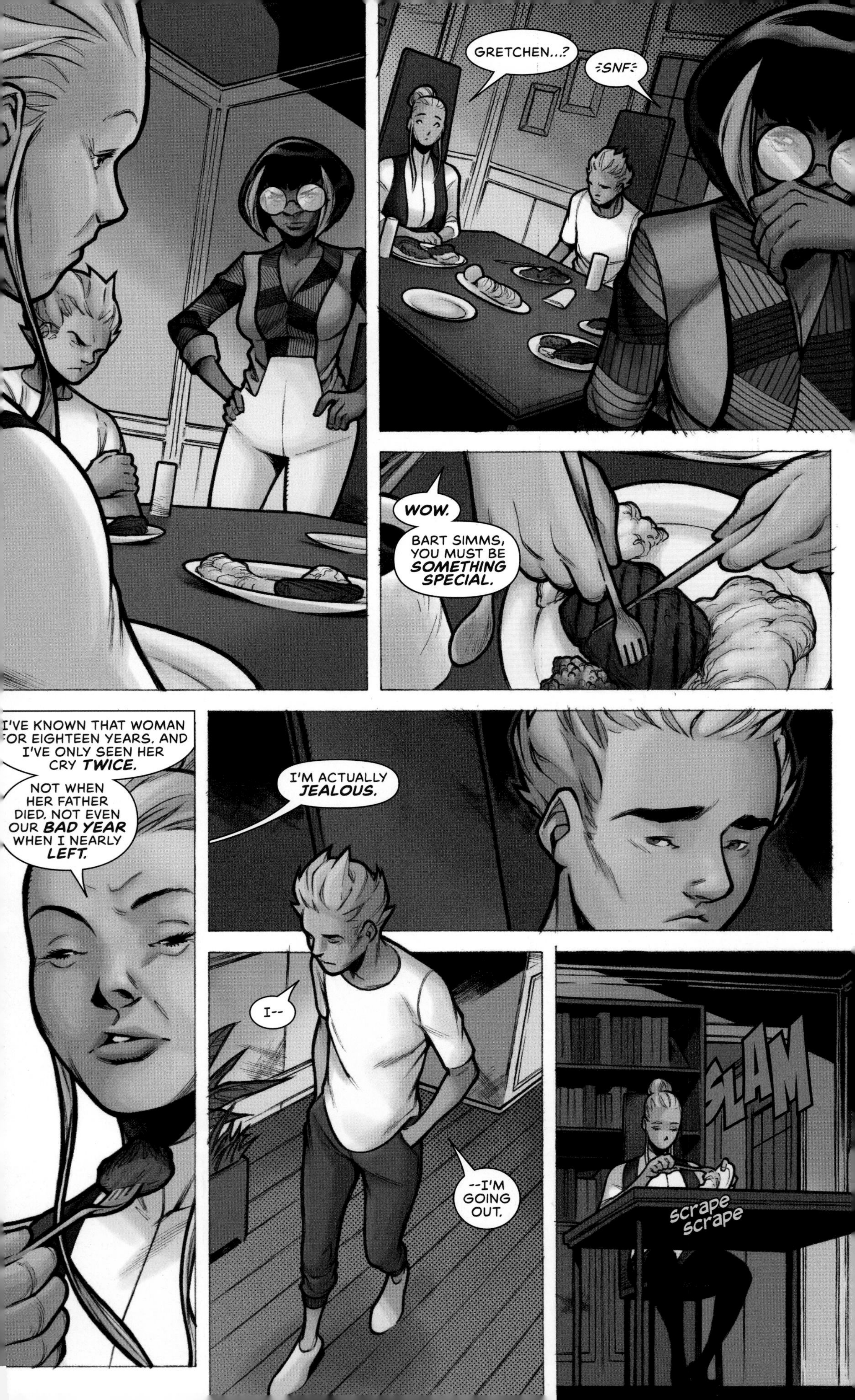
GRETCHEN...?
SNF
WOW.
BART SIMMS, YOU MUST BE SOMETHING SPECIAL.
I'VE KNOWN THAT WOMAN FOR EIGHTEEN YEARS. AND I'VE ONLY SEEN HER CRY TWICE.
NOT WHEN HER FATHER DIED. NOT EVEN OUR BAD YEAR WHEN I NEARLY LEFT.
I'M ACTUALLY JEALOUS.
I--
--I'M GOING OUT.
SLAM
scrape scrape

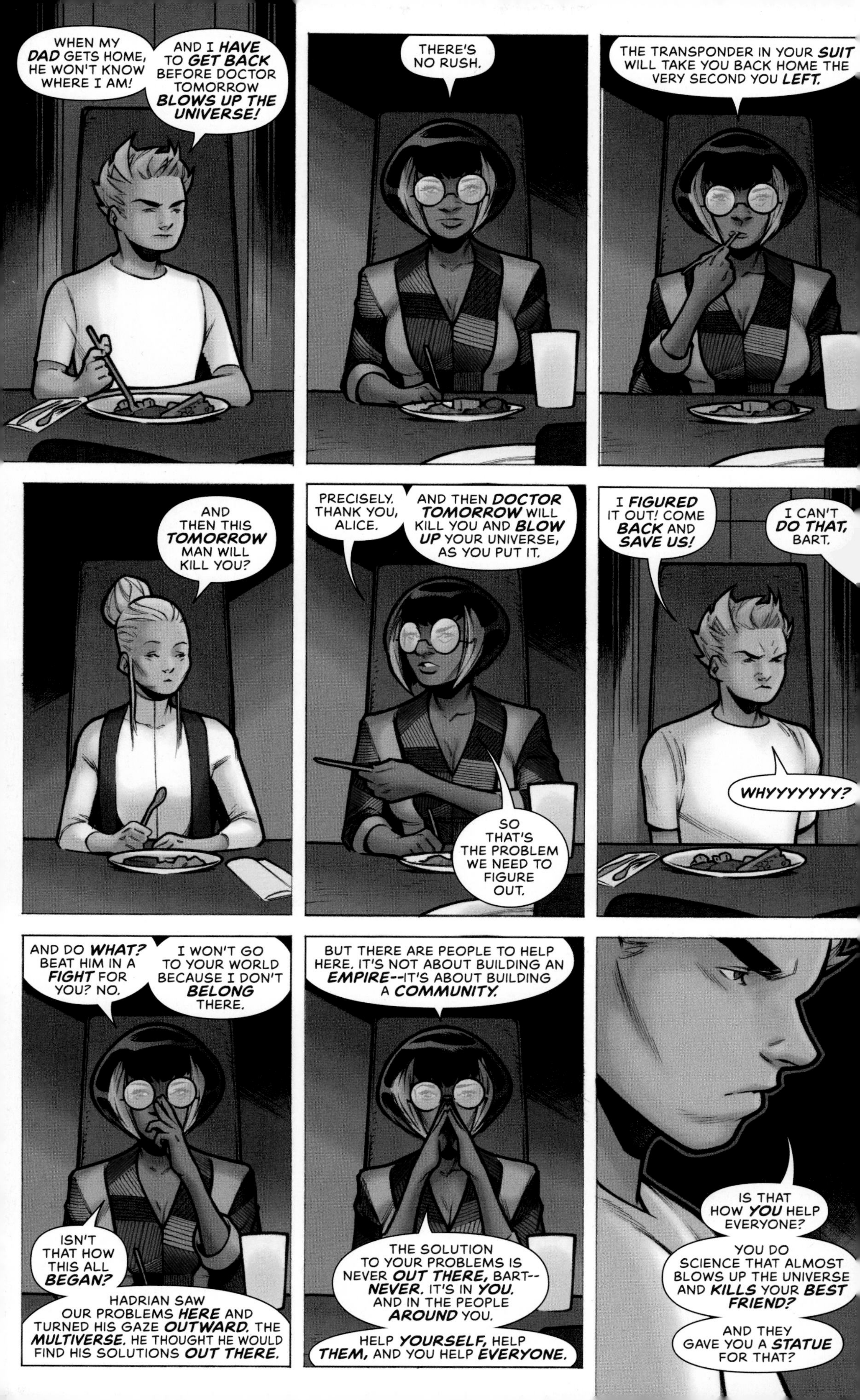
WHEN MY DAD GETS HOME, HE WON'T KNOW WHERE I AM!
AND I HAVE TO GET BACK BEFORE DOCTOR TOMORROW BLOWS UP THE UNIVERSE!
THERE'S NO RUSH.
THE TRANSPONDER IN YOUR SUIT WILL TAKE YOU BACK HOME THE VERY SECOND YOU LEFT.
AND THEN THIS TOMORROW MAN WILL KILL YOU?
PRECISELY. THANK YOU, ALICE.
AND THEN DOCTOR TOMORROW WILL KILL YOU AND BLOW UP YOUR UNIVERSE, AS YOU PUT IT.
SO THAT'S THE PROBLEM WE NEED TO FIGURE OUT.
I FIGURED IT OUT! COME BACK AND SAVE US!
I CAN'T DO THAT, BART.
WHYYYYYYY?
AND DO WHAT? BEAT HIM IN A FIGHT FOR YOU? NO.
I WON'T GO TO YOUR WORLD BECAUSE I DON'T BELONG THERE.
ISN'T THAT HOW THIS ALL BEGAN?
HADRIAN SAW OUR PROBLEMS HERE AND TURNED HIS GAZE OUTWARD. THE MULTIVERSE. HE THOUGHT HE WOULD FIND HIS SOLUTIONS OUT THERE.
BUT THERE ARE PEOPLE TO HELP HERE. IT'S NOT ABOUT BUILDING AN EMPIRE--IT'S ABOUT BUILDING A COMMUNITY.
THE SOLUTION TO YOUR PROBLEMS IS NEVER OUT THERE, BART--NEVER. IT'S IN YOU. AND IN THE PEOPLE AROUND YOU.
HELP YOURSELF, HELP THEM, AND YOU HELP EVERYONE.
IS THAT HOW YOU HELP EVERYONE?
YOU DO SCIENCE THAT ALMOST BLOWS UP THE UNIVERSE AND KILLS YOUR BEST FRIEND?
AND THEY GAVE YOU A STATUE FOR THAT?

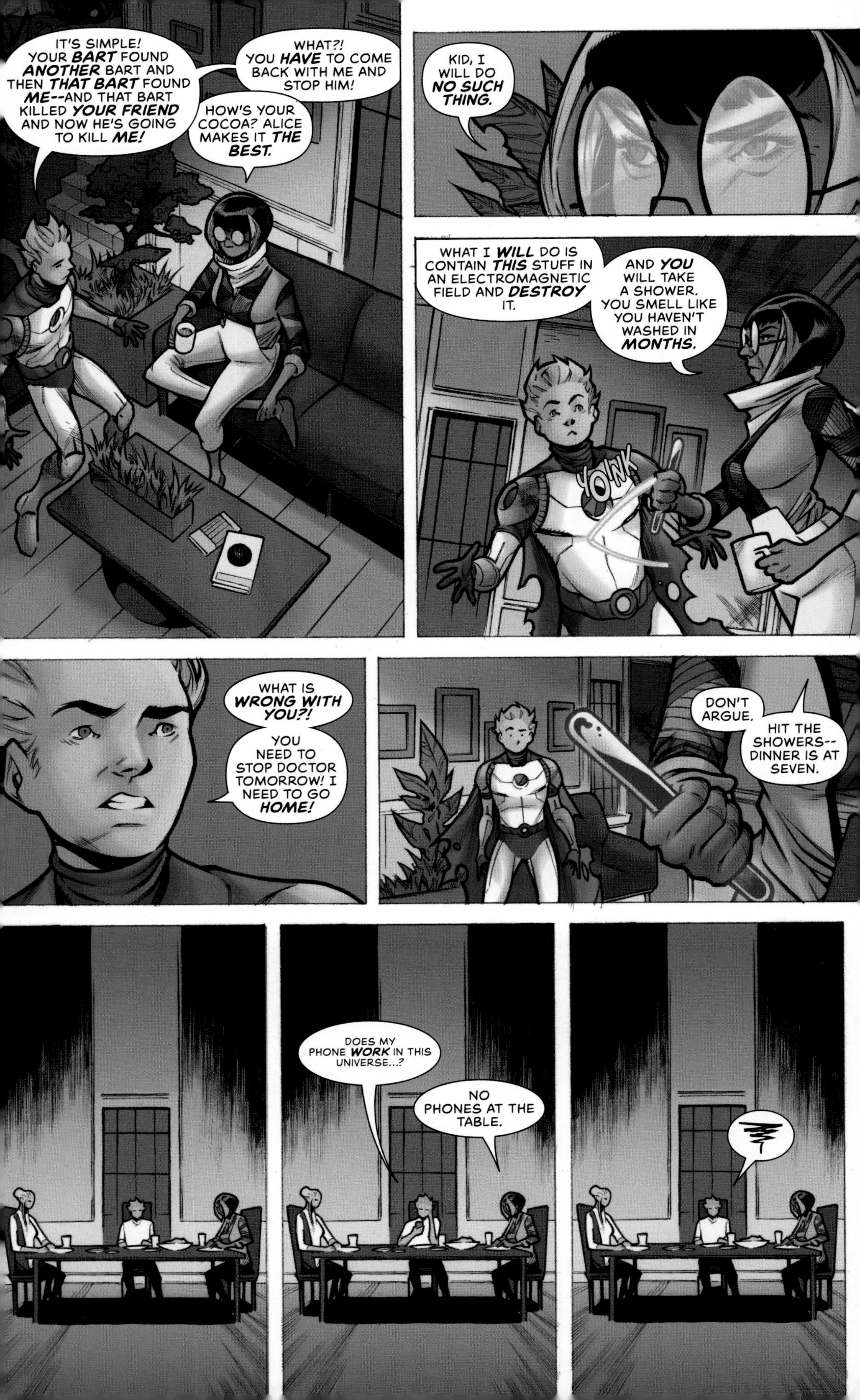
IT'S SIMPLE! YOUR BART FOUND ANOTHER BART AND THEN THAT BART FOUND ME--AND THAT BART KILLED YOUR FRIEND AND NOW HE'S GOING TO KILL ME!
WHAT?! YOU HAVE TO COME BACK WITH ME AND STOP HIM!
HOW'S YOUR COCOA? ALICE MAKES IT THE BEST.
KID, I WILL DO NO SUCH THING.
WHAT I WILL DO IS CONTAIN THIS STUFF IN AN ELECTROMAGNETIC FIELD AND DESTROY IT.
AND YOU WILL TAKE A SHOWER. YOU SMELL LIKE YOU HAVEN'T WASHED IN MONTHS.
YOINK
WHAT IS WRONG WITH YOU?!
YOU NEED TO STOP DOCTOR TOMORROW! I NEED TO GO HOME!
DON'T ARGUE.
HIT THE SHOWERS-- DINNER IS AT SEVEN.
DOES MY PHONE WORK IN THIS UNIVERSE...?
NO PHONES AT THE TABLE.

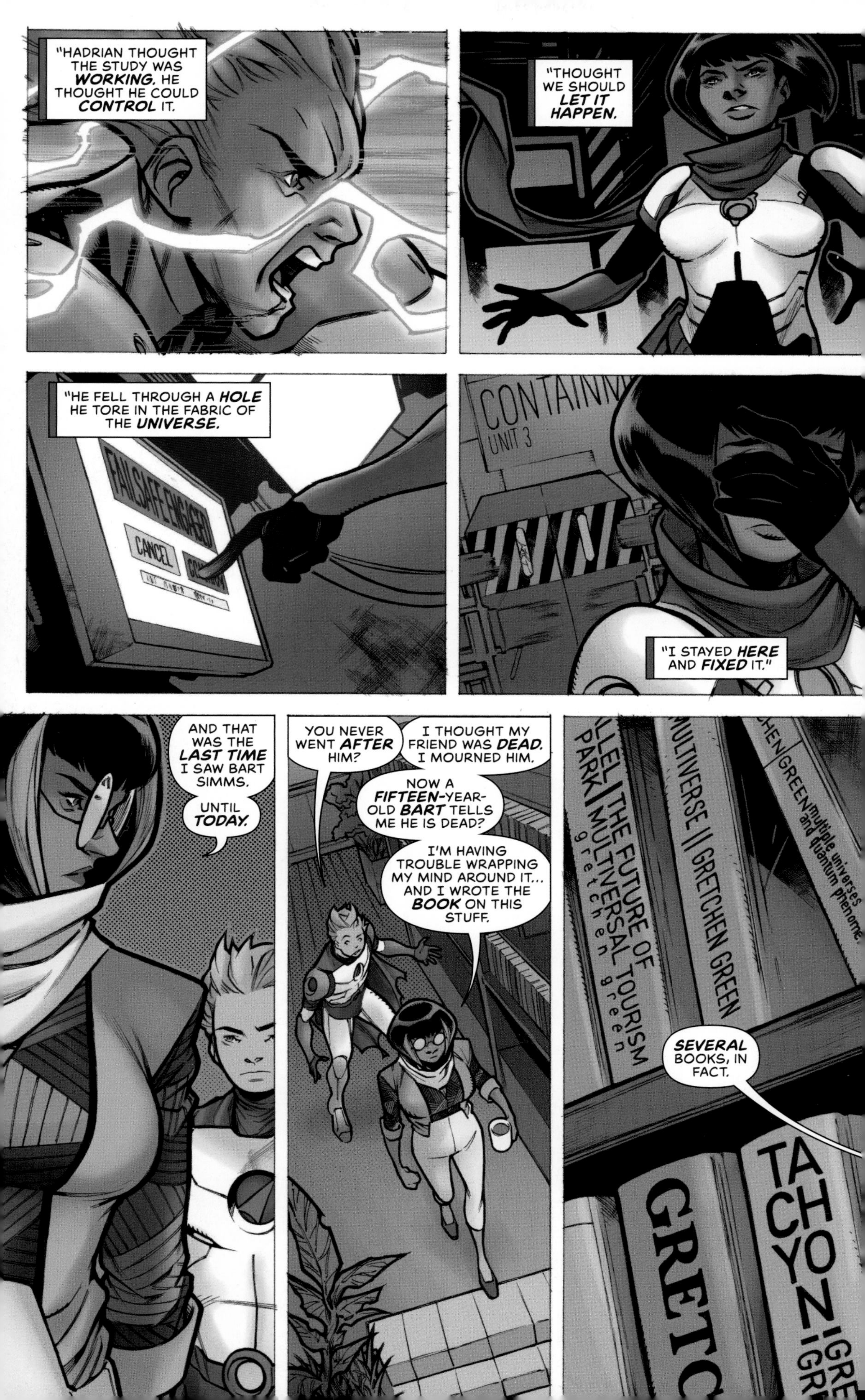
"HADRIAN THOUGHT THE STUDY WAS ***WORKING.*** HE THOUGHT HE COULD ***CONTROL*** IT.
"THOUGHT WE SHOULD ***LET IT HAPPEN.***
"HE FELL THROUGH A ***HOLE*** HE TORE IN THE FABRIC OF THE ***UNIVERSE.***
FAILSAFE ENGAGED
CANCEL
CONTAINM
UNIT 3
"I STAYED ***HERE*** AND ***FIXED*** IT."
AND THAT WAS THE ***LAST TIME*** I SAW BART SIMMS.
UNTIL ***TODAY.***
YOU NEVER WENT ***AFTER*** HIM?
I THOUGHT MY FRIEND WAS ***DEAD.*** I MOURNED HIM.
NOW A ***FIFTEEN-***YEAR-OLD ***BART*** TELLS ME HE IS DEAD?
I'M HAVING TROUBLE WRAPPING MY MIND AROUND IT... AND I WROTE THE ***BOOK*** ON THIS STUFF.
THE FUTURE OF MULTIVERSAL TOURISM
gretchen green
MULTIVERSE || GRETCHEN GREEN
multiple universes and quantum phenome
SEVERAL BOOKS, IN FACT.
TACHYON

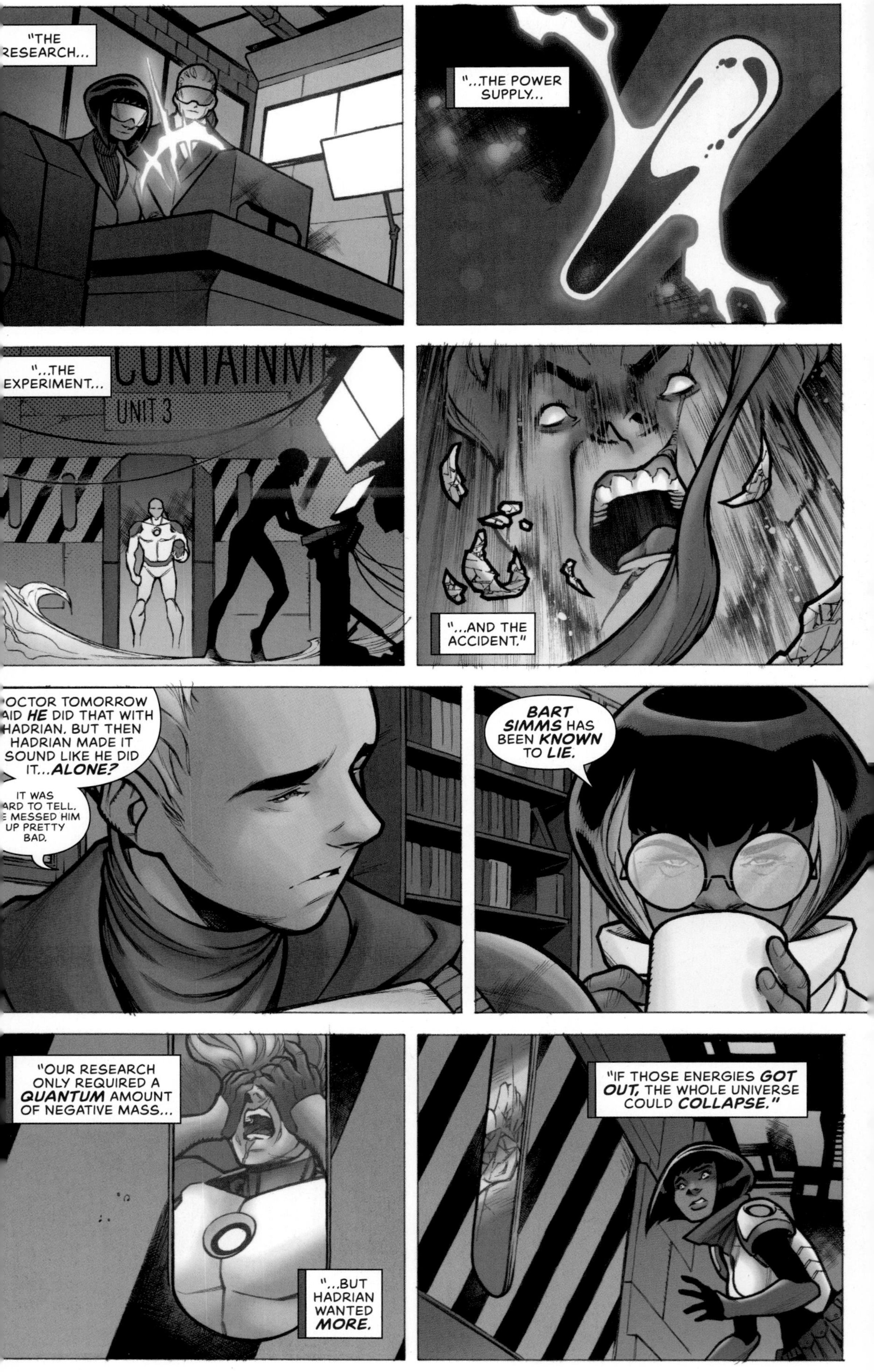

"THE
RESEARCH...
"...THE POWER SUPPLY...
CONTAINM
UNIT 3
"...THE EXPERIMENT...
"...AND THE ACCIDENT."
OCTOR TOMORROW AID HE DID THAT WITH HADRIAN. BUT THEN HADRIAN MADE IT SOUND LIKE HE DID IT...ALONE?
IT WAS ARD TO TELL. E MESSED HIM UP PRETTY BAD.
BART SIMMS HAS BEEN KNOWN TO LIE.
"OUR RESEARCH ONLY REQUIRED A QUANTUM AMOUNT OF NEGATIVE MASS...
"...BUT HADRIAN WANTED MORE.
"IF THOSE ENERGIES GOT OUT, THE WHOLE UNIVERSE COULD COLLAPSE."

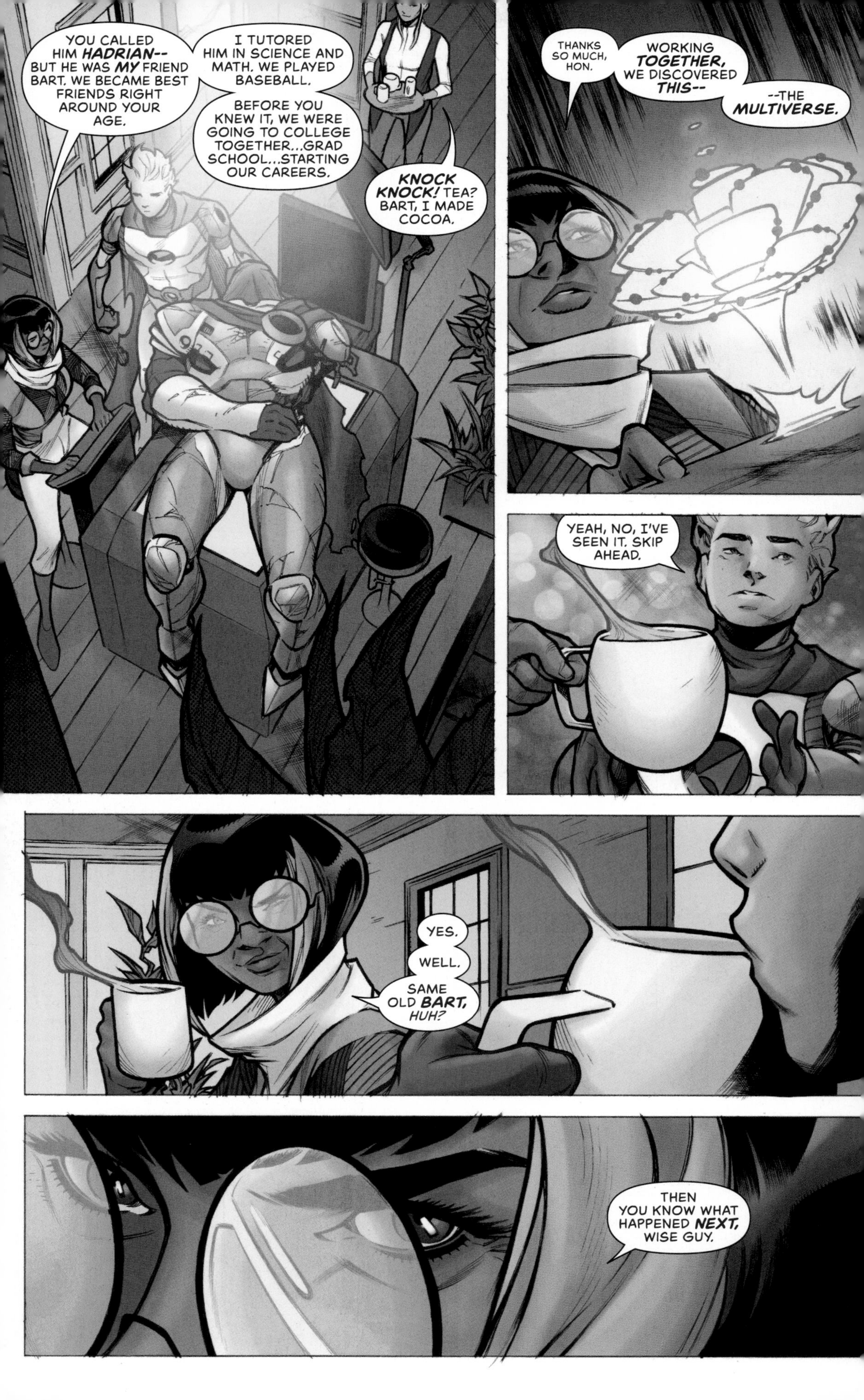
YOU CALLED HIM **HADRIAN**-- BUT HE WAS **MY** FRIEND BART. WE BECAME BEST FRIENDS RIGHT AROUND YOUR AGE.
I TUTORED HIM IN SCIENCE AND MATH. WE PLAYED BASEBALL.
BEFORE YOU KNEW IT, WE WERE GOING TO COLLEGE TOGETHER...GRAD SCHOOL...STARTING OUR CAREERS.
KNOCK KNOCK! TEA? BART, I MADE COCOA.
THANKS SO MUCH, HON.
WORKING **TOGETHER,** WE DISCOVERED **THIS**--
--THE **MULTIVERSE.**
YEAH, NO, I'VE SEEN IT. SKIP AHEAD.
YES.
WELL.
SAME OLD **BART,** *HUH?*
THEN YOU KNOW WHAT HAPPENED **NEXT,** WISE GUY.

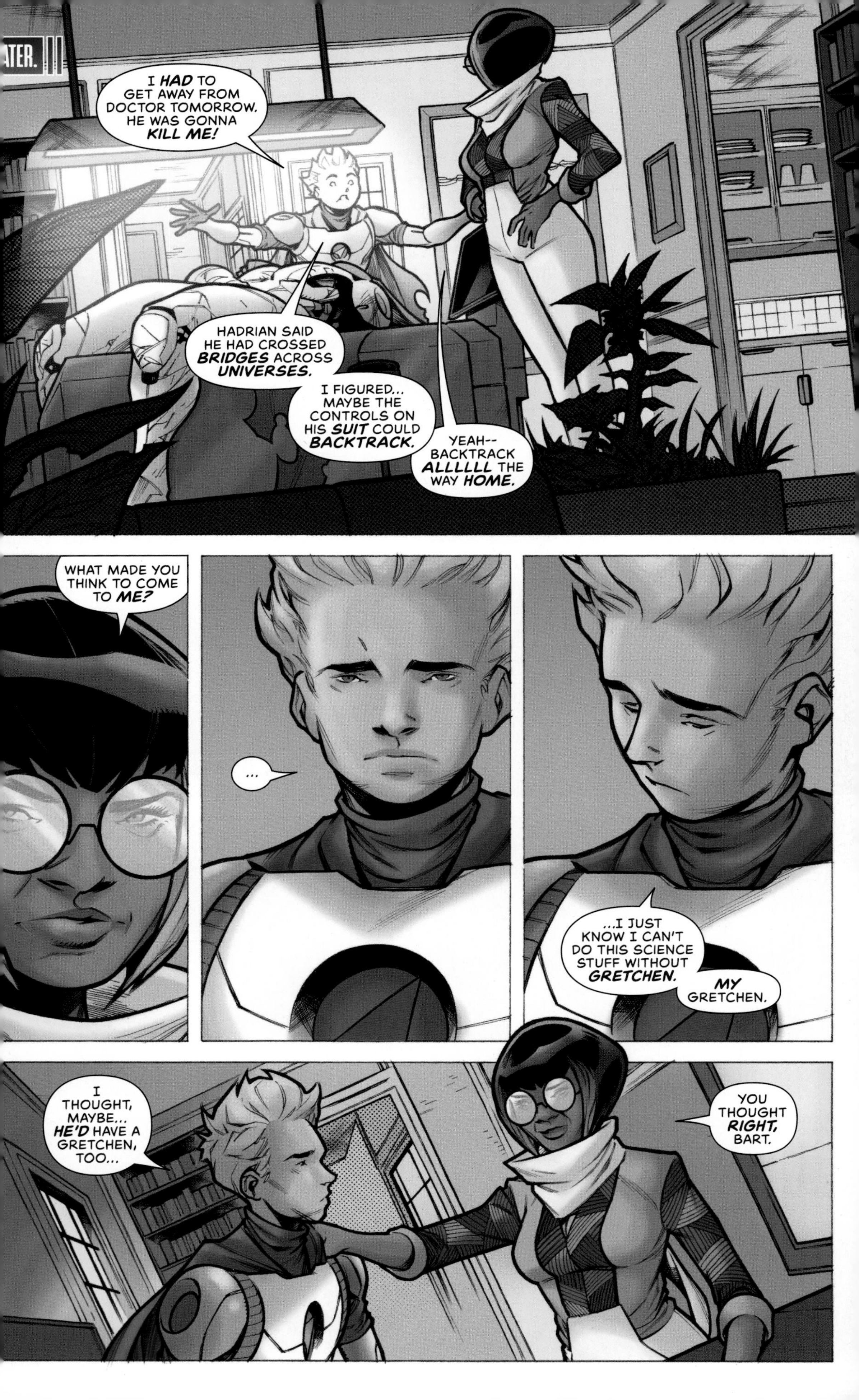
ATER.
I HAD TO GET AWAY FROM DOCTOR TOMORROW. HE WAS GONNA KILL ME!
HADRIAN SAID HE HAD CROSSED BRIDGES ACROSS UNIVERSES.
I FIGURED... MAYBE THE CONTROLS ON HIS SUIT COULD BACKTRACK.
YEAH-- BACKTRACK ALLLLLL THE WAY HOME.
WHAT MADE YOU THINK TO COME TO ME?
...
...I JUST KNOW I CAN'T DO THIS SCIENCE STUFF WITHOUT GRETCHEN.
MY GRETCHEN.
I THOUGHT, MAYBE... HE'D HAVE A GRETCHEN, TOO...
YOU THOUGHT RIGHT, BART.

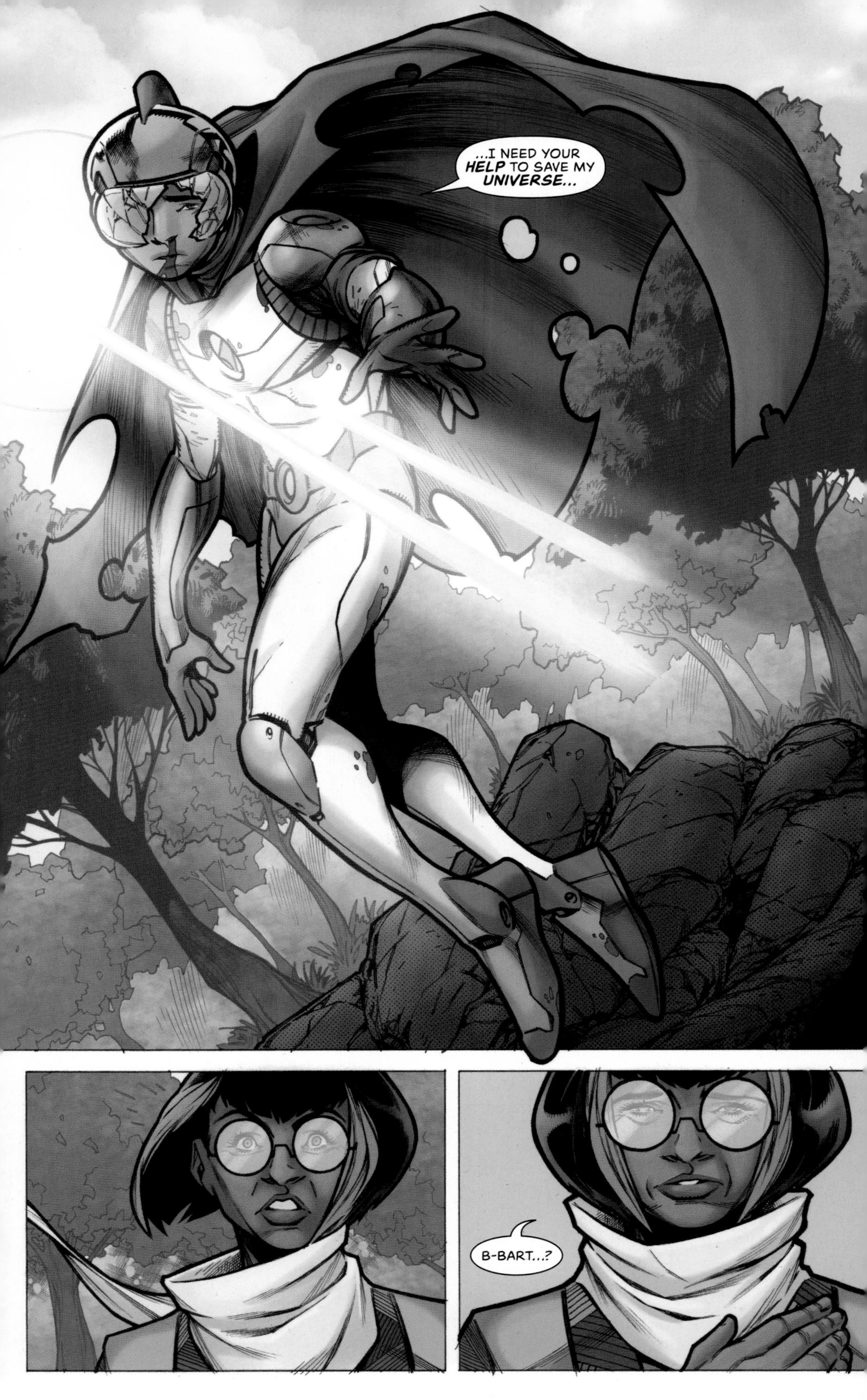
...I NEED YOUR HELP TO SAVE MY UNIVERSE...
B-BART...?

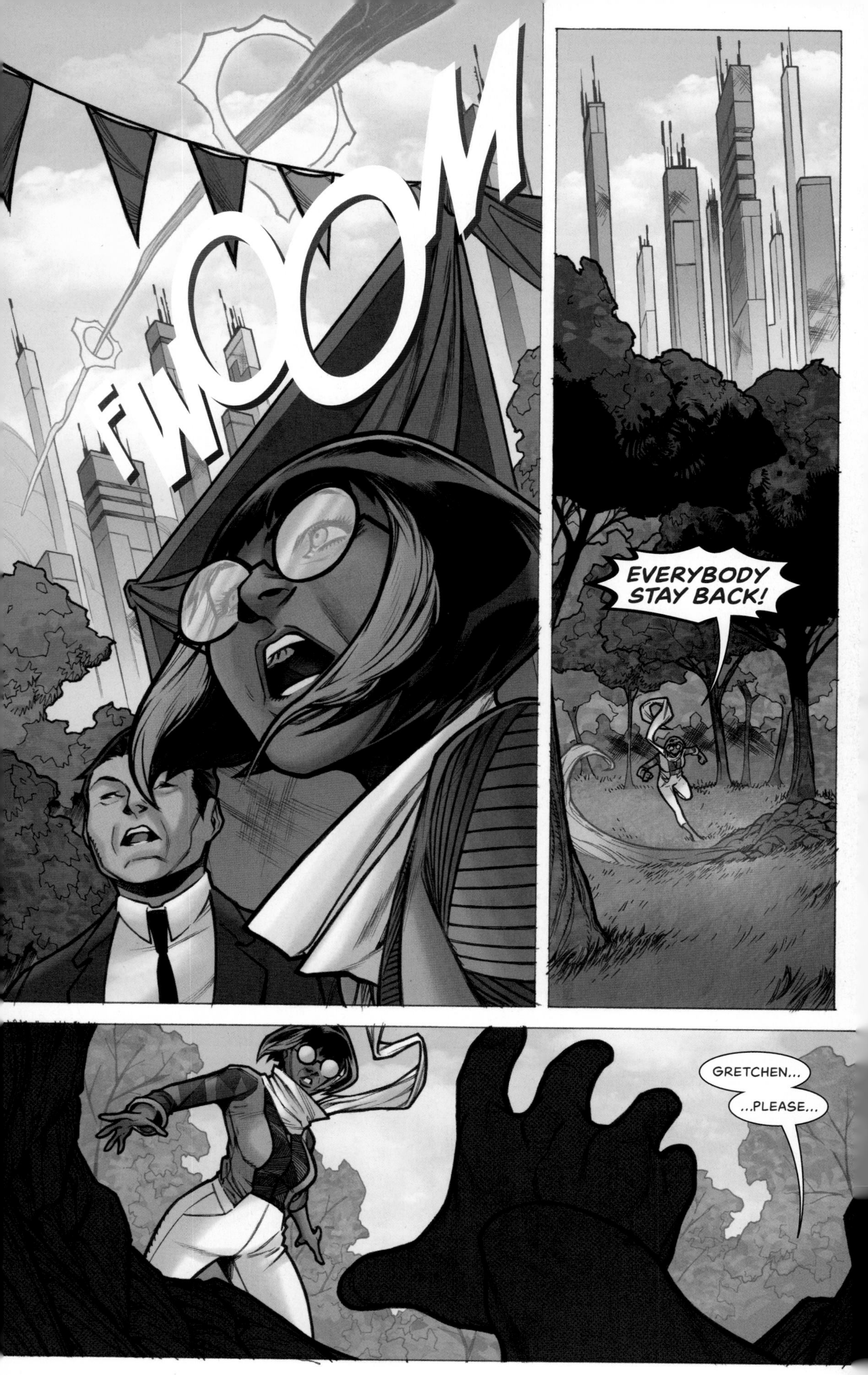
FWOOM
EVERYBODY STAY BACK!
GRETCHEN...
...PLEASE...

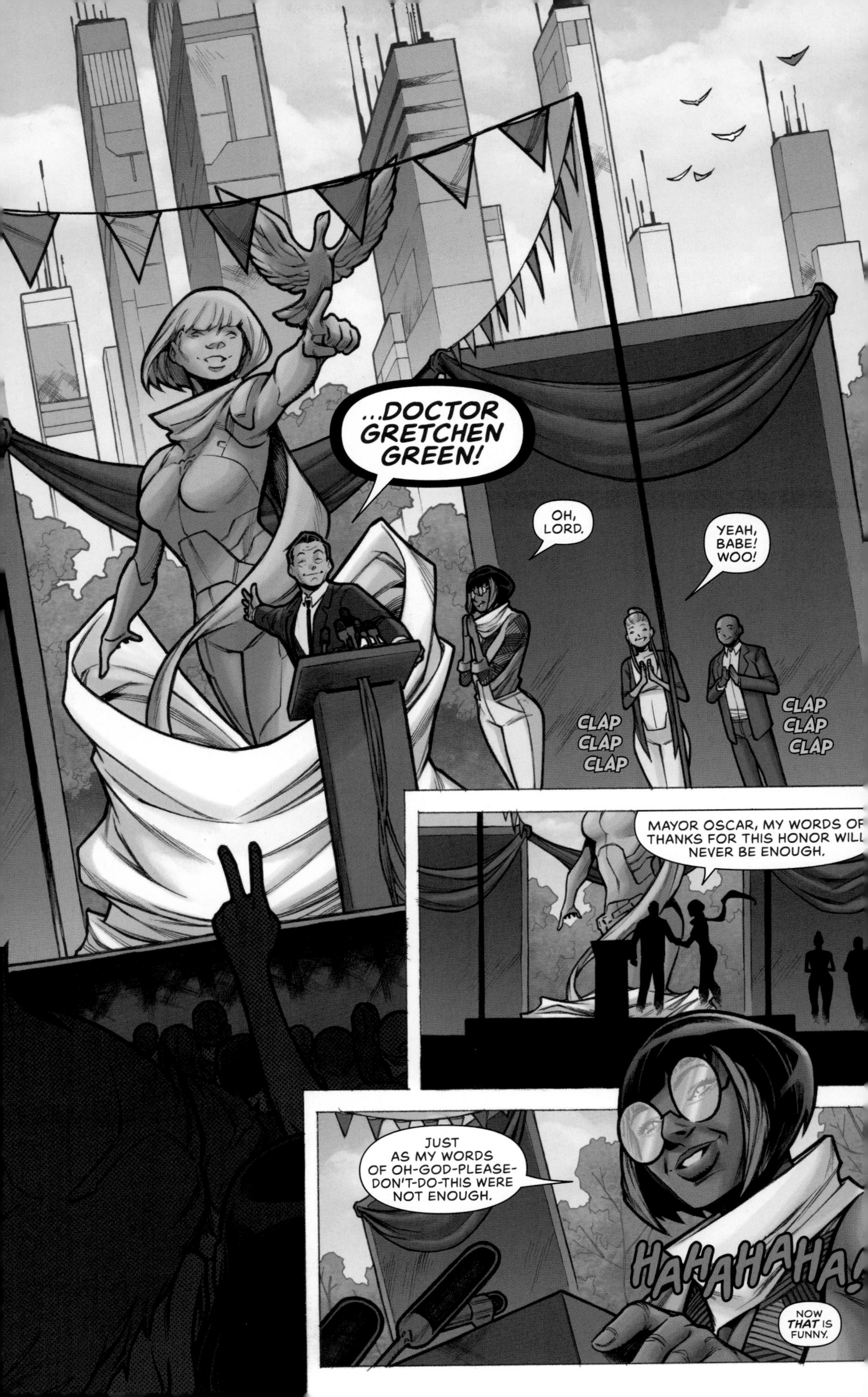
...DOCTOR GRETCHEN GREEN!
OH, LORD.
YEAH, BABE! WOO!
CLAP CLAP CLAP
CLAP CLAP CLAP
MAYOR OSCAR, MY WORDS OF THANKS FOR THIS HONOR WILL NEVER BE ENOUGH.
JUST AS MY WORDS OF OH-GOD-PLEASE-DON'T-DO-THIS WERE NOT ENOUGH.
HAHAHAHA!
NOW THAT IS FUNNY.

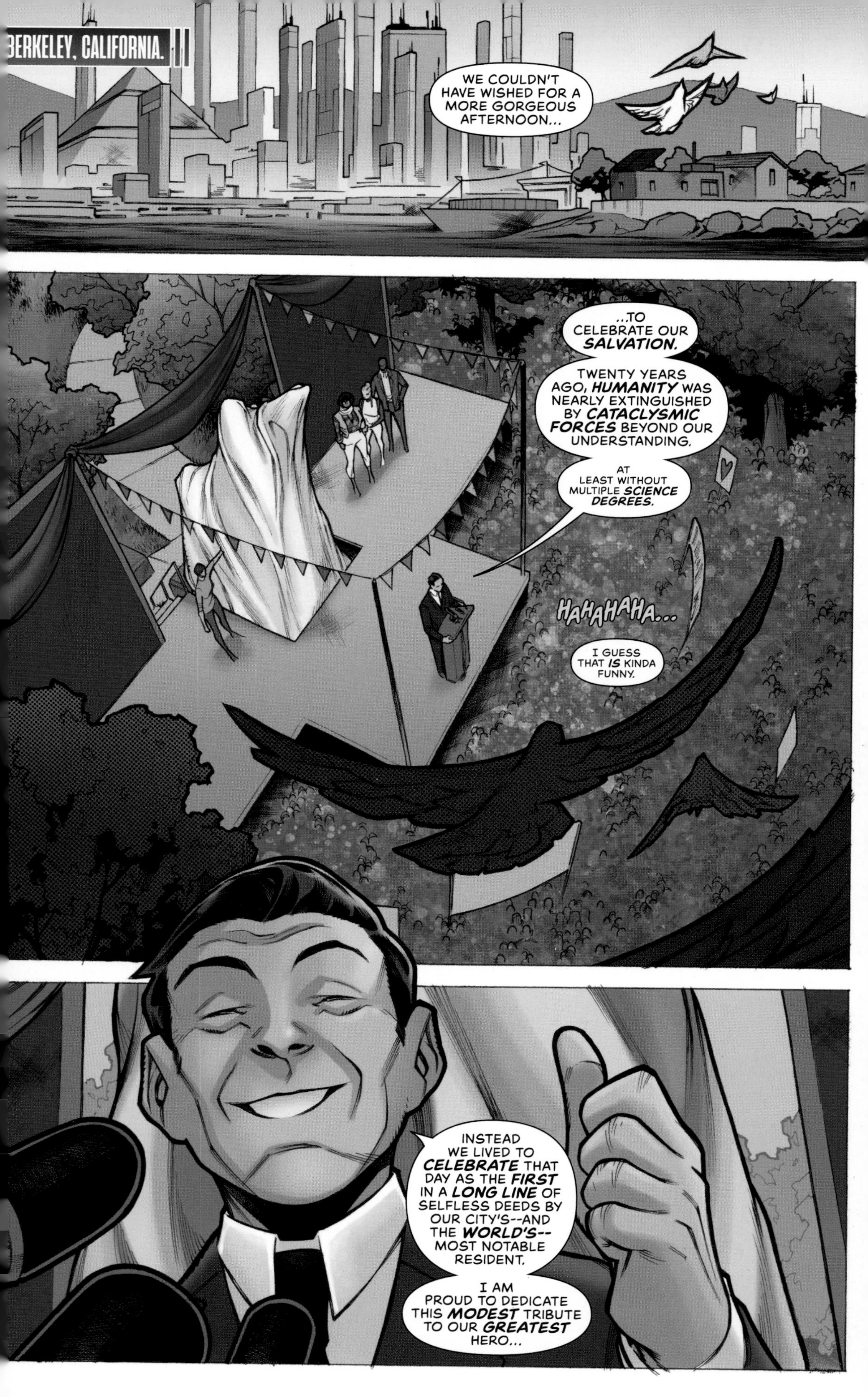
BERKELEY, CALIFORNIA.
WE COULDN'T HAVE WISHED FOR A MORE GORGEOUS AFTERNOON...
...TO CELEBRATE OUR SALVATION.
TWENTY YEARS AGO, HUMANITY WAS NEARLY EXTINGUISHED BY CATACLYSMIC FORCES BEYOND OUR UNDERSTANDING.
AT LEAST WITHOUT MULTIPLE SCIENCE DEGREES.
HAHAHAHA...
I GUESS THAT IS KINDA FUNNY.
INSTEAD WE LIVED TO CELEBRATE THAT DAY AS THE FIRST IN A LONG LINE OF SELFLESS DEEDS BY OUR CITY'S--AND THE WORLD'S--MOST NOTABLE RESIDENT.
I AM PROUD TO DEDICATE THIS MODEST TRIBUTE TO OUR GREATEST HERO...

DOCTOR TOMORROW #4

WRITER: ALEJANDRO ARBONA
ARTIST: JIM TOWE
COLORIST: KELLY FITZPATRICK
LETTERER: CLAYTON COWLES
COVER ARTISTS: DAVID LAFUENTE with GERMAN GARCIA
ASSISTANT EDITOR: DREW BAUMGARTNER
SENIOR EDITORIAL DIRECTOR: ROBERT MEYERS

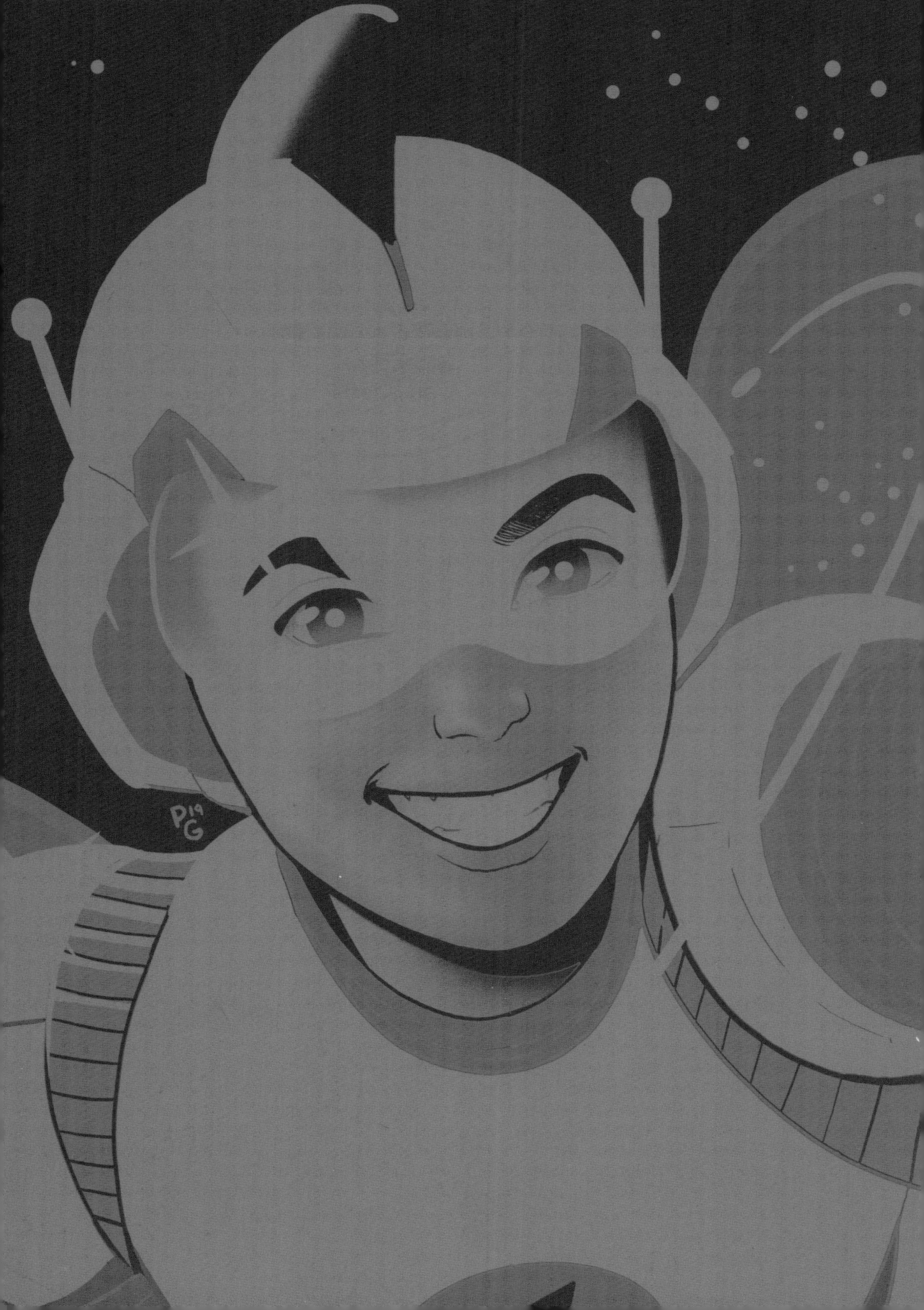

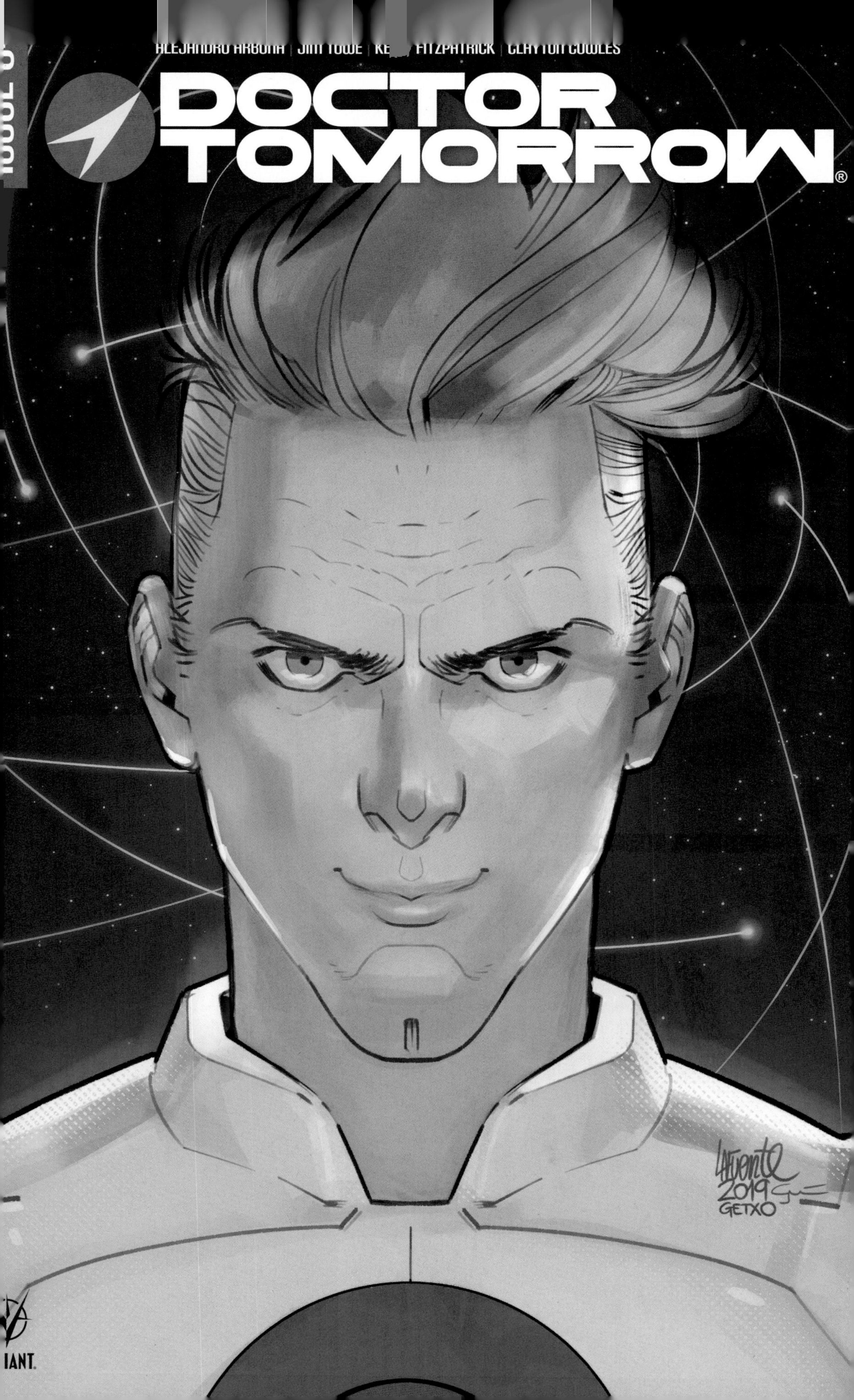

DOCTOR TOMORROW
LaFuente 2019
GETXO

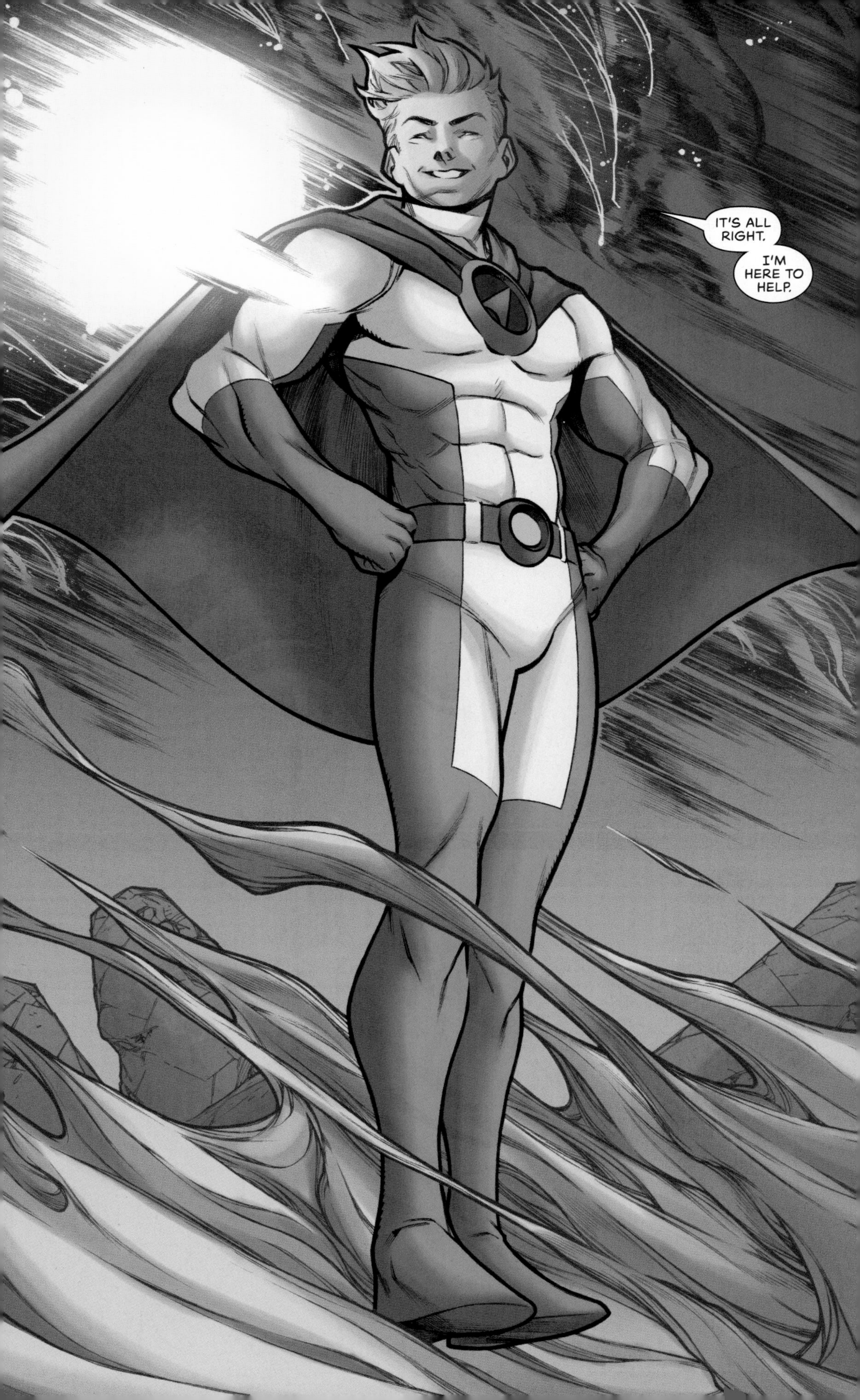
IT'S ALL RIGHT.
I'M HERE TO HELP.

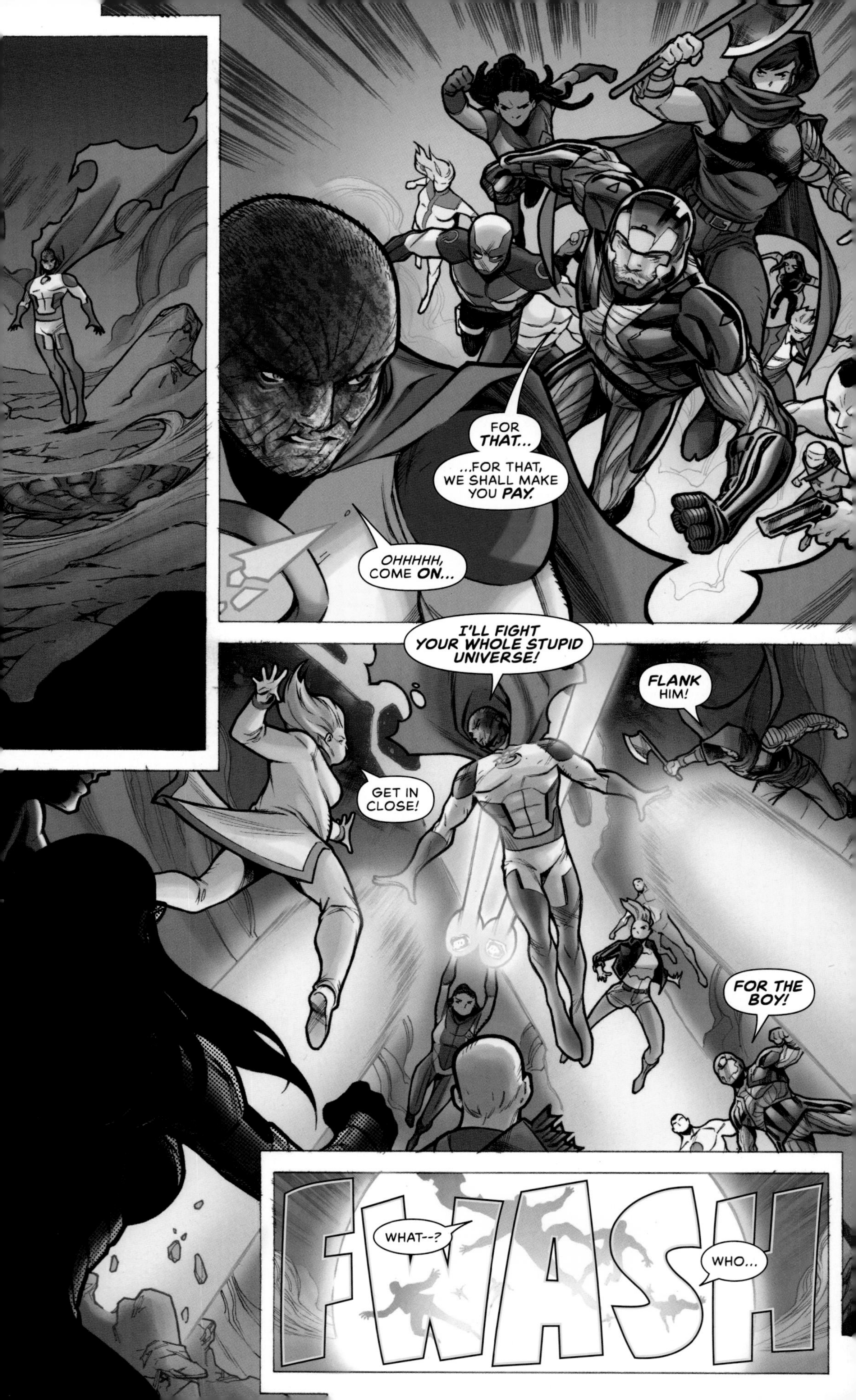
FOR THAT...
...FOR THAT, WE SHALL MAKE YOU PAY.
OHHHHH, COME ON...
I'LL FIGHT YOUR WHOLE STUPID UNIVERSE!
FLANK HIM!
GET IN CLOSE!
FOR THE BOY!
FWASH
WHAT--?
WHO...

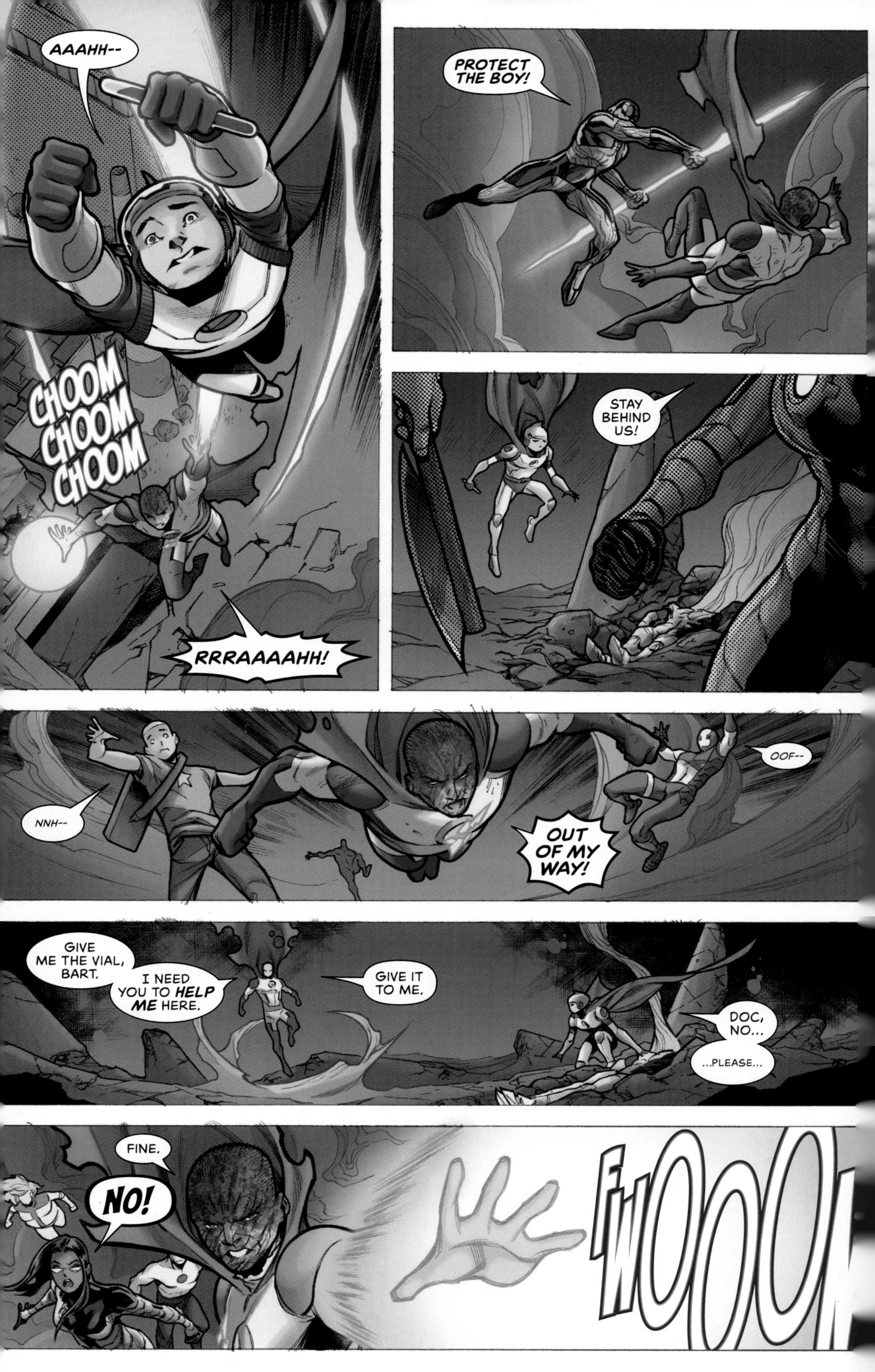
AAAHH--
CHOOM CHOOM CHOOM
RRRAAAAHH!
PROTECT THE BOY!
STAY BEHIND US!
NNH--
OUT OF MY WAY!
OOF--
GIVE ME THE VIAL, BART.
I NEED YOU TO HELP ME HERE.
GIVE IT TO ME.
DOC, NO...
...PLEASE...
FINE.
NO!
FWOOOM

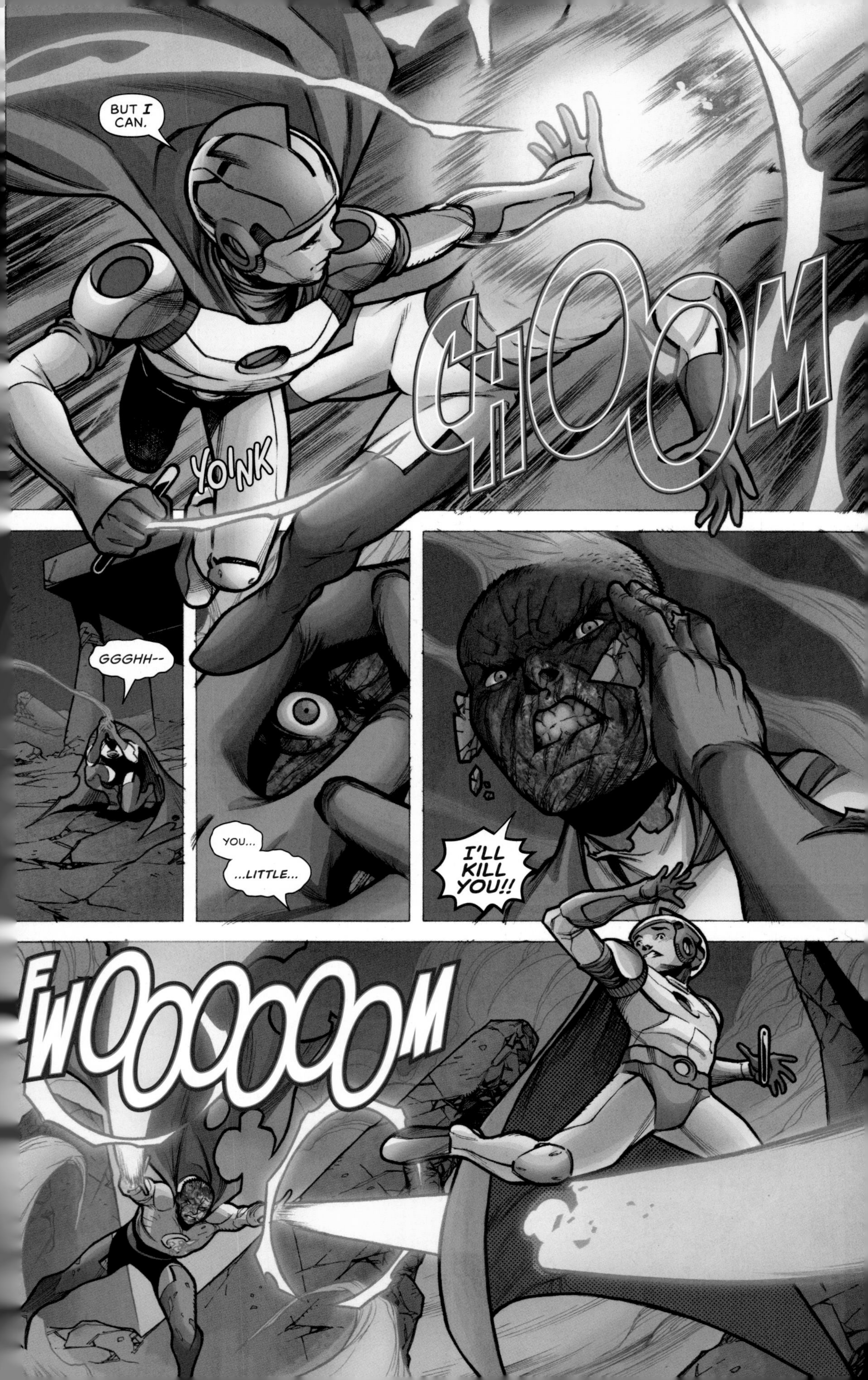
BUT I CAN.
CHOOM
YOINK
GGGHH--
YOU...
...LITTLE...
I'LL KILL YOU!!
FWOOOOOOM

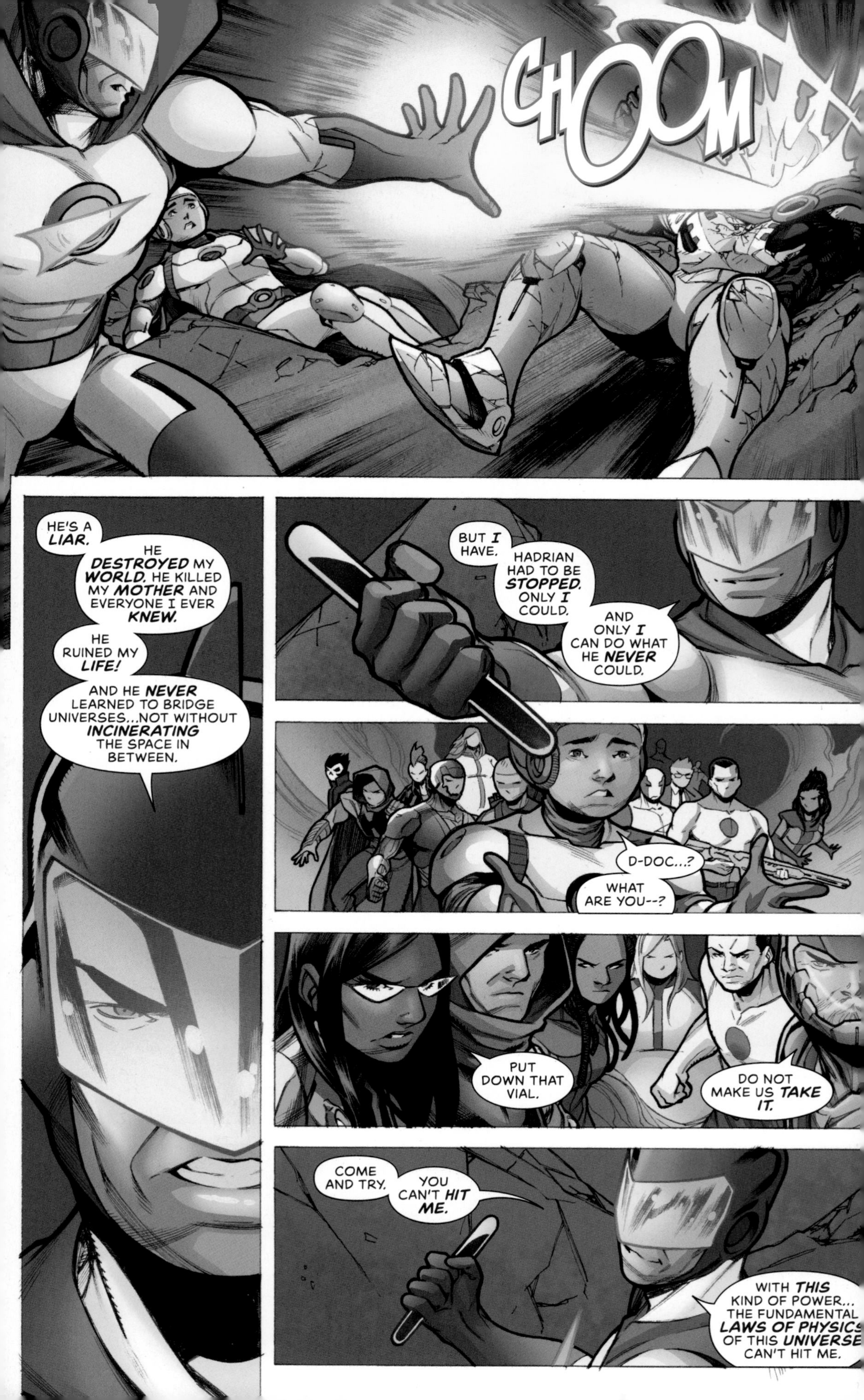
CHOOM
HE'S A LIAR.
HE DESTROYED MY WORLD. HE KILLED MY MOTHER AND EVERYONE I EVER KNEW.
HE RUINED MY LIFE!
AND HE NEVER LEARNED TO BRIDGE UNIVERSES...NOT WITHOUT INCINERATING THE SPACE IN BETWEEN.
BUT I HAVE.
HADRIAN HAD TO BE STOPPED. ONLY I COULD.
AND ONLY I CAN DO WHAT HE NEVER COULD.
D-DOC...?
WHAT ARE YOU--?
PUT DOWN THAT VIAL.
DO NOT MAKE US TAKE IT.
COME AND TRY.
YOU CAN'T HIT ME.
WITH THIS KIND OF POWER... THE FUNDAMENTAL LAWS OF PHYSICS OF THIS UNIVERSE CAN'T HIT ME.

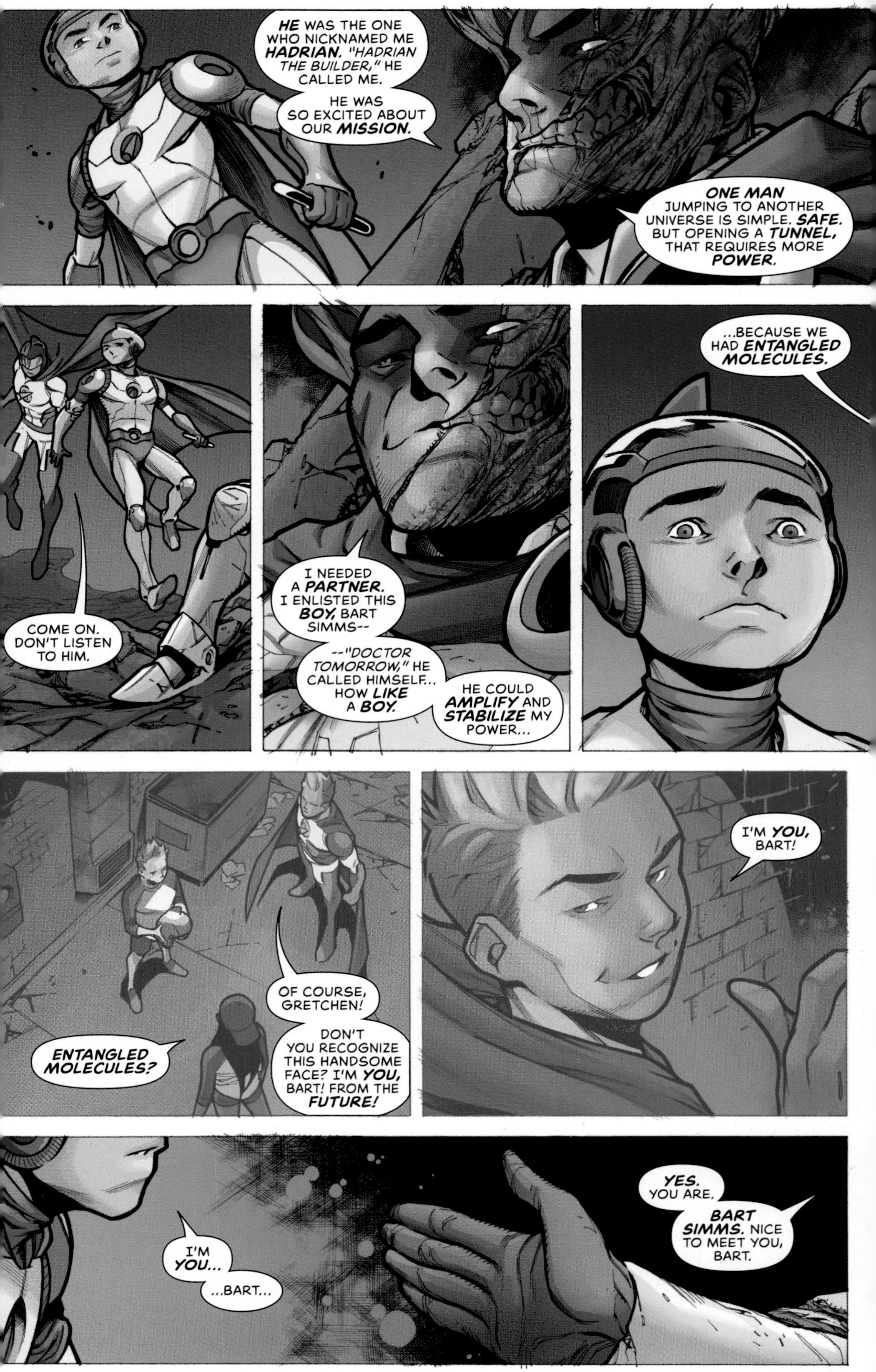
HE WAS THE ONE WHO NICKNAMED ME HADRIAN. "HADRIAN THE BUILDER," HE CALLED ME.
HE WAS SO EXCITED ABOUT OUR MISSION.
ONE MAN JUMPING TO ANOTHER UNIVERSE IS SIMPLE. SAFE. BUT OPENING A TUNNEL, THAT REQUIRES MORE POWER.
COME ON. DON'T LISTEN TO HIM.
I NEEDED A PARTNER. I ENLISTED THIS BOY, BART SIMMS--
--"DOCTOR TOMORROW," HE CALLED HIMSELF... HOW LIKE A BOY.
HE COULD AMPLIFY AND STABILIZE MY POWER...
...BECAUSE WE HAD ENTANGLED MOLECULES.
ENTANGLED MOLECULES?
OF COURSE, GRETCHEN!
DON'T YOU RECOGNIZE THIS HANDSOME FACE? I'M YOU, BART! FROM THE FUTURE!
I'M YOU, BART!
I'M YOU...
...BART...
YES. YOU ARE.
BART SIMMS. NICE TO MEET YOU, BART.

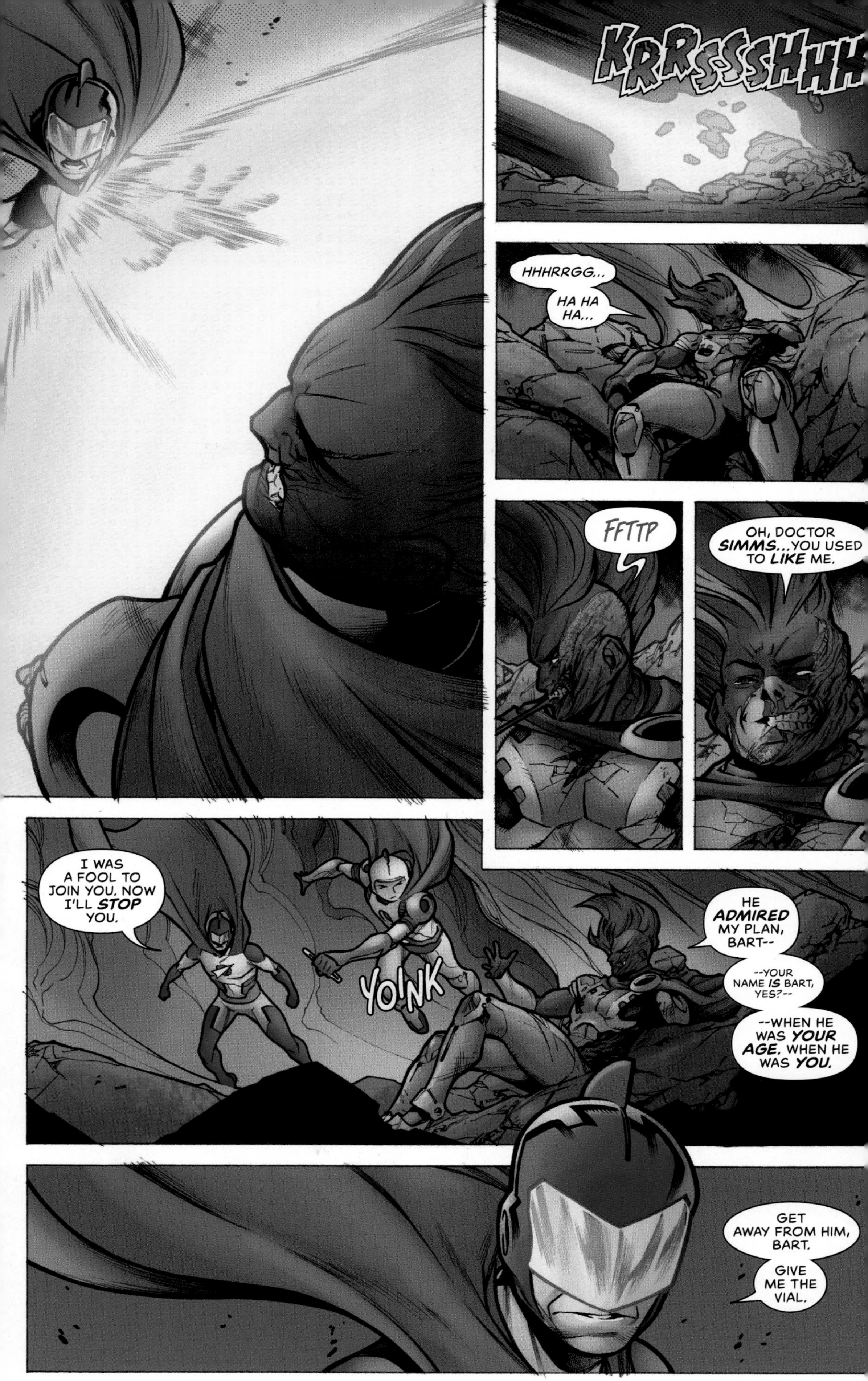
KRRSSSHHH
HHHRRGG...
HA HA HA...
FFTTP
OH, DOCTOR SIMMS...YOU USED TO LIKE ME.
I WAS A FOOL TO JOIN YOU. NOW I'LL STOP YOU.
YOINK
HE ADMIRED MY PLAN, BART--
--YOUR NAME IS BART, YES?--
--WHEN HE WAS YOUR AGE. WHEN HE WAS YOU.
GET AWAY FROM HIM, BART.
GIVE ME THE VIAL.

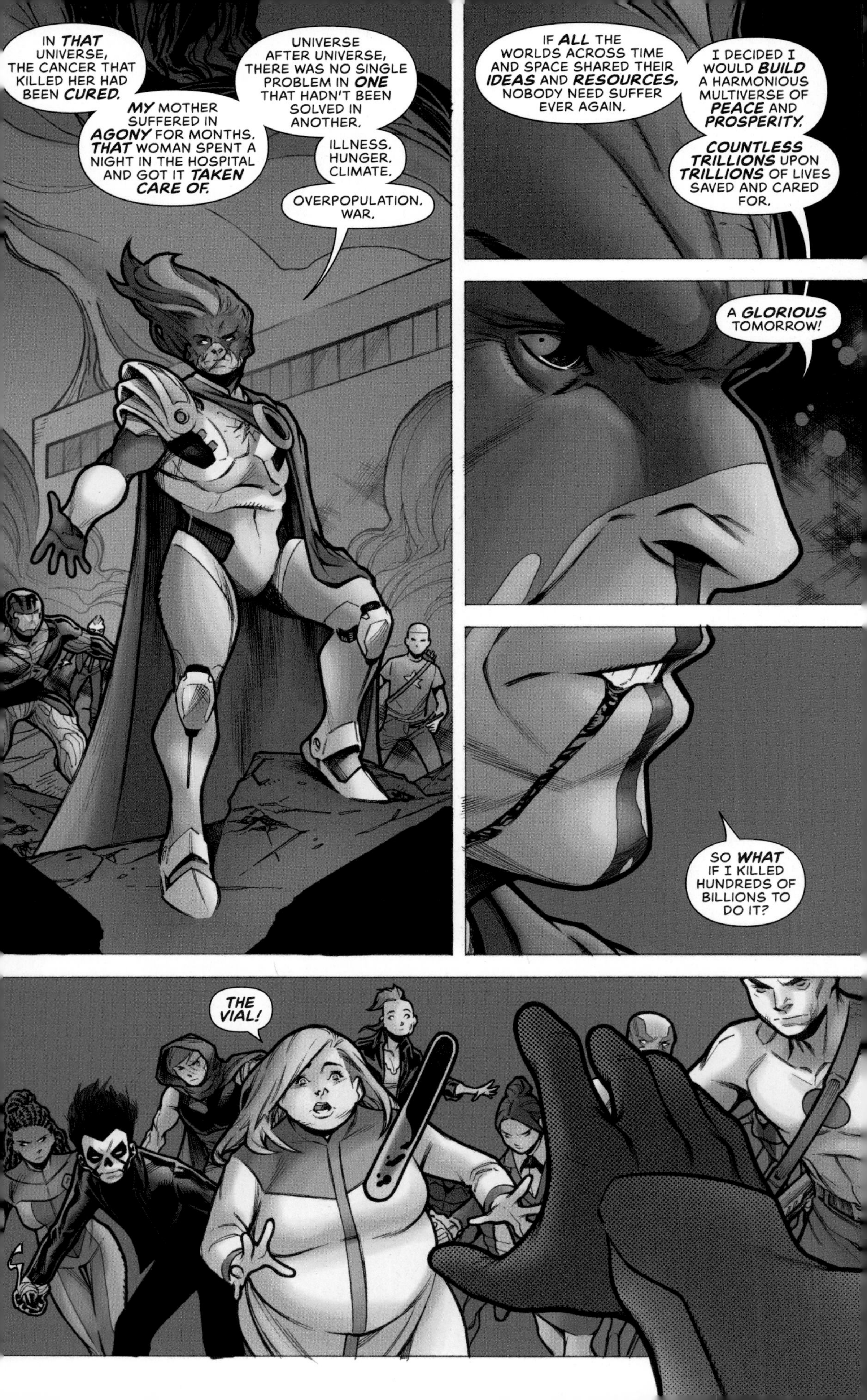
IN **THAT** UNIVERSE, THE CANCER THAT KILLED HER HAD BEEN **CURED.**
MY MOTHER SUFFERED IN **AGONY** FOR MONTHS. **THAT** WOMAN SPENT A NIGHT IN THE HOSPITAL AND GOT IT **TAKEN CARE OF.**
UNIVERSE AFTER UNIVERSE, THERE WAS NO SINGLE PROBLEM IN **ONE** THAT HADN'T BEEN SOLVED IN ANOTHER.
ILLNESS. HUNGER. CLIMATE.
OVERPOPULATION. WAR.
IF **ALL** THE WORLDS ACROSS TIME AND SPACE SHARED THEIR **IDEAS** AND **RESOURCES,** NOBODY NEED SUFFER EVER AGAIN.
I DECIDED I WOULD **BUILD** A HARMONIOUS MULTIVERSE OF **PEACE** AND **PROSPERITY.**
COUNTLESS TRILLIONS UPON **TRILLIONS** OF LIVES SAVED AND CARED FOR.
A **GLORIOUS** TOMORROW!
SO **WHAT** IF I KILLED HUNDREDS OF BILLIONS TO DO IT?
THE VIAL!

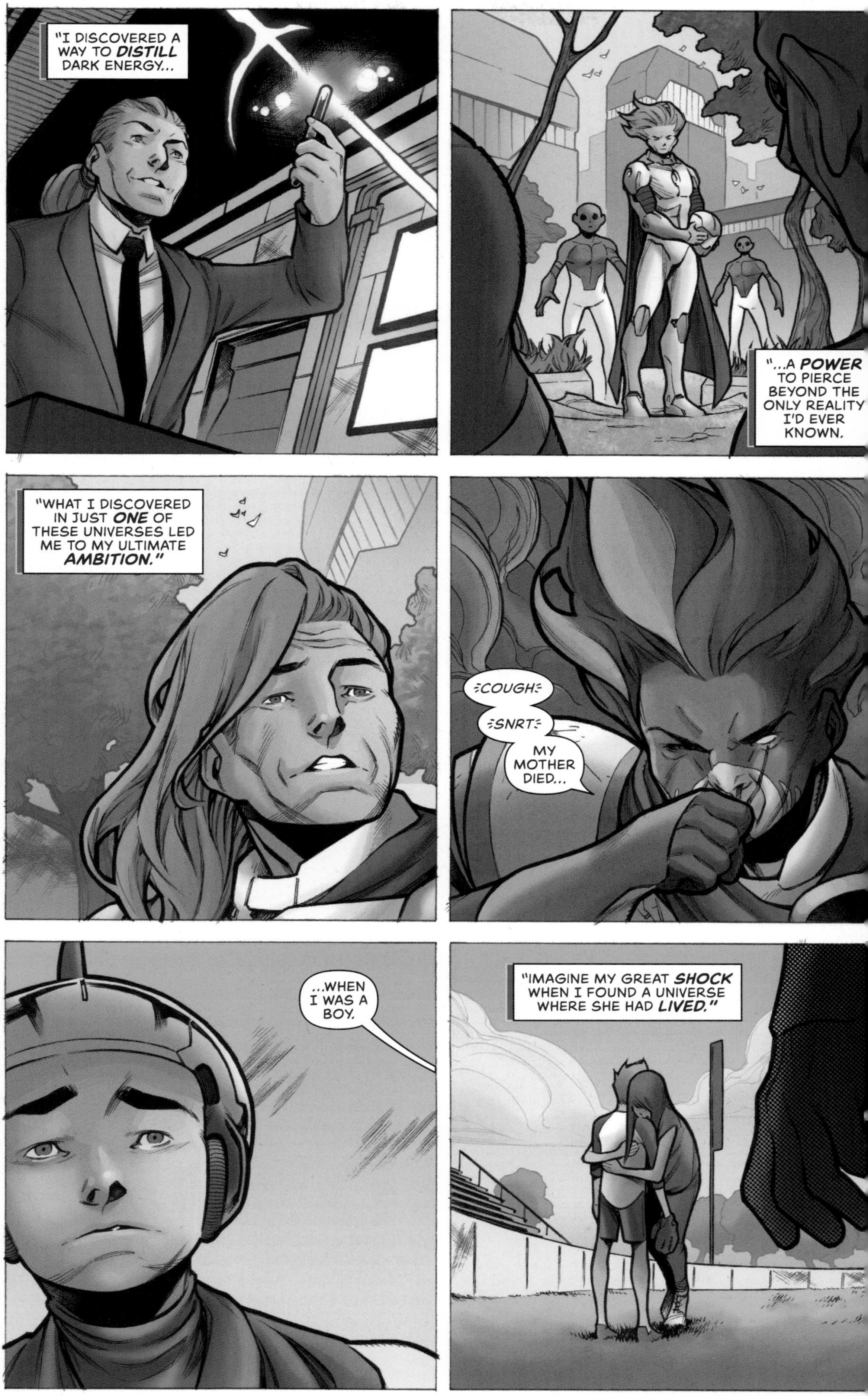
"I DISCOVERED A WAY TO DISTILL DARK ENERGY...
"...A POWER TO PIERCE BEYOND THE ONLY REALITY I'D EVER KNOWN.
"WHAT I DISCOVERED IN JUST ONE OF THESE UNIVERSES LED ME TO MY ULTIMATE AMBITION."
COUGH
SNRT
MY MOTHER DIED...
...WHEN I WAS A BOY.
"IMAGINE MY GREAT SHOCK WHEN I FOUND A UNIVERSE WHERE SHE HAD LIVED."

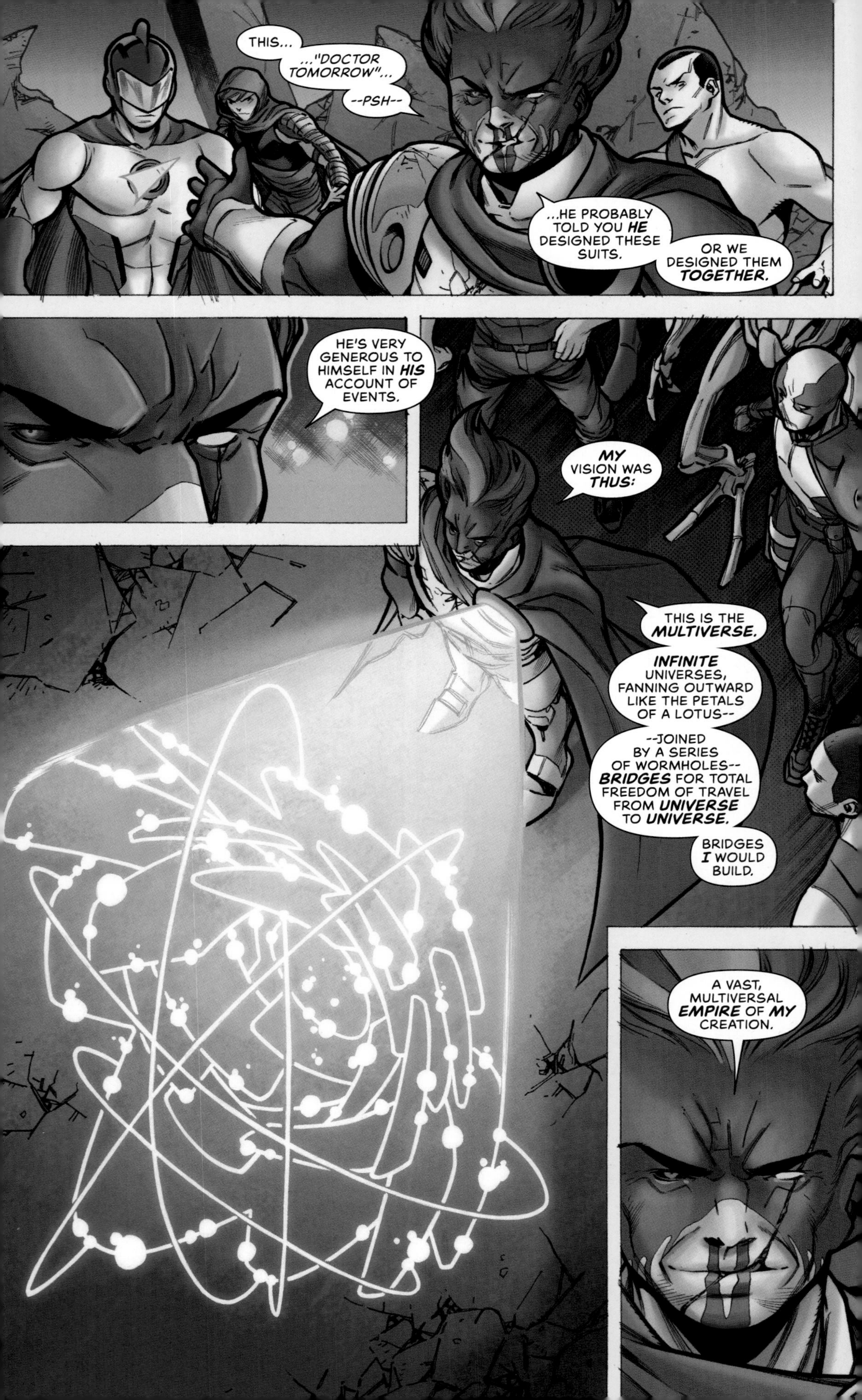
THIS...
..."DOCTOR TOMORROW"...
--PSH--
...HE PROBABLY TOLD YOU **HE** DESIGNED THESE SUITS.
OR WE DESIGNED THEM ***TOGETHER.***
HE'S VERY GENEROUS TO HIMSELF IN ***HIS*** ACCOUNT OF EVENTS.
MY VISION WAS ***THUS:***
THIS IS THE ***MULTIVERSE.***
INFINITE UNIVERSES, FANNING OUTWARD LIKE THE PETALS OF A LOTUS--
--JOINED BY A SERIES OF WORMHOLES--***BRIDGES*** FOR TOTAL FREEDOM OF TRAVEL FROM ***UNIVERSE*** TO ***UNIVERSE.***
BRIDGES ***I*** WOULD BUILD.
A VAST, MULTIVERSAL ***EMPIRE*** OF ***MY*** CREATION.

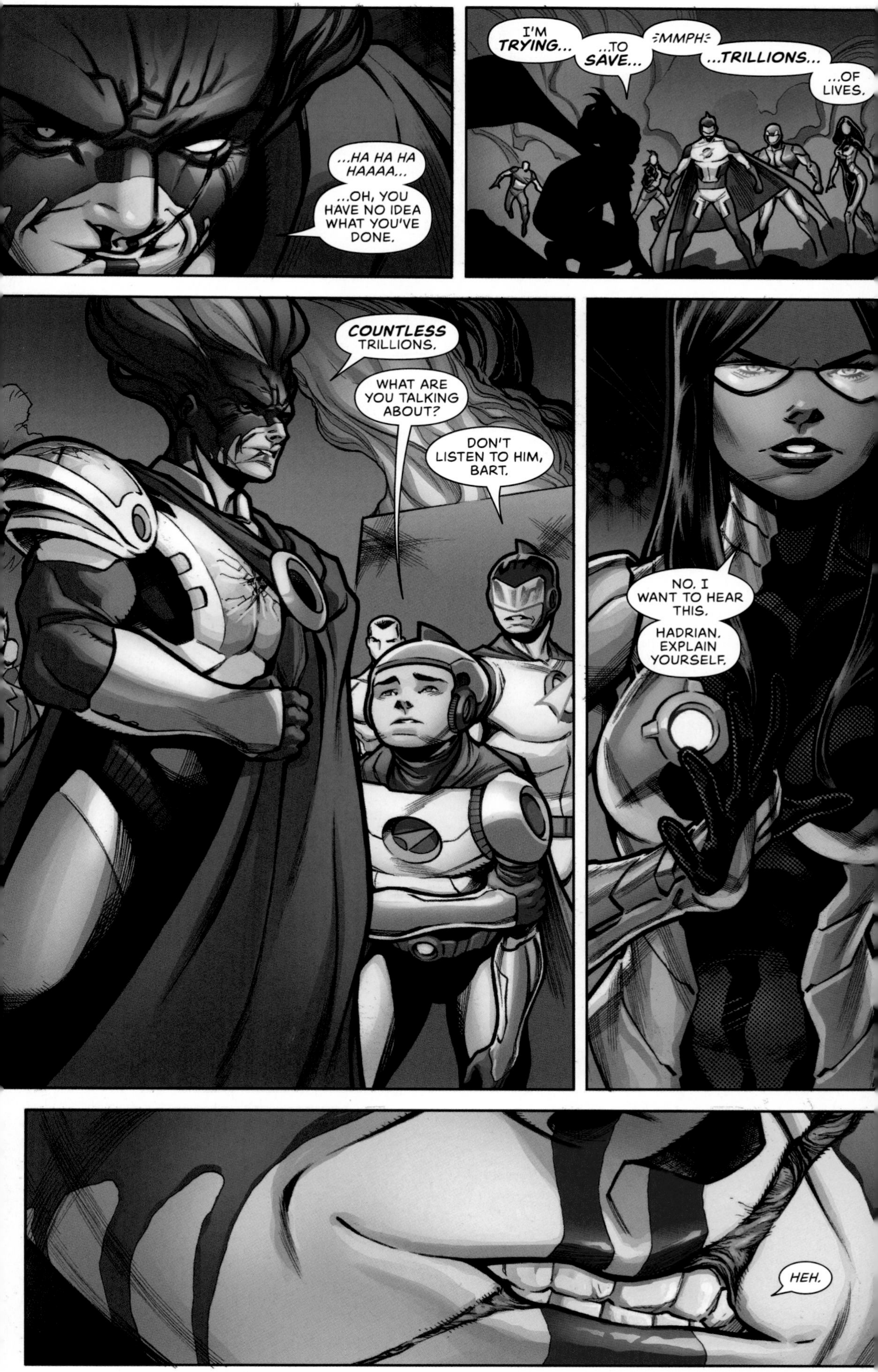
...HA HA HA HAAAA...
...OH, YOU HAVE NO IDEA WHAT YOU'VE DONE.
I'M TRYING...
...TO SAVE...
MMPH
...TRILLIONS...
...OF LIVES.
COUNTLESS TRILLIONS.
WHAT ARE YOU TALKING ABOUT?
DON'T LISTEN TO HIM, BART.
NO. I WANT TO HEAR THIS.
HADRIAN. EXPLAIN YOURSELF.
HEH.

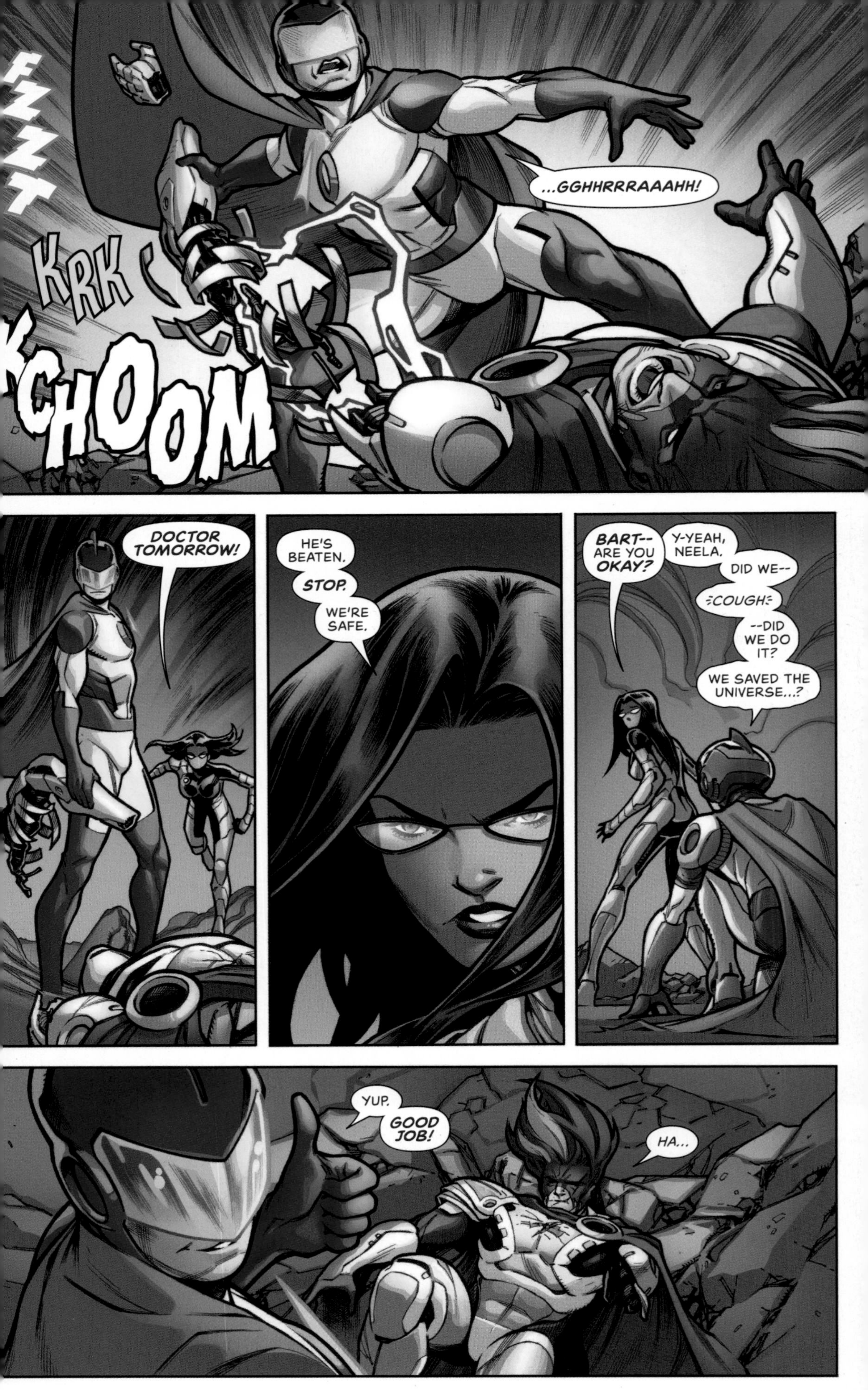
FZZZT
...GGHHRRRAAAHH!
KRK
CHOOM
DOCTOR TOMORROW!
HE'S BEATEN.
STOP.
WE'RE SAFE.
BART-- ARE YOU OKAY?
Y-YEAH, NEELA.
DID WE--
COUGH
--DID WE DO IT?
WE SAVED THE UNIVERSE...?
YUP.
GOOD JOB!
HA...

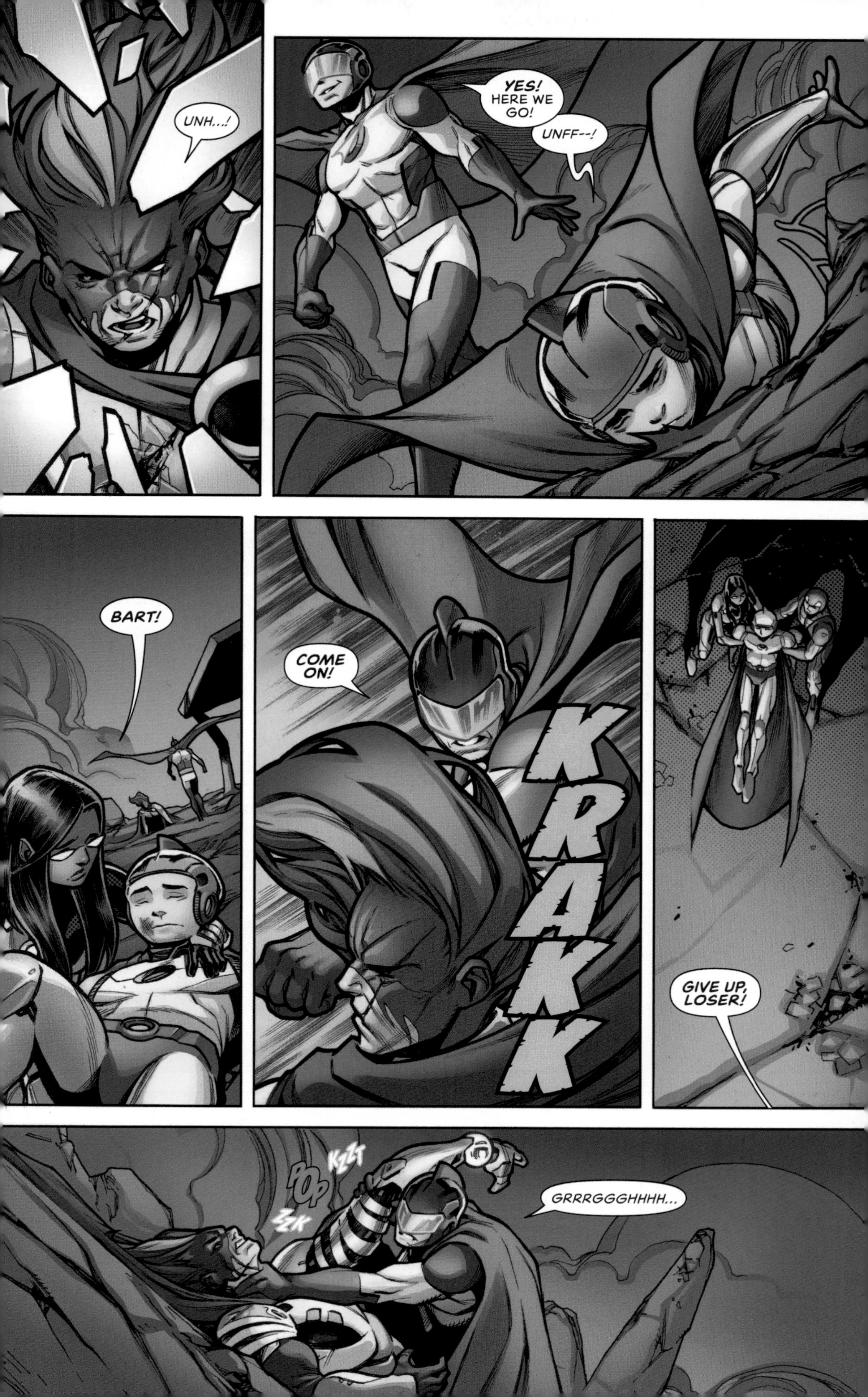
UNH...!
YES! HERE WE GO!
UNFF--!
BART!
COME ON!
KRAKK
GIVE UP, LOSER!
POP
KZZT
ZZK
GRRRGGGHHHH...

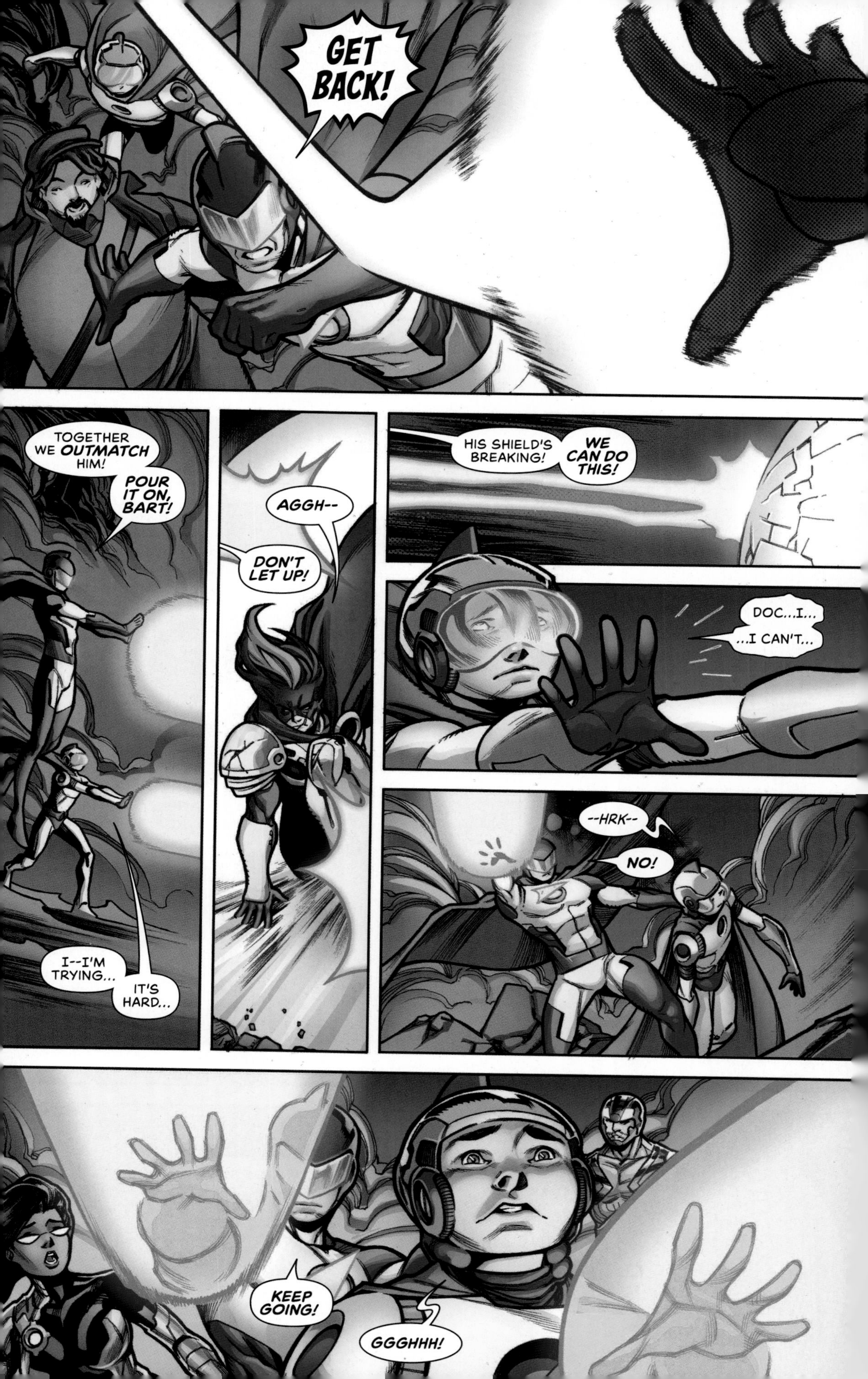
GET BACK!
TOGETHER WE OUTMATCH HIM!
POUR IT ON, BART!
I--I'M TRYING...
IT'S HARD...
AGGH--
DON'T LET UP!
HIS SHIELD'S BREAKING!
WE CAN DO THIS!
DOC...I...
...I CAN'T...
--HRK--
NO!
KEEP GOING!
GGGHHH!

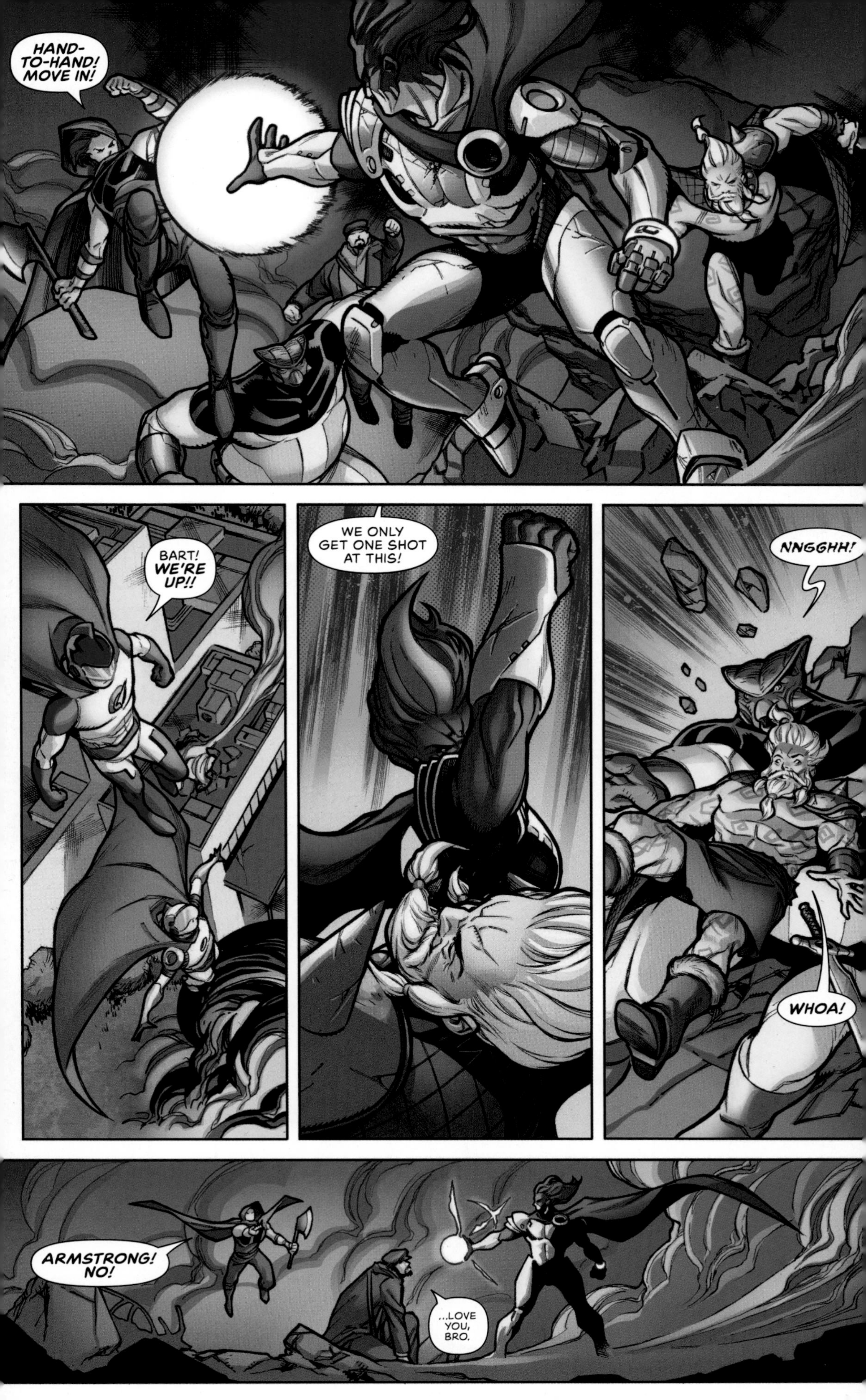
HAND-TO-HAND! MOVE IN!
BART! WE'RE UP!!
WE ONLY GET ONE SHOT AT THIS!
NNGGHH!
WHOA!
ARMSTRONG! NO!
...LOVE YOU, BRO.

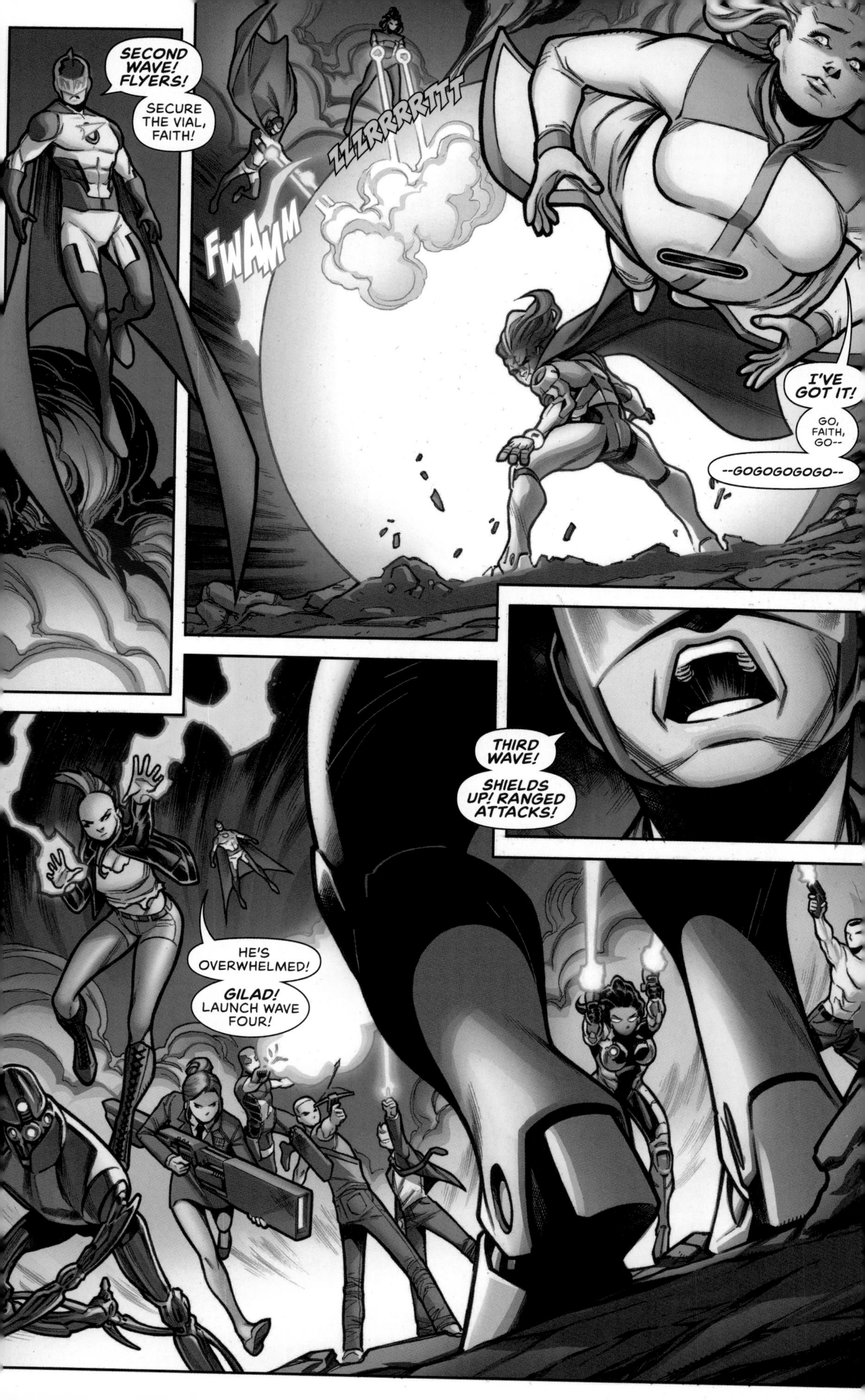
SECOND WAVE! FLYERS!
SECURE THE VIAL, FAITH!
ZZZRRRRRTTT
FWAMM
I'VE GOT IT!
GO, FAITH, GO--
--GOGOGOGOGO--
THIRD WAVE!
SHIELDS UP! RANGED ATTACKS!
HE'S OVERWHELMED!
GILAD! LAUNCH WAVE FOUR!

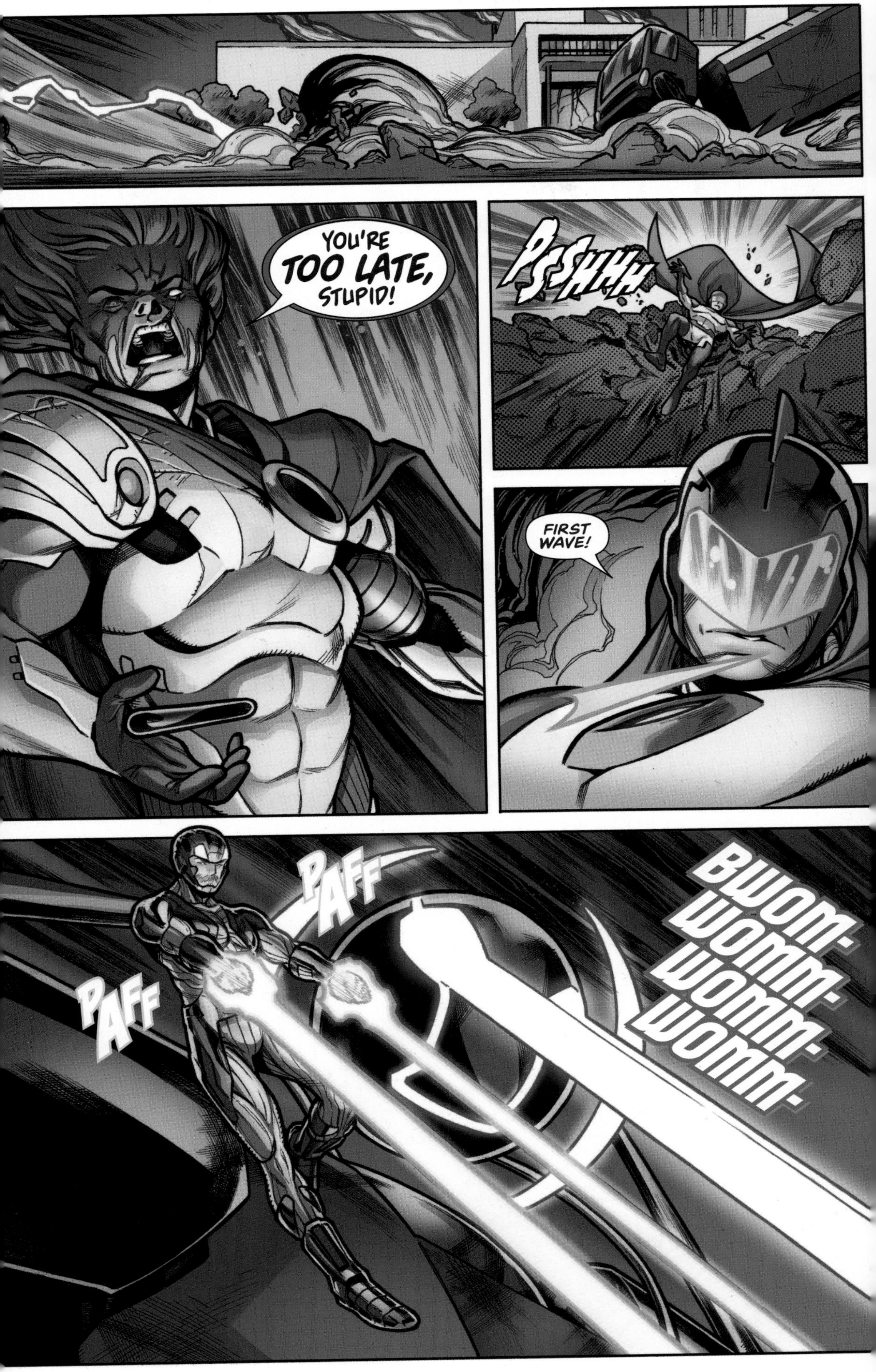
YOU'RE TOO LATE, STUPID!
PSSHHH
FIRST WAVE!
PAFF
PAFF
BWOM-WOMM-WOMM-WOMM-

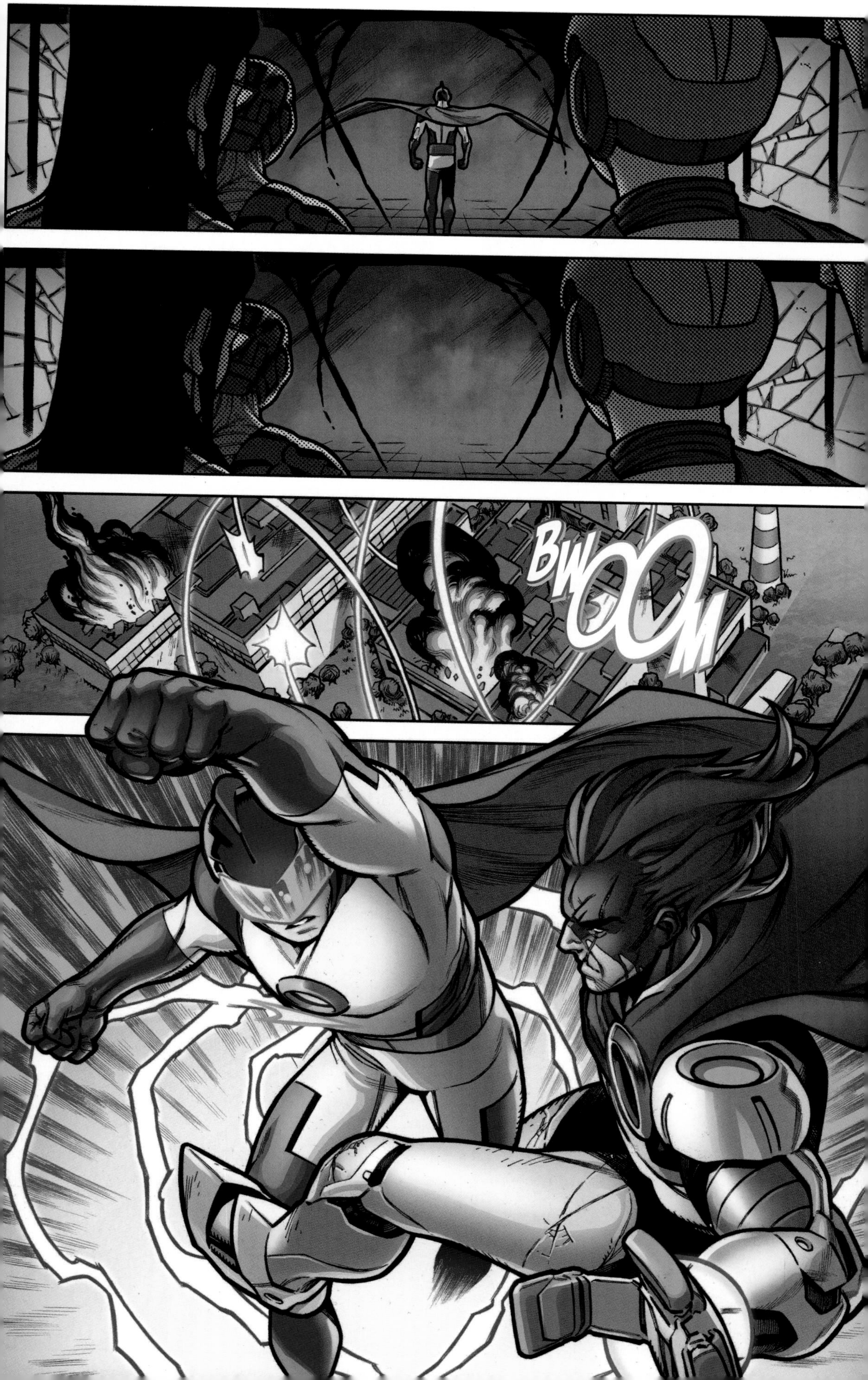
BWOOOM

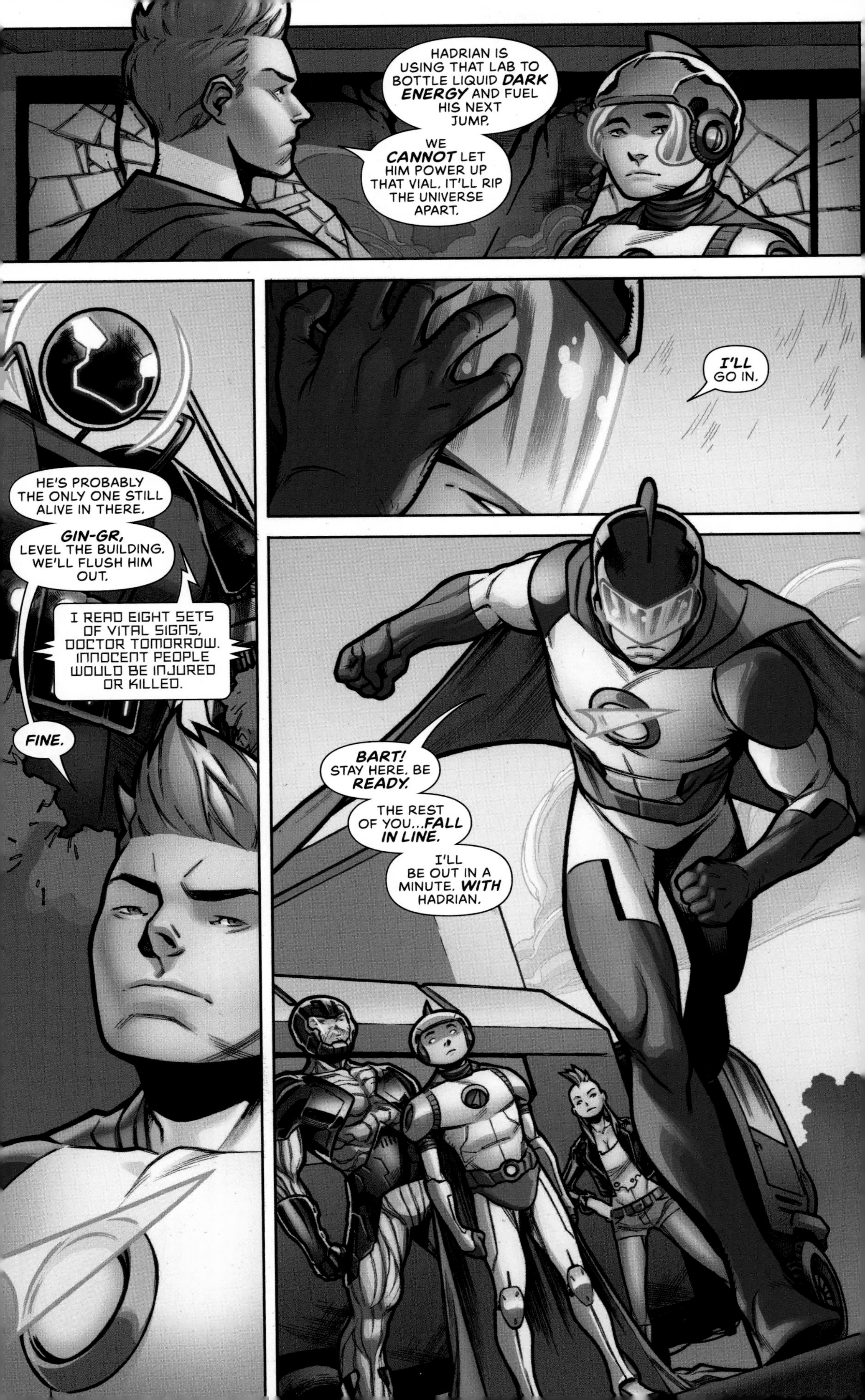
HADRIAN IS USING THAT LAB TO BOTTLE LIQUID DARK ENERGY AND FUEL HIS NEXT JUMP.
WE CANNOT LET HIM POWER UP THAT VIAL. IT'LL RIP THE UNIVERSE APART.
I'LL GO IN.
HE'S PROBABLY THE ONLY ONE STILL ALIVE IN THERE.
GIN-GR, LEVEL THE BUILDING. WE'LL FLUSH HIM OUT.
I READ EIGHT SETS OF VITAL SIGNS, DOCTOR TOMORROW. INNOCENT PEOPLE WOULD BE INJURED OR KILLED.
FINE.
BART! STAY HERE. BE READY.
THE REST OF YOU...FALL IN LINE.
I'LL BE OUT IN A MINUTE. WITH HADRIAN.

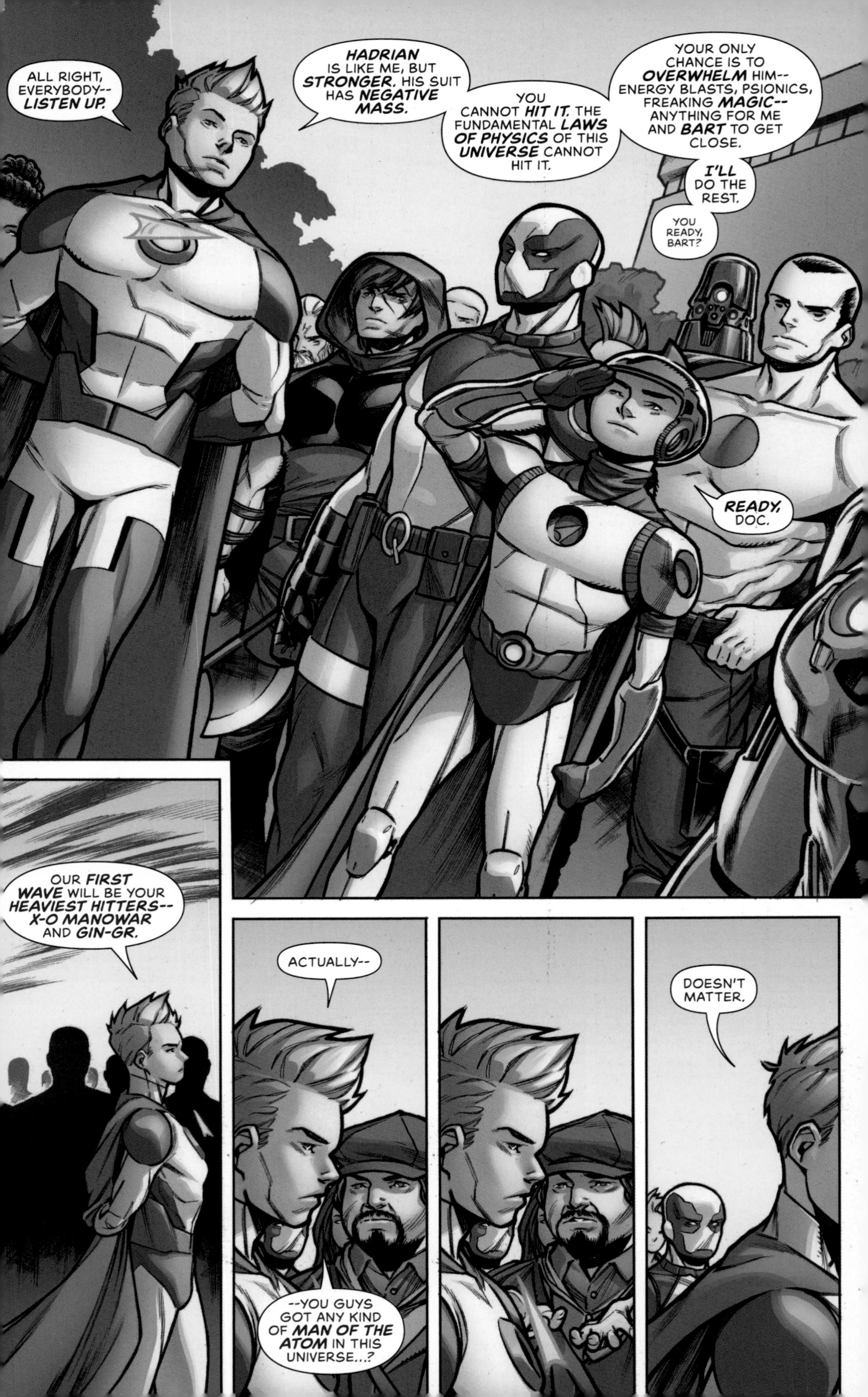
ALL RIGHT, EVERYBODY-- LISTEN UP.
HADRIAN IS LIKE ME, BUT STRONGER. HIS SUIT HAS NEGATIVE MASS.
YOU CANNOT HIT IT. THE FUNDAMENTAL LAWS OF PHYSICS OF THIS UNIVERSE CANNOT HIT IT.
YOUR ONLY CHANCE IS TO OVERWHELM HIM-- ENERGY BLASTS, PSIONICS, FREAKING MAGIC-- ANYTHING FOR ME AND BART TO GET CLOSE.
I'LL DO THE REST.
YOU READY, BART?
READY, DOC.
OUR FIRST WAVE WILL BE YOUR HEAVIEST HITTERS-- X-O MANOWAR AND GIN-GR.
ACTUALLY--
--YOU GUYS GOT ANY KIND OF MAN OF THE ATOM IN THIS UNIVERSE...?
DOESN'T MATTER.

DOCTOR TOMORROW #3

WRITER: ALEJANDRO ARBONA
ARTIST: JIM TOWE
COLORISTS: DIEGO RODRIGUEZ and KELLY FITZPATRICK
LETTERER: CLAYTON COWLES
COVER ARTIST: MICHAEL WALSH
ASSISTANT EDITOR: DREW BAUMGARTNER
SENIOR EDITORIAL DIRECTOR: ROBERT MEYERS

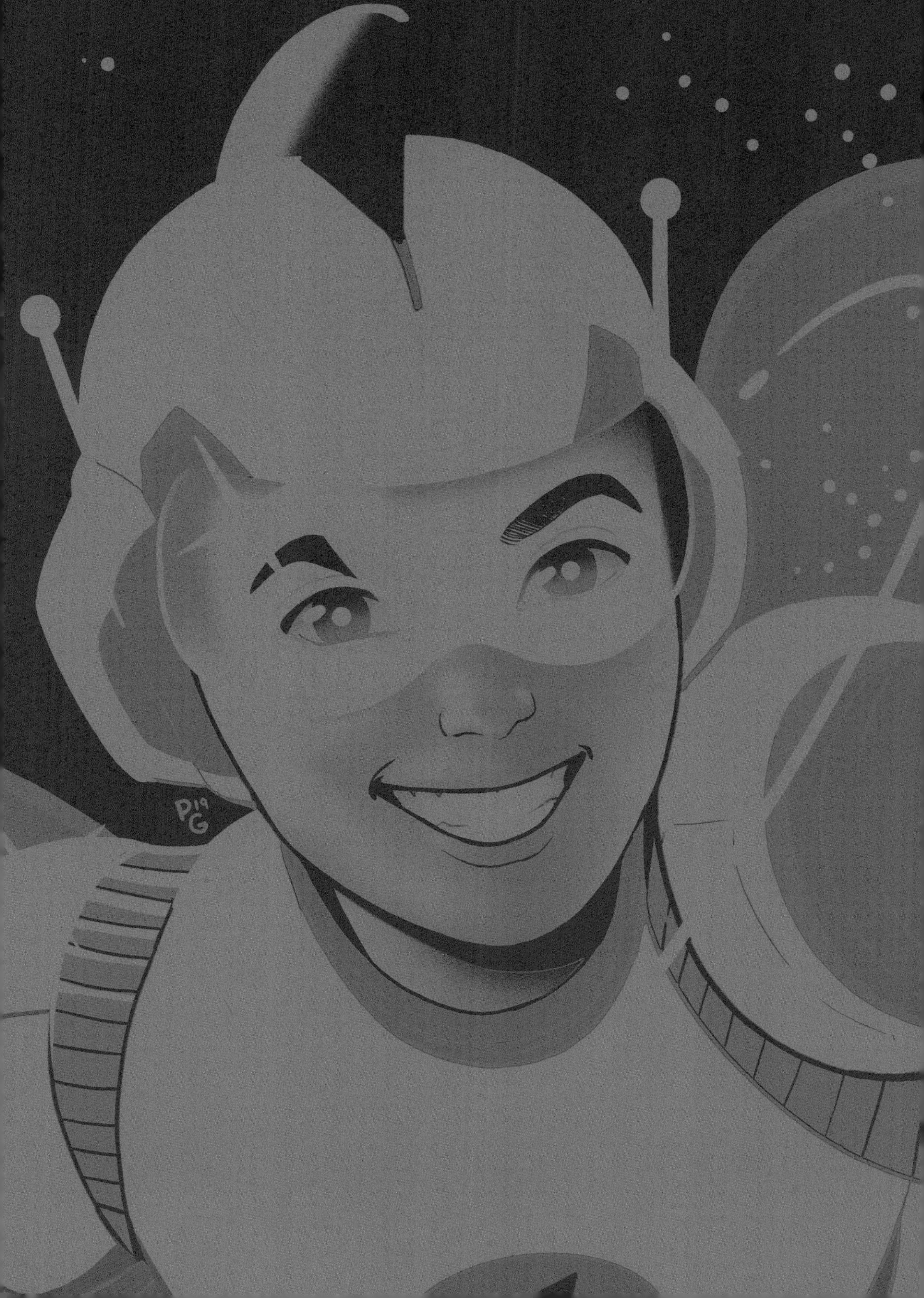

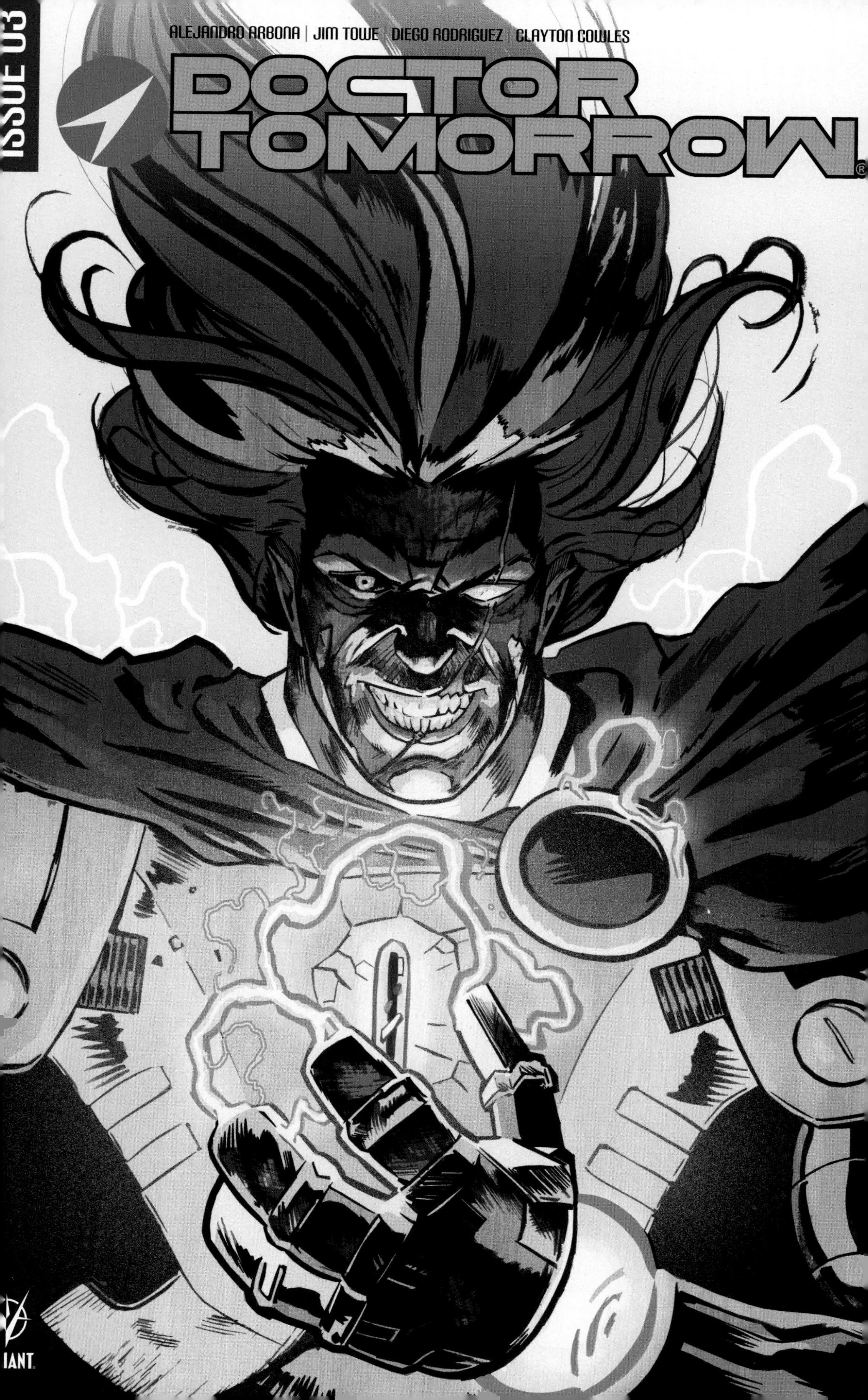
ISSUE 03
ALEJANDRO ARBONA | JIM TOWE | DIEGO RODRIGUEZ | CLAYTON COWLES
DOCTOR TOMORROW

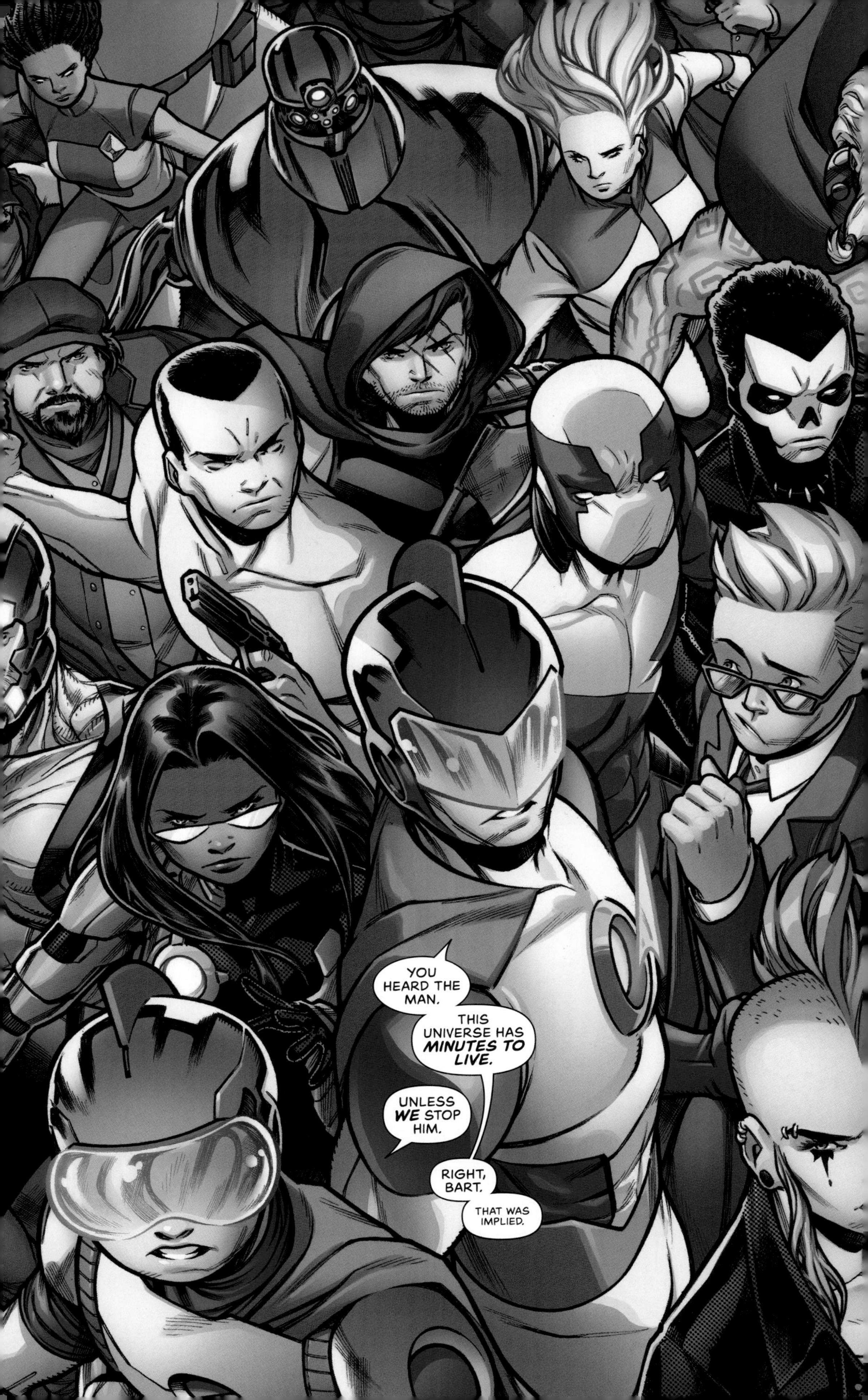
YOU HEARD THE MAN.
THIS UNIVERSE HAS *MINUTES TO LIVE.*
UNLESS *WE* STOP HIM.
RIGHT, BART.
THAT WAS IMPLIED.

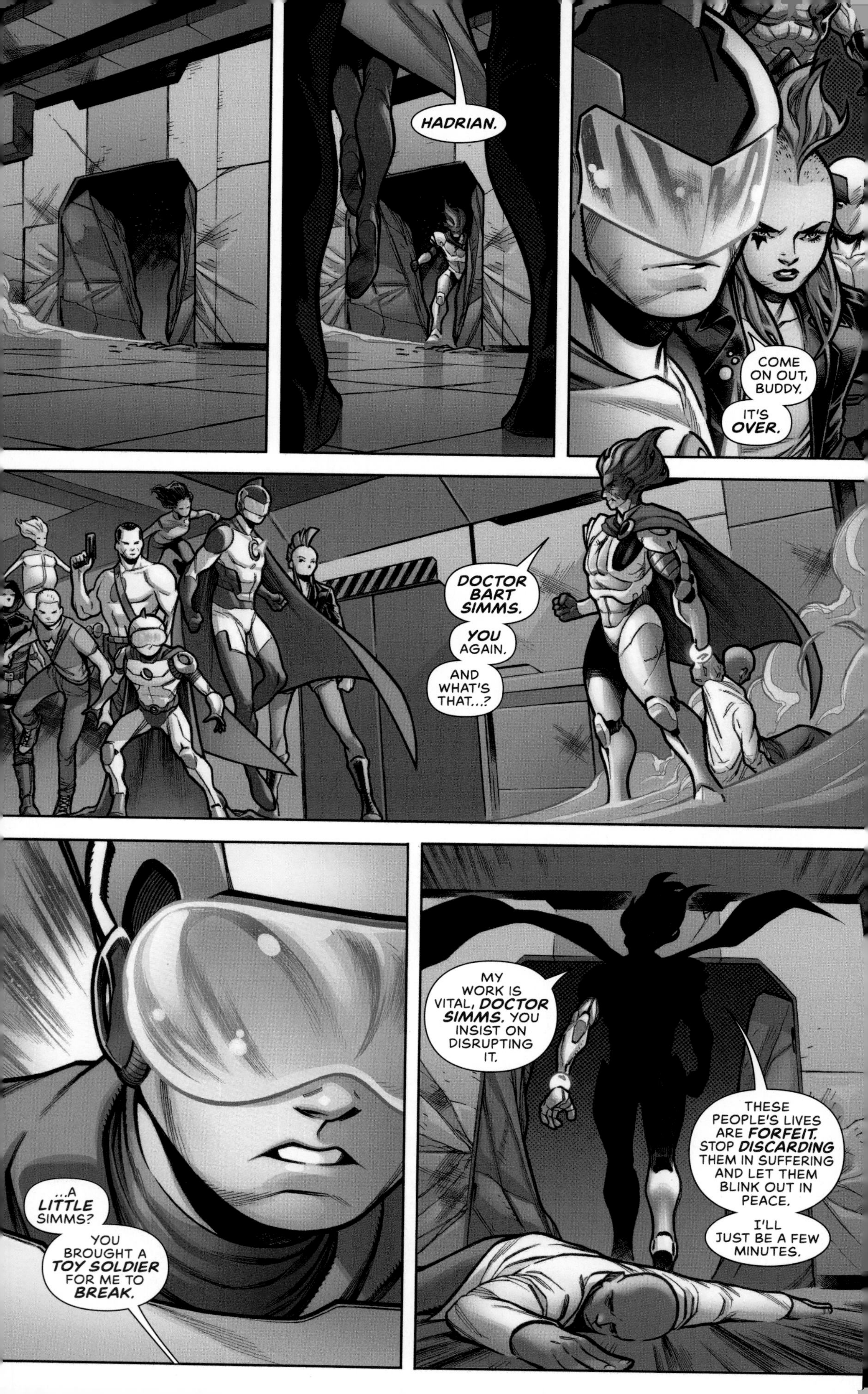
HADRIAN.
COME ON OUT, BUDDY.
IT'S OVER.
DOCTOR BART SIMMS.
YOU AGAIN.
AND WHAT'S THAT...?
...A LITTLE SIMMS?
YOU BROUGHT A TOY SOLDIER FOR ME TO BREAK.
MY WORK IS VITAL, DOCTOR SIMMS. YOU INSIST ON DISRUPTING IT.
THESE PEOPLE'S LIVES ARE FORFEIT. STOP DISCARDING THEM IN SUFFERING AND LET THEM BLINK OUT IN PEACE.
I'LL JUST BE A FEW MINUTES.

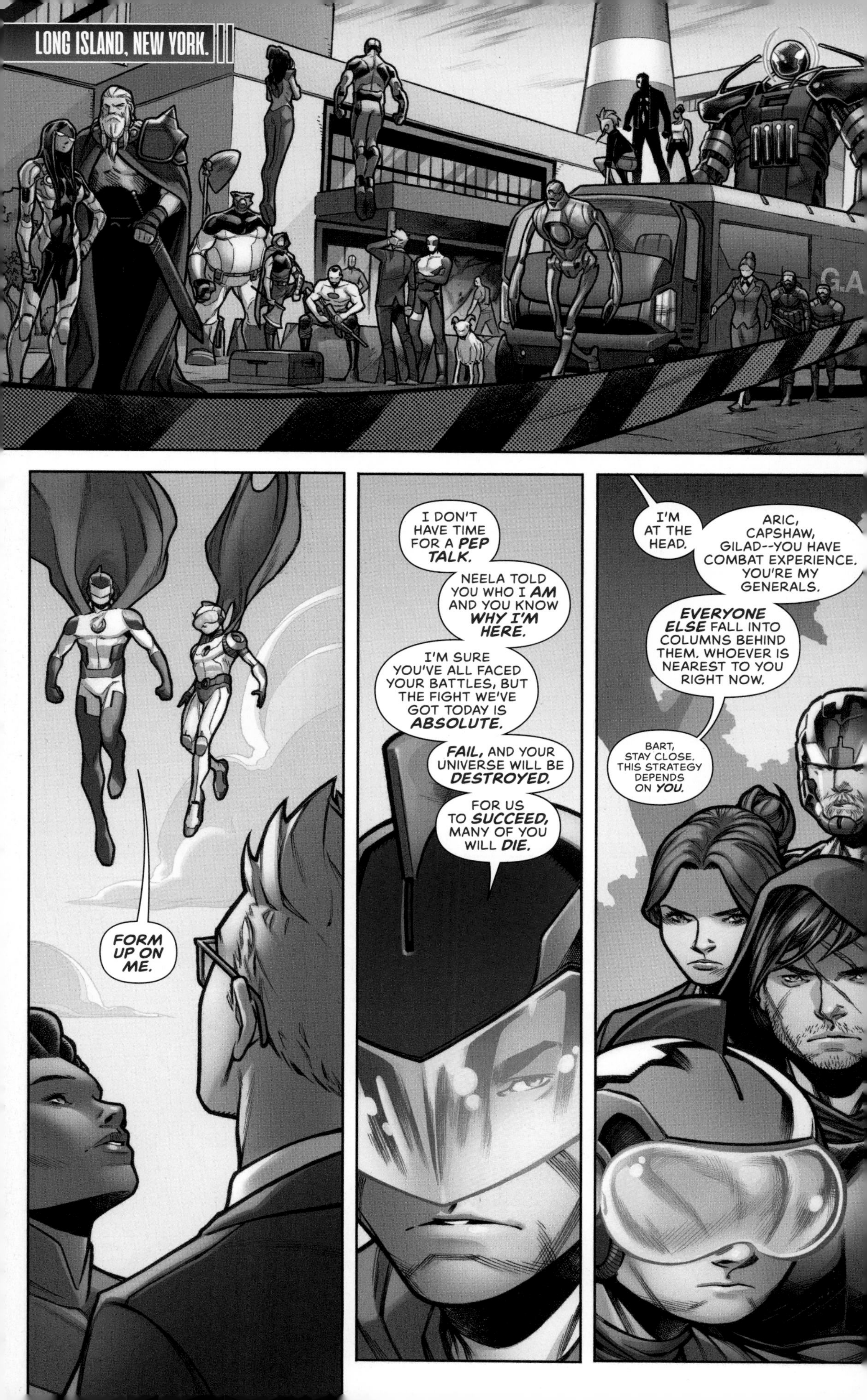
LONG ISLAND, NEW YORK.
G.A
FORM UP ON ME.
I DON'T HAVE TIME FOR A PEP TALK.
NEELA TOLD YOU WHO I AM AND YOU KNOW WHY I'M HERE.
I'M SURE YOU'VE ALL FACED YOUR BATTLES, BUT THE FIGHT WE'VE GOT TODAY IS ABSOLUTE.
FAIL, AND YOUR UNIVERSE WILL BE DESTROYED.
FOR US TO SUCCEED, MANY OF YOU WILL DIE.
I'M AT THE HEAD.
ARIC, CAPSHAW, GILAD--YOU HAVE COMBAT EXPERIENCE. YOU'RE MY GENERALS.
EVERYONE ELSE FALL INTO COLUMNS BEHIND THEM. WHOEVER IS NEAREST TO YOU RIGHT NOW.
BART, STAY CLOSE. THIS STRATEGY DEPENDS ON YOU.

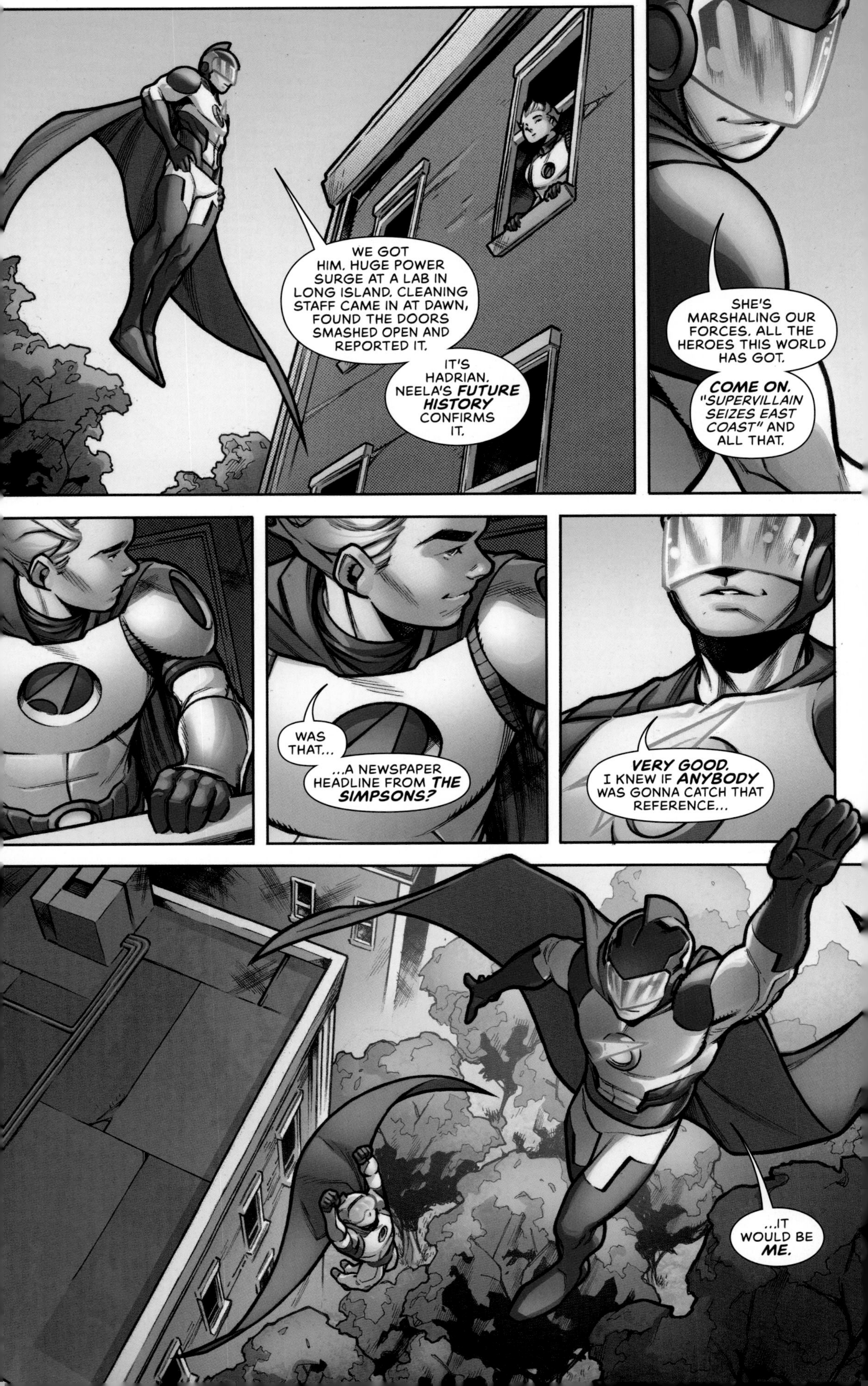
WE GOT HIM. HUGE POWER SURGE AT A LAB IN LONG ISLAND. CLEANING STAFF CAME IN AT DAWN, FOUND THE DOORS SMASHED OPEN AND REPORTED IT.
IT'S HADRIAN. NEELA'S *FUTURE HISTORY* CONFIRMS IT.
SHE'S MARSHALING OUR FORCES. ALL THE HEROES THIS WORLD HAS GOT.
COME ON. *"SUPERVILLAIN SEIZES EAST COAST"* AND ALL THAT.
WAS THAT...
...A NEWSPAPER HEADLINE FROM *THE SIMPSONS?*
VERY GOOD. I KNEW IF *ANYBODY* WAS GONNA CATCH THAT REFERENCE...
...IT WOULD BE *ME.*

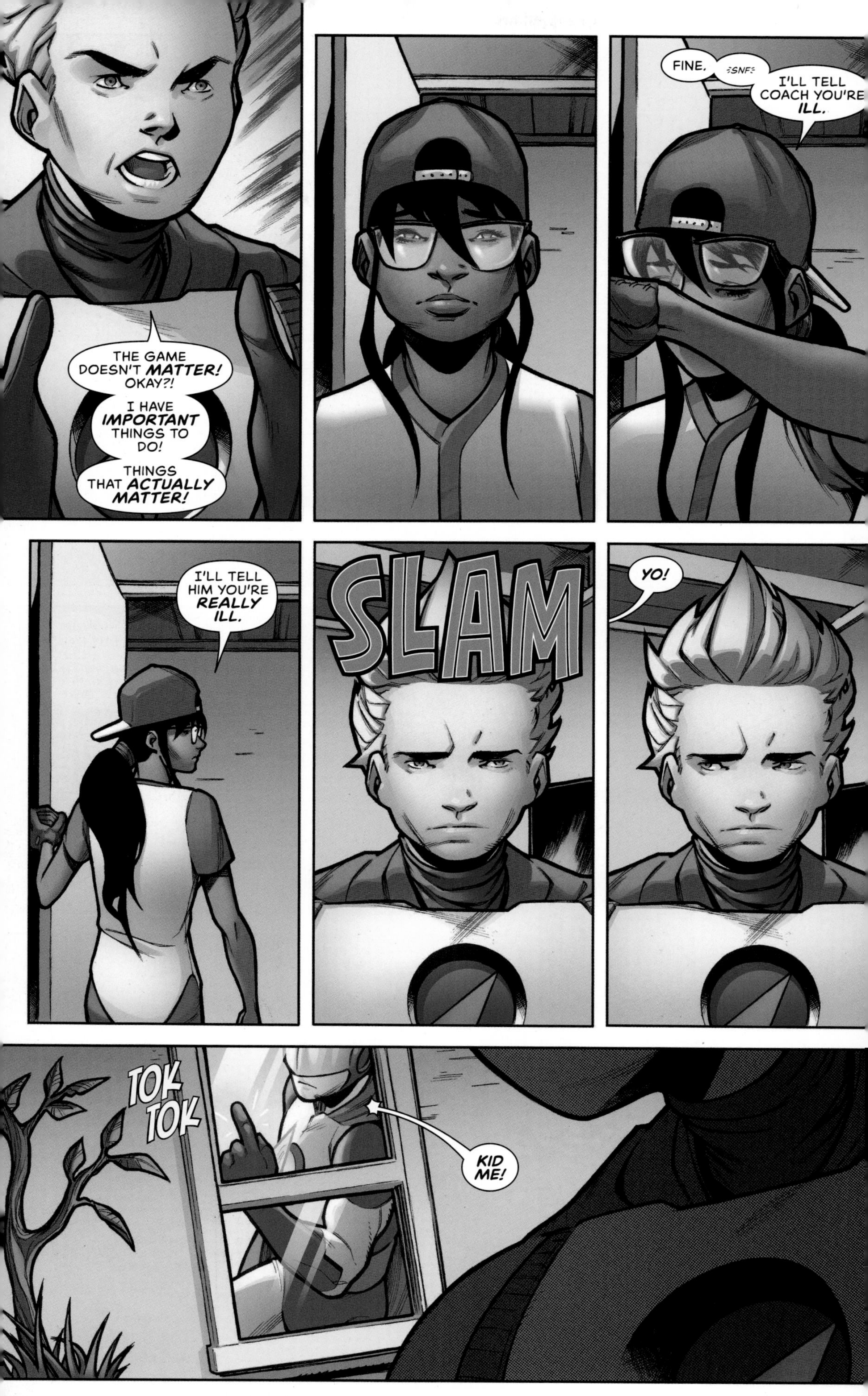
THE GAME DOESN'T MATTER! OKAY?!
I HAVE IMPORTANT THINGS TO DO!
THINGS THAT ACTUALLY MATTER!
FINE.
SNF
I'LL TELL COACH YOU'RE ILL.
I'LL TELL HIM YOU'RE REALLY ILL.
SLAM
YO!
TOK TOK
KID ME!

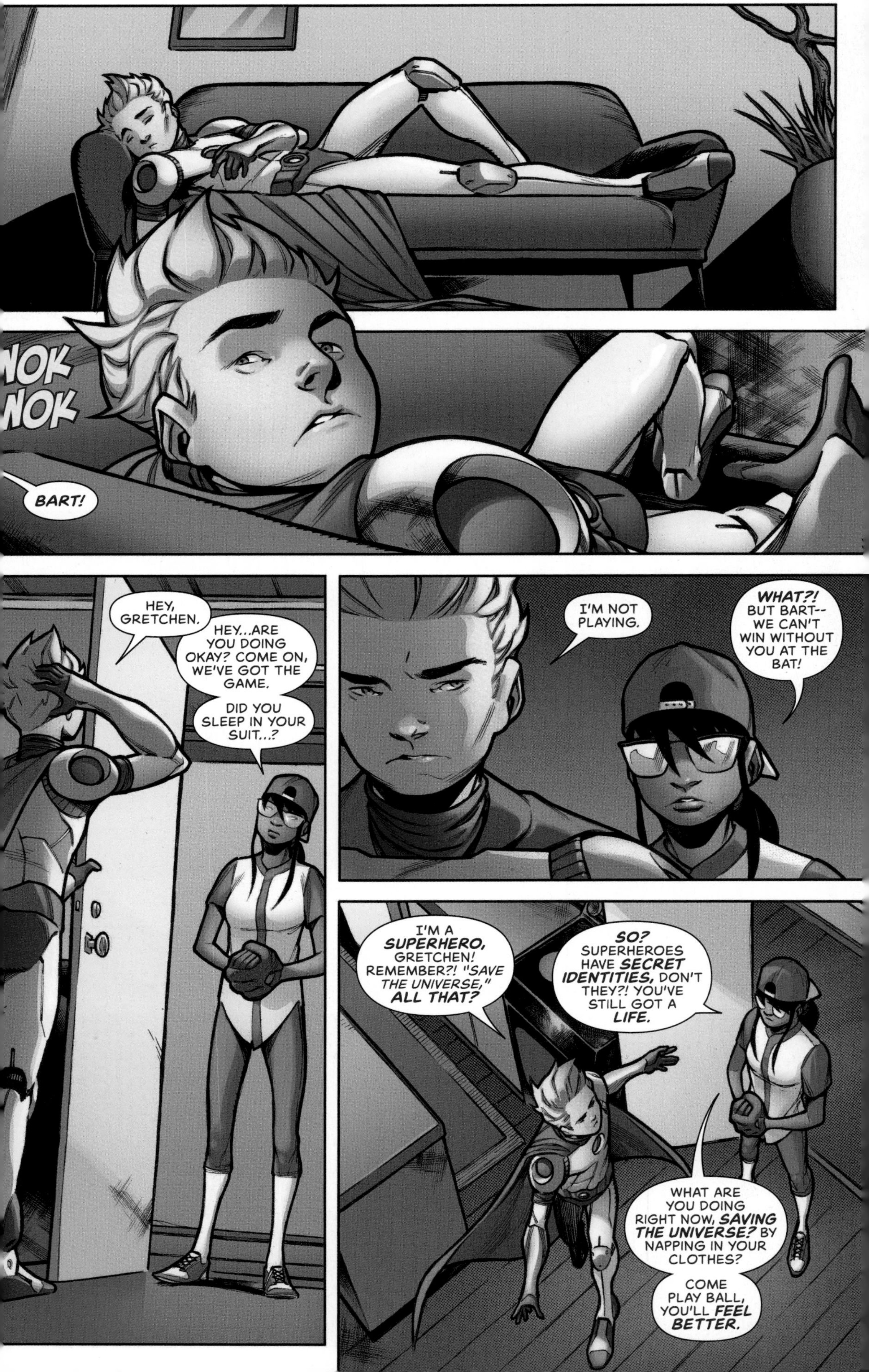
NOK
NOK
BART!
HEY, GRETCHEN.
HEY...ARE YOU DOING OKAY? COME ON, WE'VE GOT THE GAME.
DID YOU SLEEP IN YOUR SUIT...?
I'M NOT PLAYING.
WHAT?! BUT BART-- WE CAN'T WIN WITHOUT YOU AT THE BAT!
I'M A SUPERHERO, GRETCHEN! REMEMBER?! "SAVE THE UNIVERSE," ALL THAT?
SO? SUPERHEROES HAVE SECRET IDENTITIES, DON'T THEY?! YOU'VE STILL GOT A LIFE.
WHAT ARE YOU DOING RIGHT NOW, SAVING THE UNIVERSE? BY NAPPING IN YOUR CLOTHES?
COME PLAY BALL, YOU'LL FEEL BETTER.

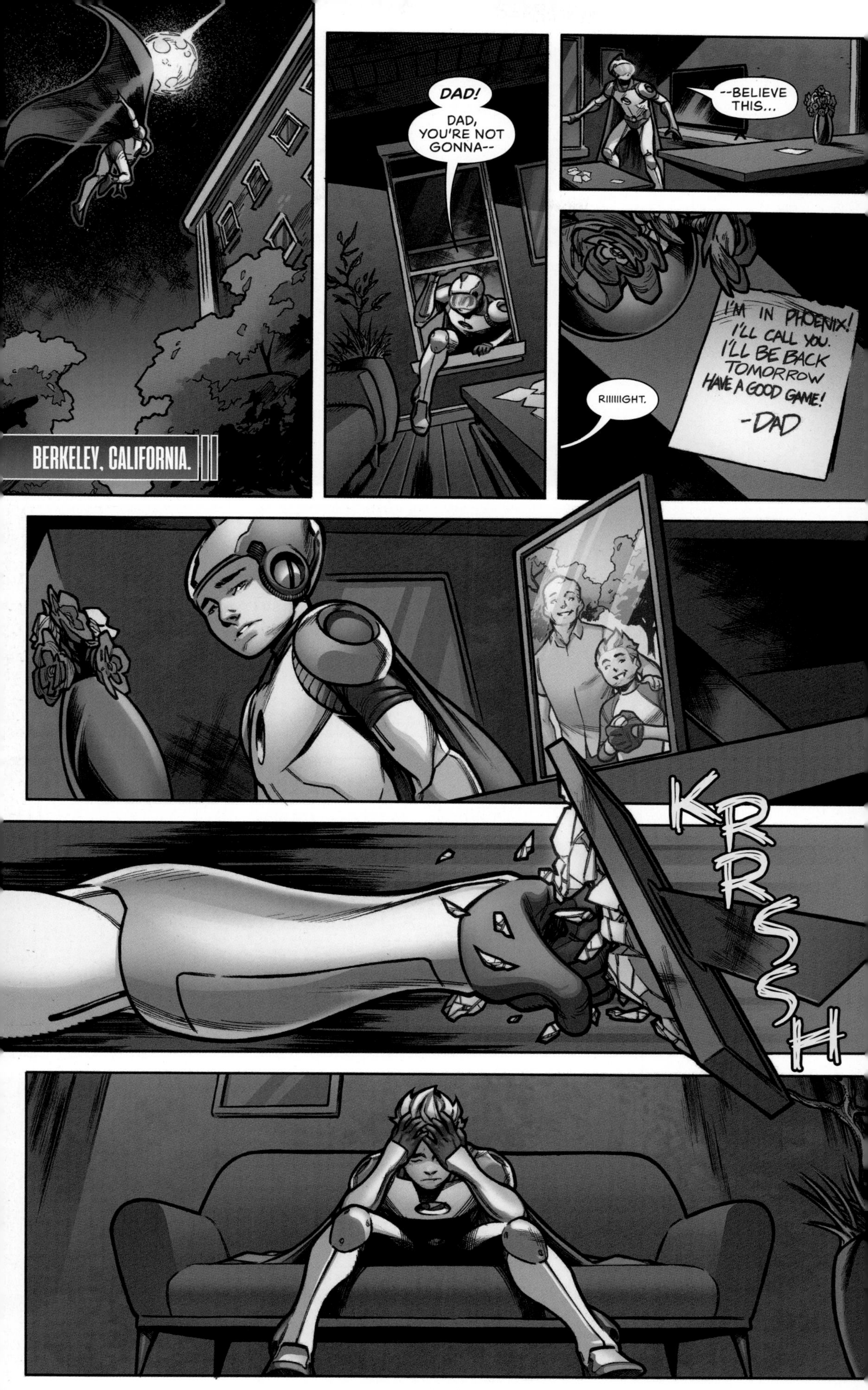
BERKELEY, CALIFORNIA.
DAD!
DAD, YOU'RE NOT GONNA--
--BELIEVE THIS...
I'M IN PHOENIX! I'LL CALL YOU. I'LL BE BACK TOMORROW HAVE A GOOD GAME! -DAD
RIIIIIGHT.
KRRSSH

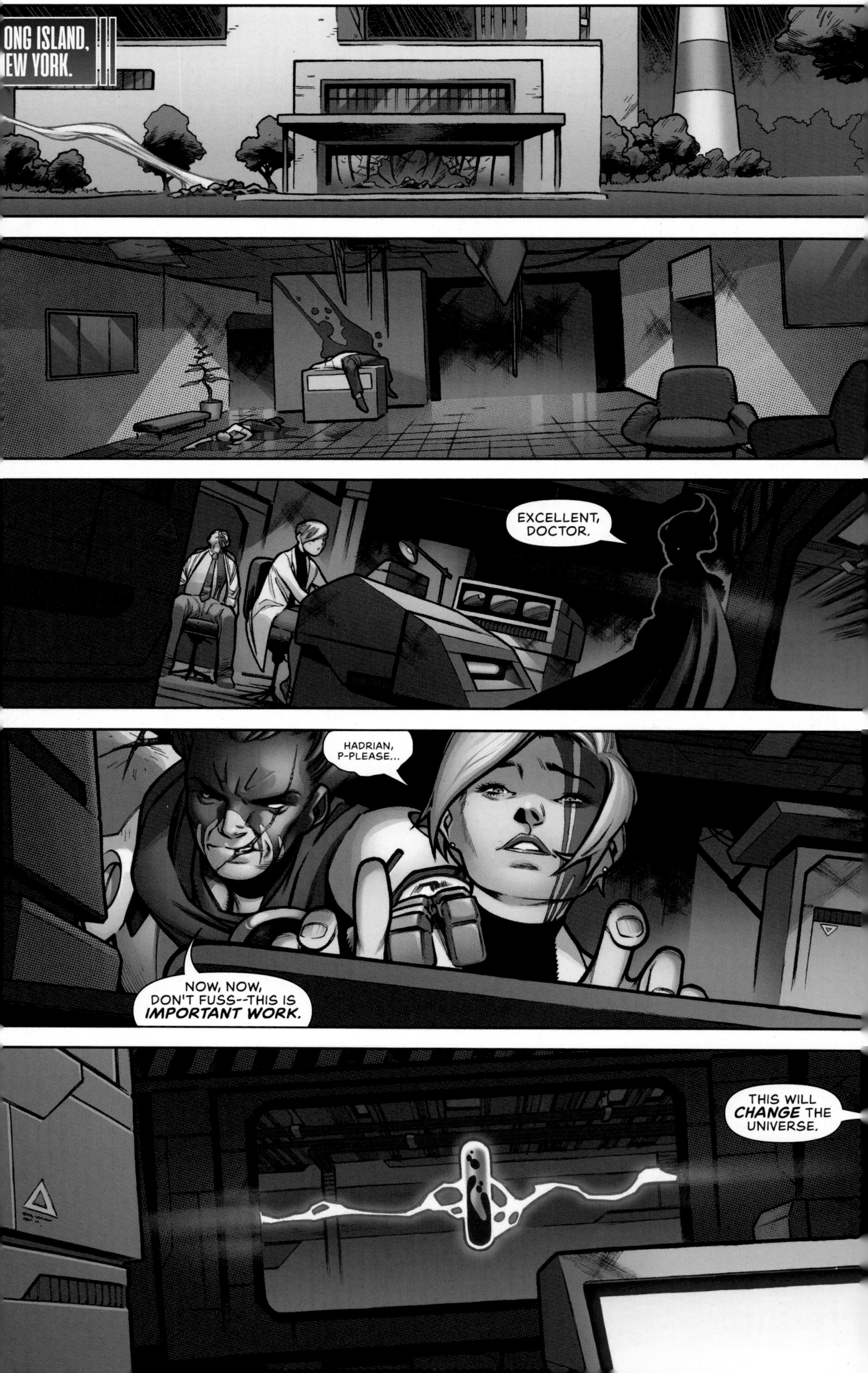
ONG ISLAND,
EW YORK.
EXCELLENT, DOCTOR.
HADRIAN, P-PLEASE...
NOW, NOW, DON'T FUSS--THIS IS IMPORTANT WORK.
THIS WILL CHANGE THE UNIVERSE.

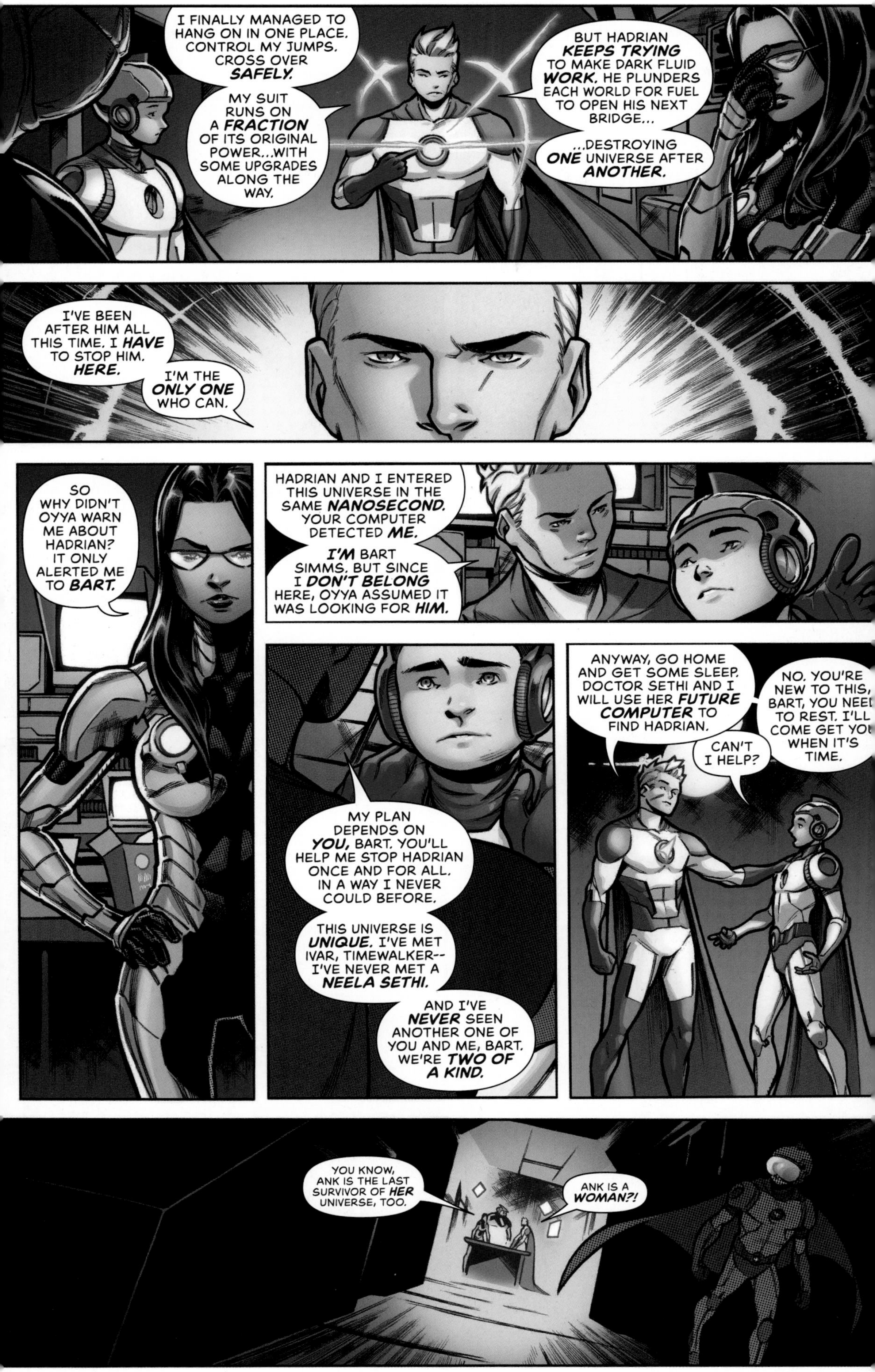
I FINALLY MANAGED TO HANG ON IN ONE PLACE. CONTROL MY JUMPS. CROSS OVER SAFELY.
MY SUIT RUNS ON A FRACTION OF ITS ORIGINAL POWER...WITH SOME UPGRADES ALONG THE WAY.
BUT HADRIAN KEEPS TRYING TO MAKE DARK FLUID WORK. HE PLUNDERS EACH WORLD FOR FUEL TO OPEN HIS NEXT BRIDGE...
...DESTROYING ONE UNIVERSE AFTER ANOTHER.
I'VE BEEN AFTER HIM ALL THIS TIME. I HAVE TO STOP HIM. HERE.
I'M THE ONLY ONE WHO CAN.
SO WHY DIDN'T OYYA WARN ME ABOUT HADRIAN? IT ONLY ALERTED ME TO BART.
HADRIAN AND I ENTERED THIS UNIVERSE IN THE SAME NANOSECOND. YOUR COMPUTER DETECTED ME.
I'M BART SIMMS. BUT SINCE I DON'T BELONG HERE, OYYA ASSUMED IT WAS LOOKING FOR HIM.
MY PLAN DEPENDS ON YOU, BART. YOU'LL HELP ME STOP HADRIAN ONCE AND FOR ALL. IN A WAY I NEVER COULD BEFORE.
THIS UNIVERSE IS UNIQUE. I'VE MET IVAR, TIMEWALKER-- I'VE NEVER MET A NEELA SETHI.
AND I'VE NEVER SEEN ANOTHER ONE OF YOU AND ME, BART. WE'RE TWO OF A KIND.
ANYWAY, GO HOME AND GET SOME SLEEP. DOCTOR SETHI AND I WILL USE HER FUTURE COMPUTER TO FIND HADRIAN.
CAN'T I HELP?
NO. YOU'RE NEW TO THIS, BART, YOU NEED TO REST. I'LL COME GET YOU WHEN IT'S TIME.
YOU KNOW, ANK IS THE LAST SURVIVOR OF HER UNIVERSE, TOO.
ANK IS A WOMAN?!

"I WAS A POST-DOC IN ASTROPHYSICS, RESEARCHING DARK ENERGY."

"MY MENTOR..."

"...WAS HADRIAN."

"I WISH WE'D NEVER MET."

"COMBINING OUR RESEARCH, WE ARRIVED TOGETHER AT OUR GREATEST CREATION..."

"...DARK FLUID."

"NEGATIVE MASS."

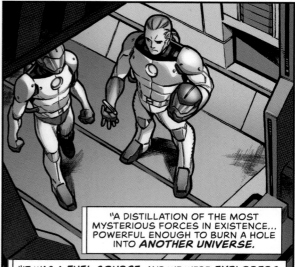

"A DISTILLATION OF THE MOST MYSTERIOUS FORCES IN EXISTENCE... POWERFUL ENOUGH TO BURN A HOLE INTO ANOTHER UNIVERSE."

"IT WAS A FUEL SOURCE, AND WE WERE EXPLORERS. WE MADE SUITS TO CHANNEL ITS POWER. A SMALL AMOUNT COULD BE SAFELY CONTAINED..."

"...BUT HADRIAN WANTED MORE."

"THE UNIVERSE WAS INCINERATED AROUND US AND WE FELL THROUGH THE VOID."

"NO PATH HAD EVER BEEN FORGED TO TRAVEL BETWEEN WORLDS AND WE PLUMMETED THROUGH COUNTLESS PARALLEL REALITIES."

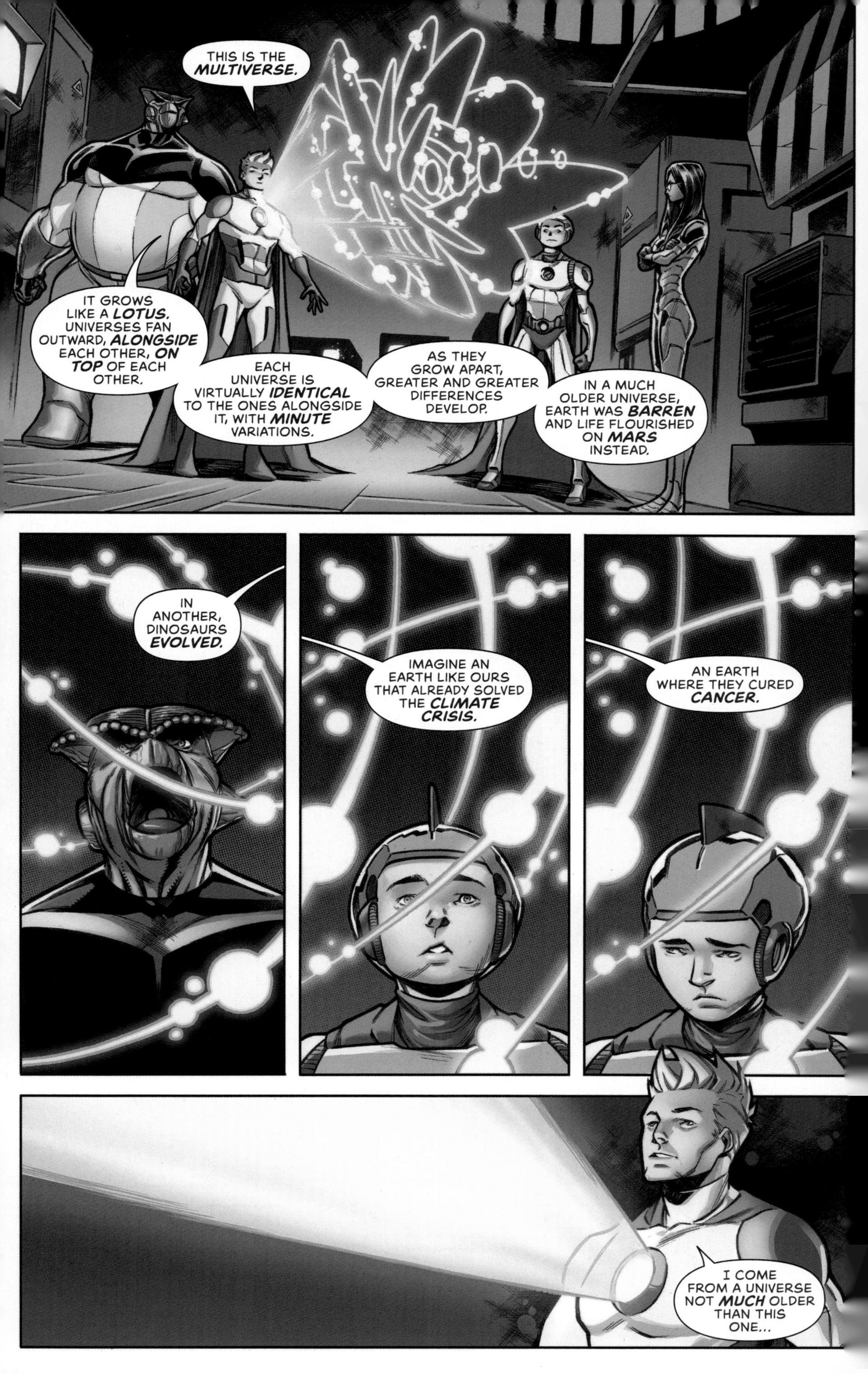
THIS IS THE **MULTIVERSE.**
IT GROWS LIKE A **LOTUS.** UNIVERSES FAN OUTWARD, **ALONGSIDE** EACH OTHER, **ON TOP** OF EACH OTHER.
EACH UNIVERSE IS VIRTUALLY **IDENTICAL** TO THE ONES ALONGSIDE IT, WITH **MINUTE** VARIATIONS.
AS THEY GROW APART, GREATER AND GREATER DIFFERENCES DEVELOP.
IN A MUCH OLDER UNIVERSE, EARTH WAS **BARREN** AND LIFE FLOURISHED ON **MARS** INSTEAD.
IN ANOTHER, DINOSAURS **EVOLVED.**
IMAGINE AN EARTH LIKE OURS THAT ALREADY SOLVED THE **CLIMATE CRISIS.**
AN EARTH WHERE THEY CURED **CANCER.**
I COME FROM A UNIVERSE NOT **MUCH** OLDER THAN THIS ONE...

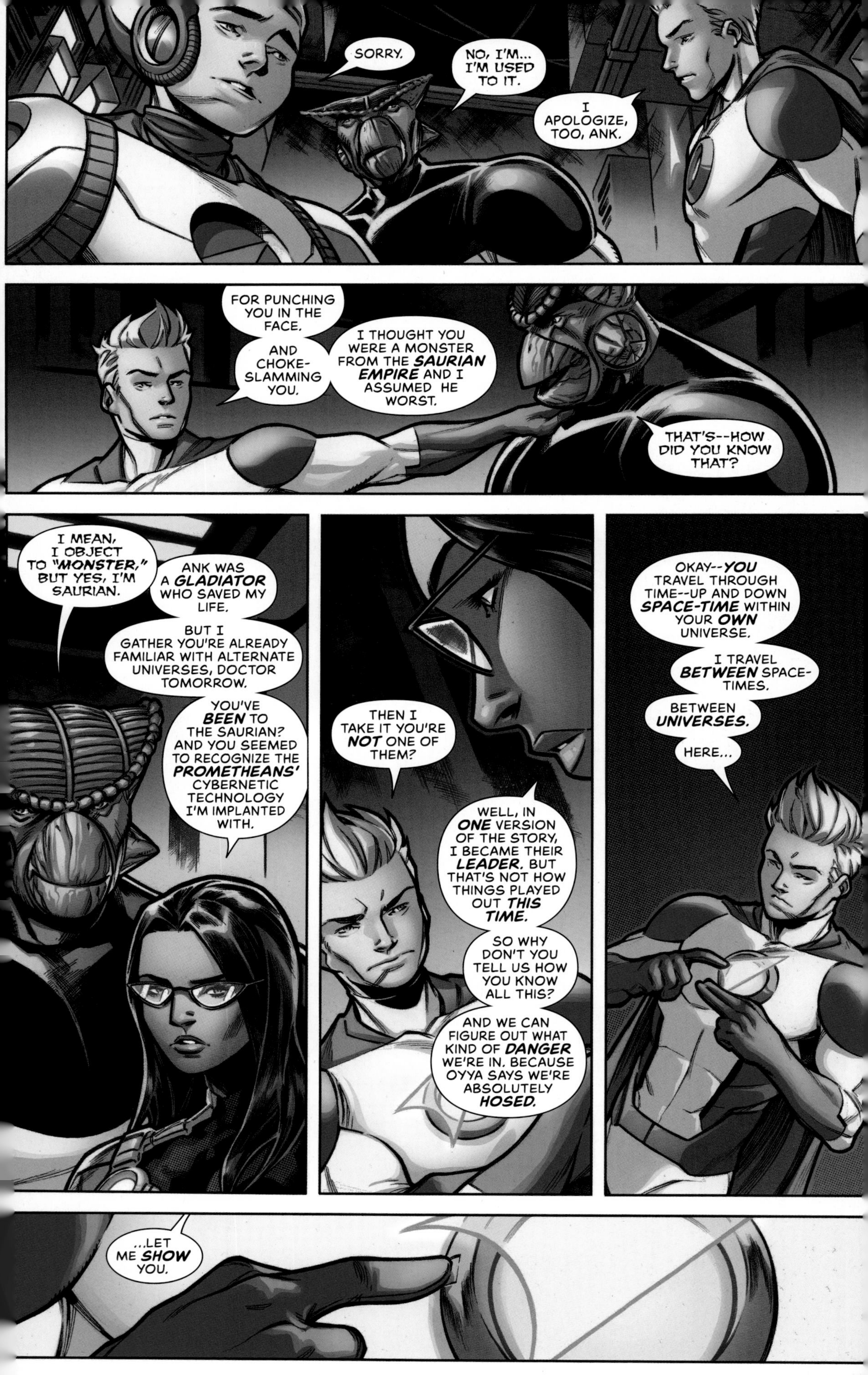
SORRY.
NO, I'M... I'M USED TO IT.
I APOLOGIZE, TOO, ANK.
FOR PUNCHING YOU IN THE FACE.
AND CHOKE-SLAMMING YOU.
I THOUGHT YOU WERE A MONSTER FROM THE SAURIAN EMPIRE AND I ASSUMED HE WORST.
THAT'S--HOW DID YOU KNOW THAT?
I MEAN, I OBJECT TO "MONSTER," BUT YES, I'M SAURIAN.
ANK WAS A GLADIATOR WHO SAVED MY LIFE.
BUT I GATHER YOU'RE ALREADY FAMILIAR WITH ALTERNATE UNIVERSES, DOCTOR TOMORROW.
YOU'VE BEEN TO THE SAURIAN? AND YOU SEEMED TO RECOGNIZE THE PROMETHEANS' CYBERNETIC TECHNOLOGY I'M IMPLANTED WITH.
THEN I TAKE IT YOU'RE NOT ONE OF THEM?
WELL, IN ONE VERSION OF THE STORY, I BECAME THEIR LEADER. BUT THAT'S NOT HOW THINGS PLAYED OUT THIS TIME.
SO WHY DON'T YOU TELL US HOW YOU KNOW ALL THIS?
AND WE CAN FIGURE OUT WHAT KIND OF DANGER WE'RE IN. BECAUSE OYYA SAYS WE'RE ABSOLUTELY HOSED.
OKAY--YOU TRAVEL THROUGH TIME--UP AND DOWN SPACE-TIME WITHIN YOUR OWN UNIVERSE.
I TRAVEL BETWEEN SPACE-TIMES.
BETWEEN UNIVERSES.
HERE...
...LET ME SHOW YOU.

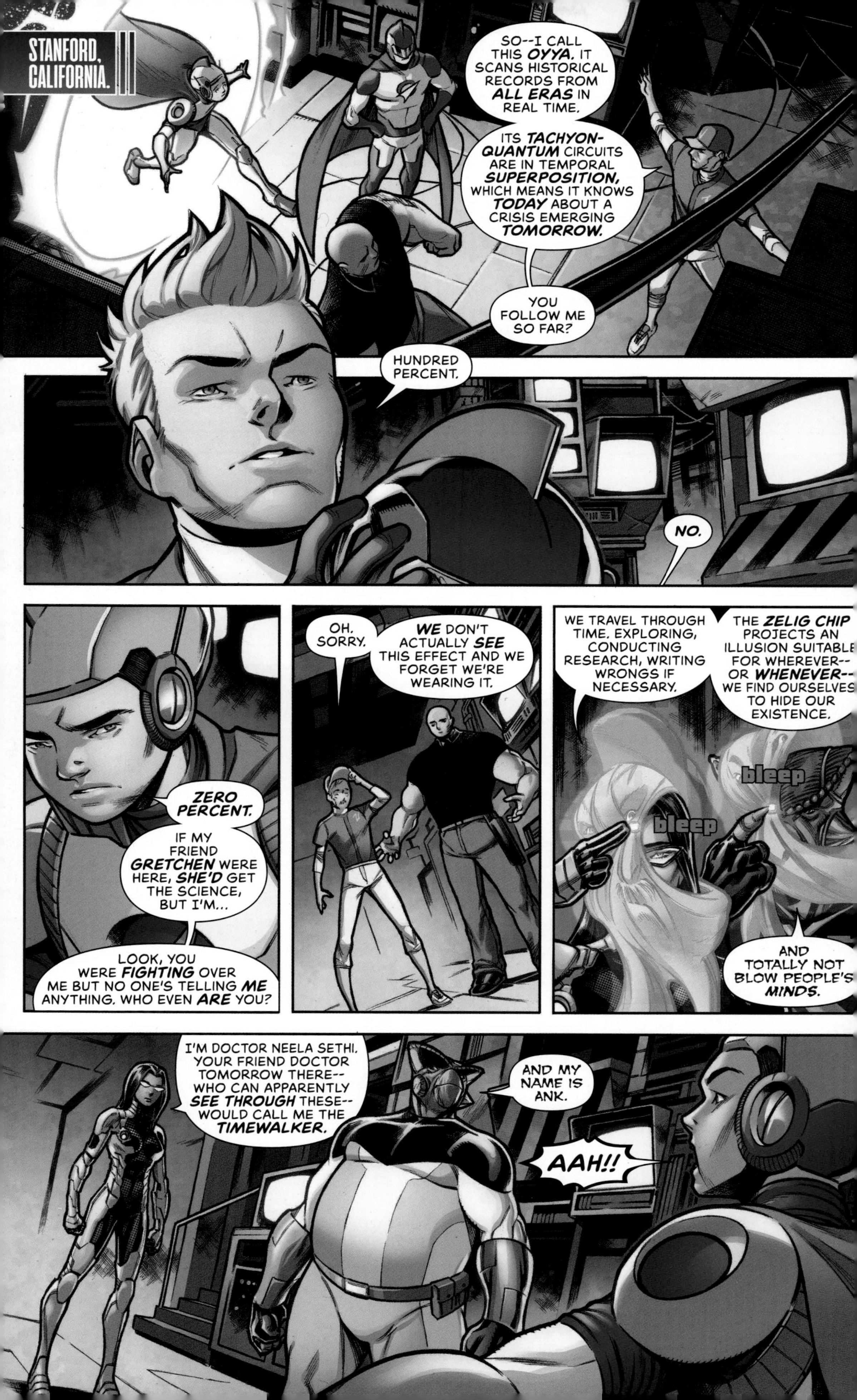
STANFORD, CALIFORNIA.
SO--I CALL THIS OYYA. IT SCANS HISTORICAL RECORDS FROM ALL ERAS IN REAL TIME.
ITS TACHYON-QUANTUM CIRCUITS ARE IN TEMPORAL SUPERPOSITION, WHICH MEANS IT KNOWS TODAY ABOUT A CRISIS EMERGING TOMORROW.
YOU FOLLOW ME SO FAR?
HUNDRED PERCENT.
NO.
ZERO PERCENT.
IF MY FRIEND GRETCHEN WERE HERE, SHE'D GET THE SCIENCE, BUT I'M...
LOOK, YOU WERE FIGHTING OVER ME BUT NO ONE'S TELLING ME ANYTHING. WHO EVEN ARE YOU?
OH. SORRY.
WE DON'T ACTUALLY SEE THIS EFFECT AND WE FORGET WE'RE WEARING IT.
WE TRAVEL THROUGH TIME. EXPLORING, CONDUCTING RESEARCH, WRITING WRONGS IF NECESSARY.
THE ZELIG CHIP PROJECTS AN ILLUSION SUITABLE FOR WHEREVER-- OR WHENEVER-- WE FIND OURSELVES TO HIDE OUR EXISTENCE.
bleep
bleep
AND TOTALLY NOT BLOW PEOPLE'S MINDS.
I'M DOCTOR NEELA SETHI. YOUR FRIEND DOCTOR TOMORROW THERE-- WHO CAN APPARENTLY SEE THROUGH THESE-- WOULD CALL ME THE TIMEWALKER.
AND MY NAME IS ANK.
AAH!!

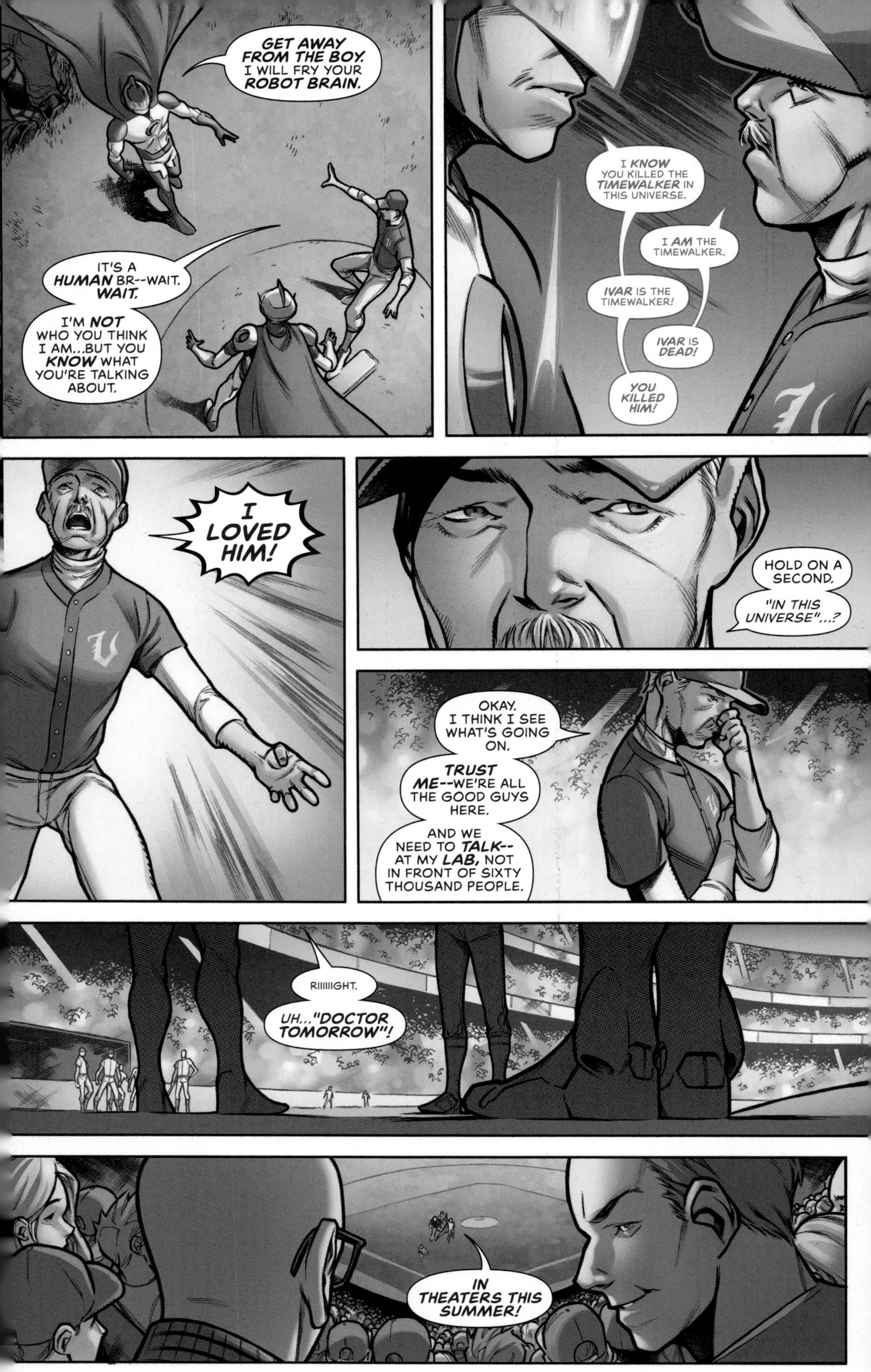
GET AWAY FROM THE BOY. I WILL FRY YOUR ROBOT BRAIN.
IT'S A HUMAN BR--WAIT. WAIT.
I'M NOT WHO YOU THINK I AM...BUT YOU KNOW WHAT YOU'RE TALKING ABOUT.
I KNOW YOU KILLED THE TIMEWALKER IN THIS UNIVERSE.
I AM THE TIMEWALKER.
IVAR IS THE TIMEWALKER!
IVAR IS DEAD!
YOU KILLED HIM!
I LOVED HIM!
HOLD ON A SECOND.
"IN THIS UNIVERSE"...?
OKAY. I THINK I SEE WHAT'S GOING ON.
TRUST ME--WE'RE ALL THE GOOD GUYS HERE.
AND WE NEED TO TALK--AT MY LAB, NOT IN FRONT OF SIXTY THOUSAND PEOPLE.
RIIIIIIGHT.
UH..."DOCTOR TOMORROW"!
IN THEATERS THIS SUMMER!

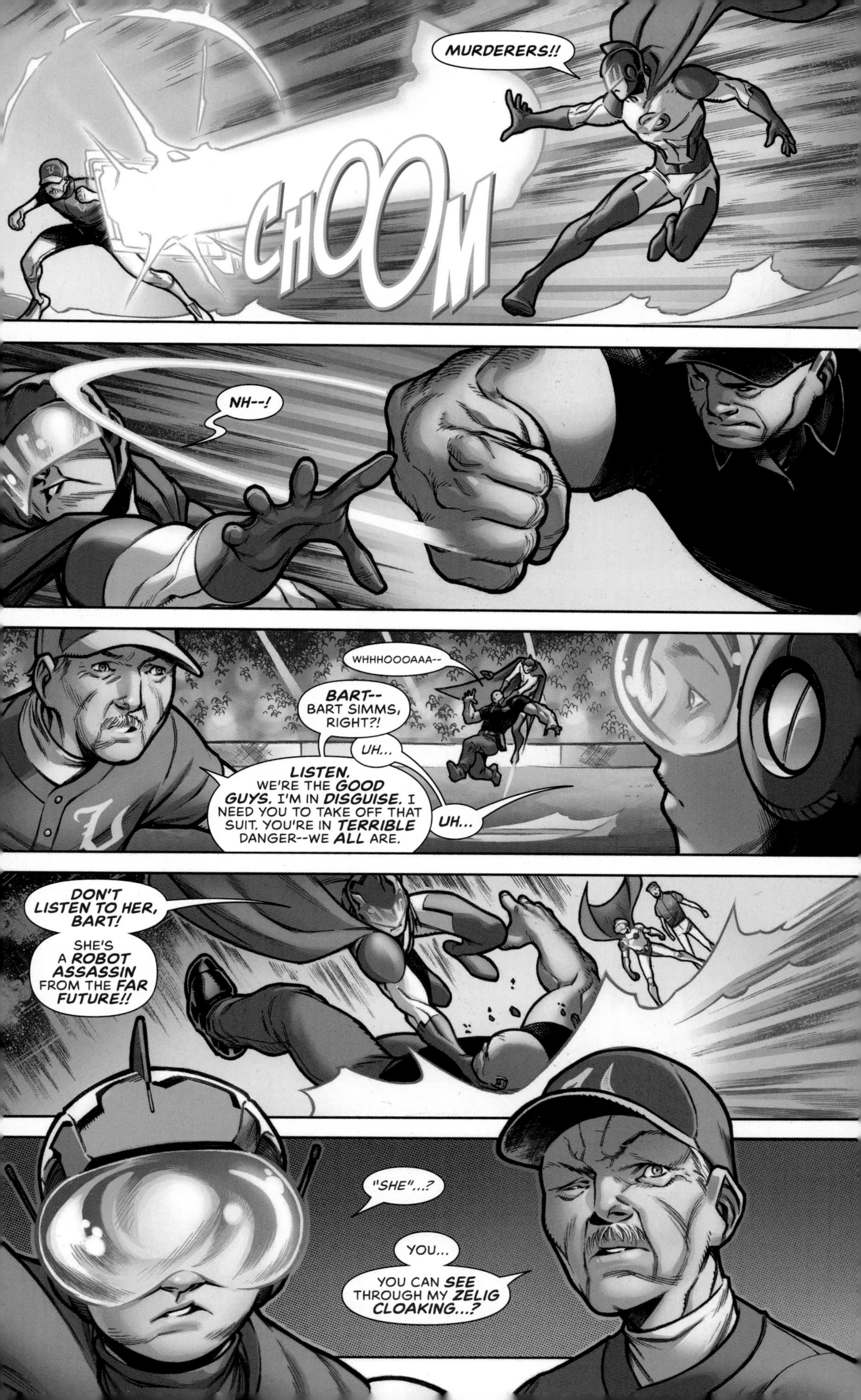
MURDERERS!!
CHOOOM
NH--!
WHHHOOOAAA--
BART--
BART SIMMS, RIGHT?!
UH...
LISTEN.
WE'RE THE GOOD GUYS. I'M IN DISGUISE. I NEED YOU TO TAKE OFF THAT SUIT. YOU'RE IN TERRIBLE DANGER--WE ALL ARE.
UH...
DON'T LISTEN TO HER, BART!
SHE'S A ROBOT ASSASSIN FROM THE FAR FUTURE!!
"SHE"...?
YOU...
YOU CAN SEE THROUGH MY ZELIG CLOAKING...?

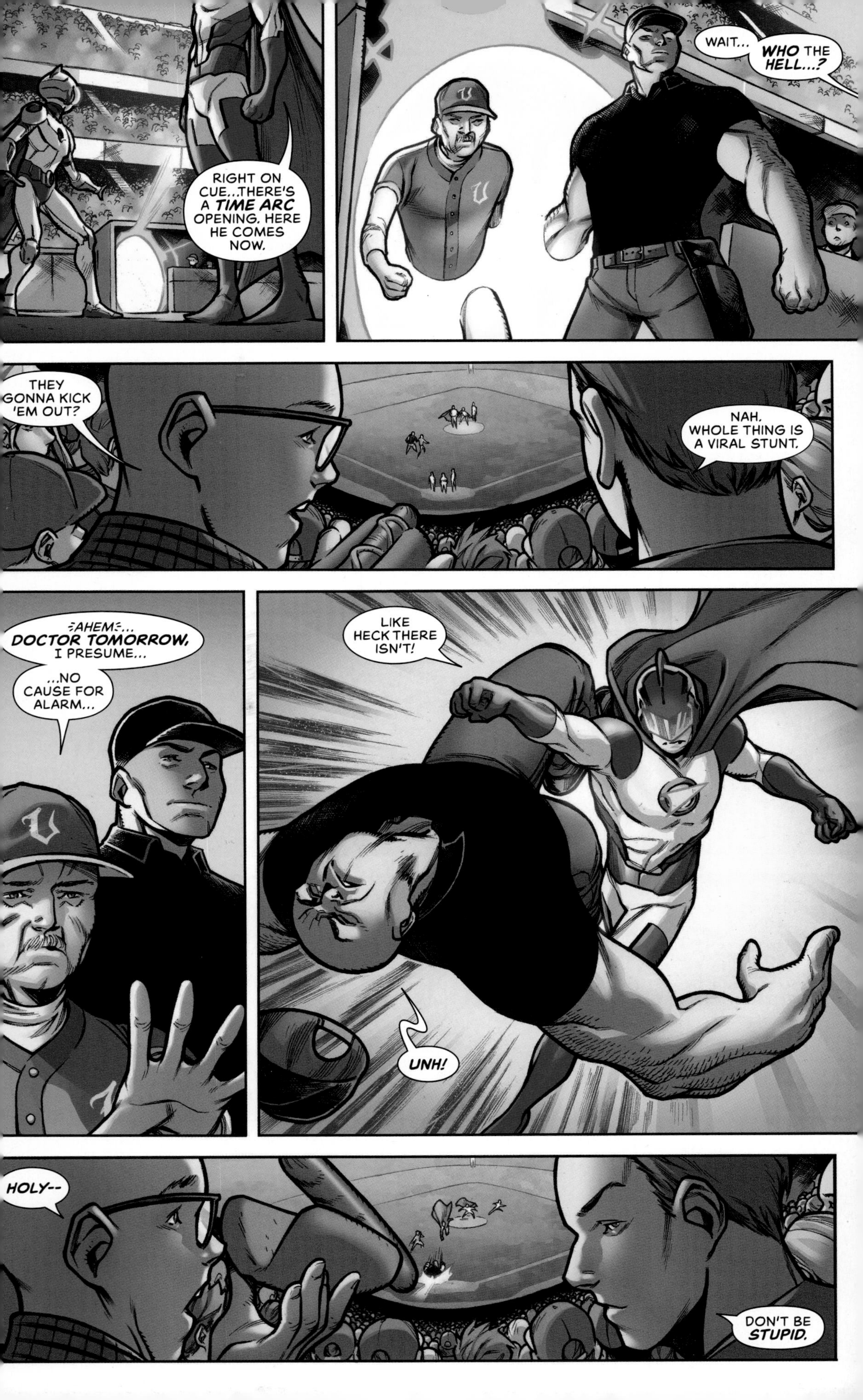

RIGHT ON CUE...THERE'S A TIME ARC OPENING. HERE HE COMES NOW.
WAIT... WHO THE HELL...?
THEY GONNA KICK 'EM OUT?
NAH. WHOLE THING IS A VIRAL STUNT.
AHEM... DOCTOR TOMORROW, I PRESUME...
...NO CAUSE FOR ALARM...
LIKE HECK THERE ISN'T!
UNH!
HOLY--
DON'T BE STUPID.

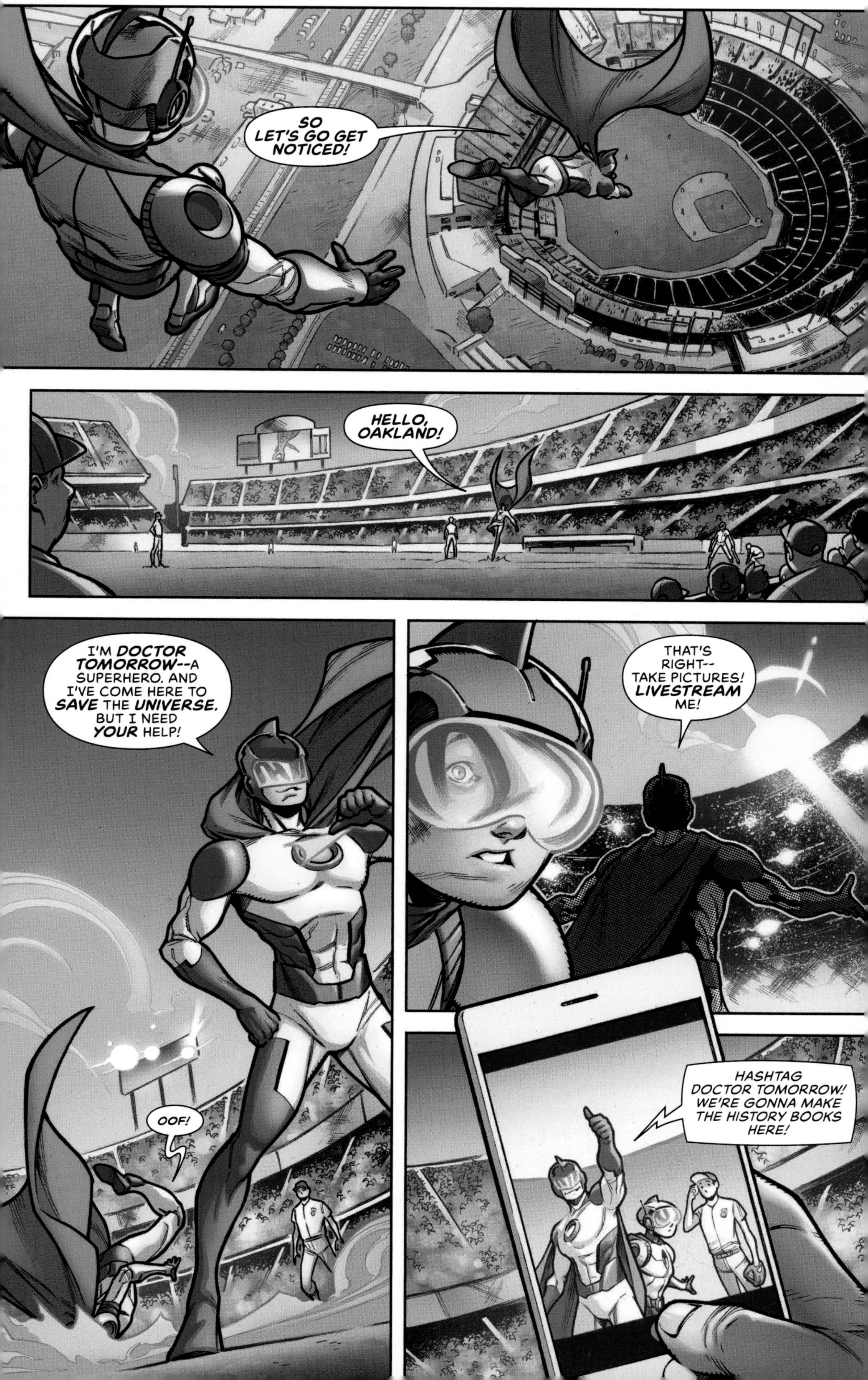
SO LET'S GO GET NOTICED!
HELLO, OAKLAND!
I'M DOCTOR TOMORROW--A SUPERHERO, AND I'VE COME HERE TO SAVE THE UNIVERSE. BUT I NEED YOUR HELP!
OOF!
THAT'S RIGHT-- TAKE PICTURES! LIVESTREAM ME!
HASHTAG DOCTOR TOMORROW! WE'RE GONNA MAKE THE HISTORY BOOKS HERE!

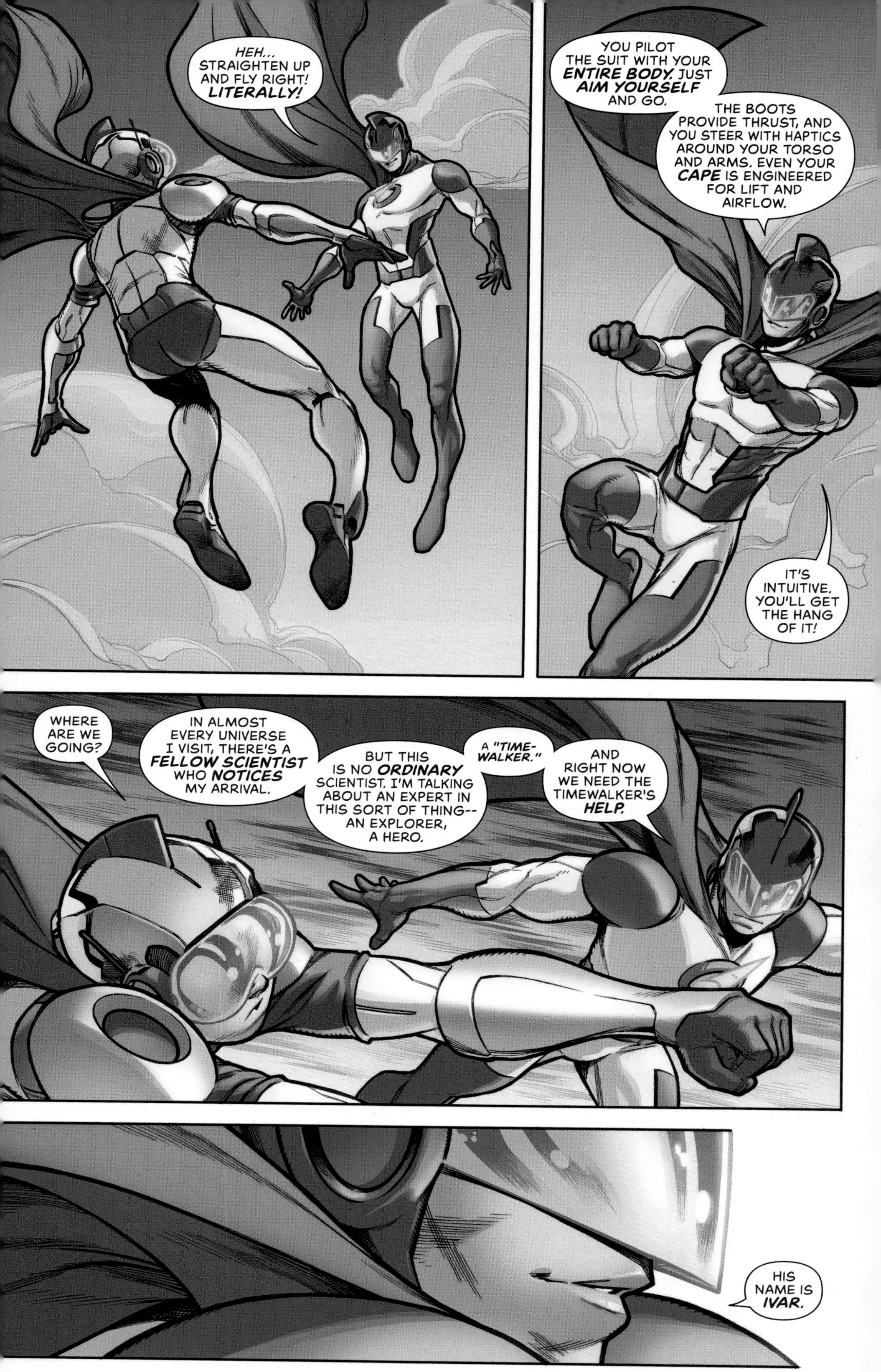
HEH... STRAIGHTEN UP AND FLY RIGHT! LITERALLY!
YOU PILOT THE SUIT WITH YOUR ENTIRE BODY. JUST AIM YOURSELF AND GO.
THE BOOTS PROVIDE THRUST, AND YOU STEER WITH HAPTICS AROUND YOUR TORSO AND ARMS. EVEN YOUR CAPE IS ENGINEERED FOR LIFT AND AIRFLOW.
IT'S INTUITIVE. YOU'LL GET THE HANG OF IT!
WHERE ARE WE GOING?
IN ALMOST EVERY UNIVERSE I VISIT, THERE'S A FELLOW SCIENTIST WHO NOTICES MY ARRIVAL.
BUT THIS IS NO ORDINARY SCIENTIST. I'M TALKING ABOUT AN EXPERT IN THIS SORT OF THING-- AN EXPLORER, A HERO.
A "TIME-WALKER."
AND RIGHT NOW WE NEED THE TIMEWALKER'S HELP.
HIS NAME IS IVAR.

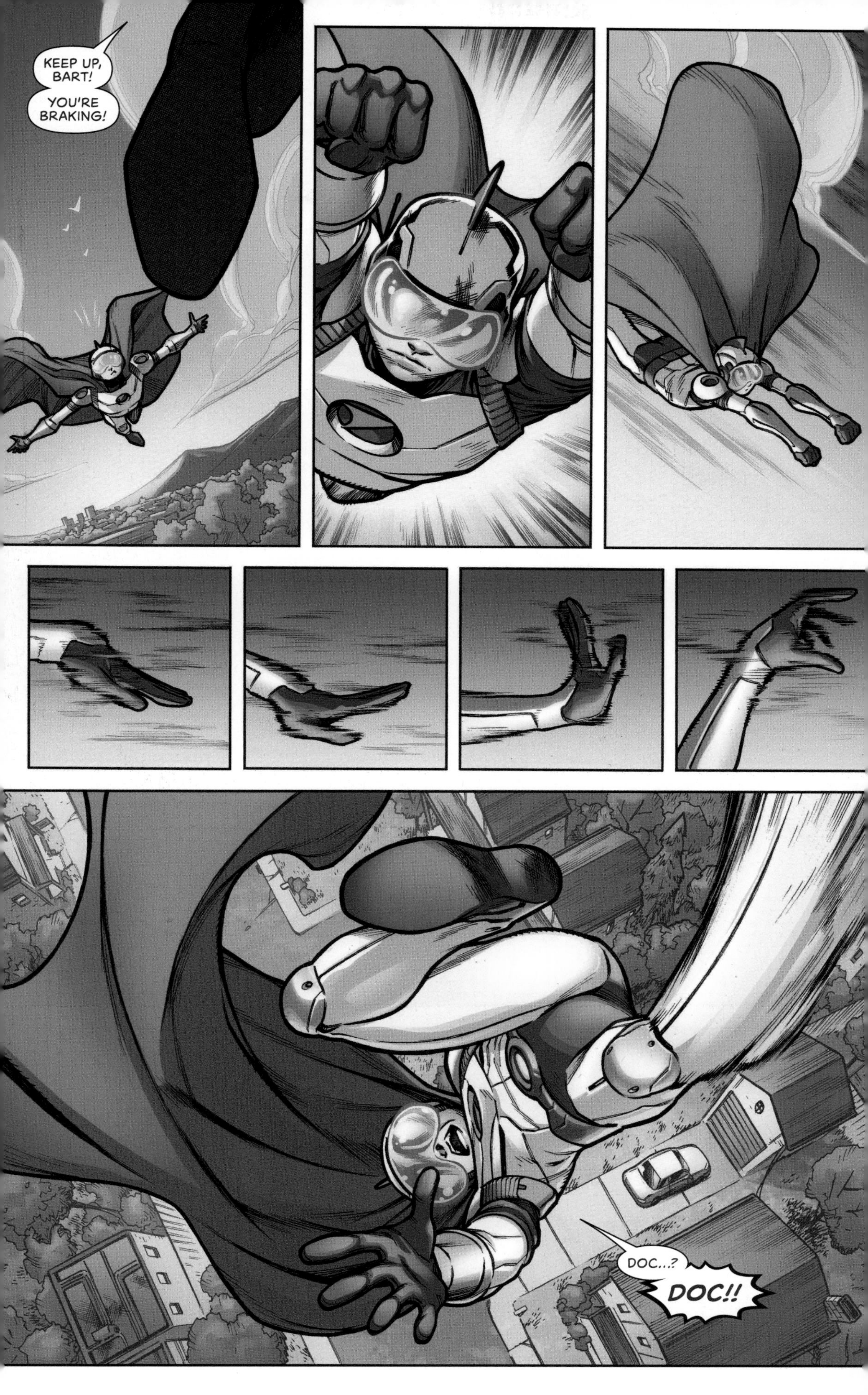
KEEP UP, BART!
YOU'RE BRAKING!
DOC...?
DOC!!

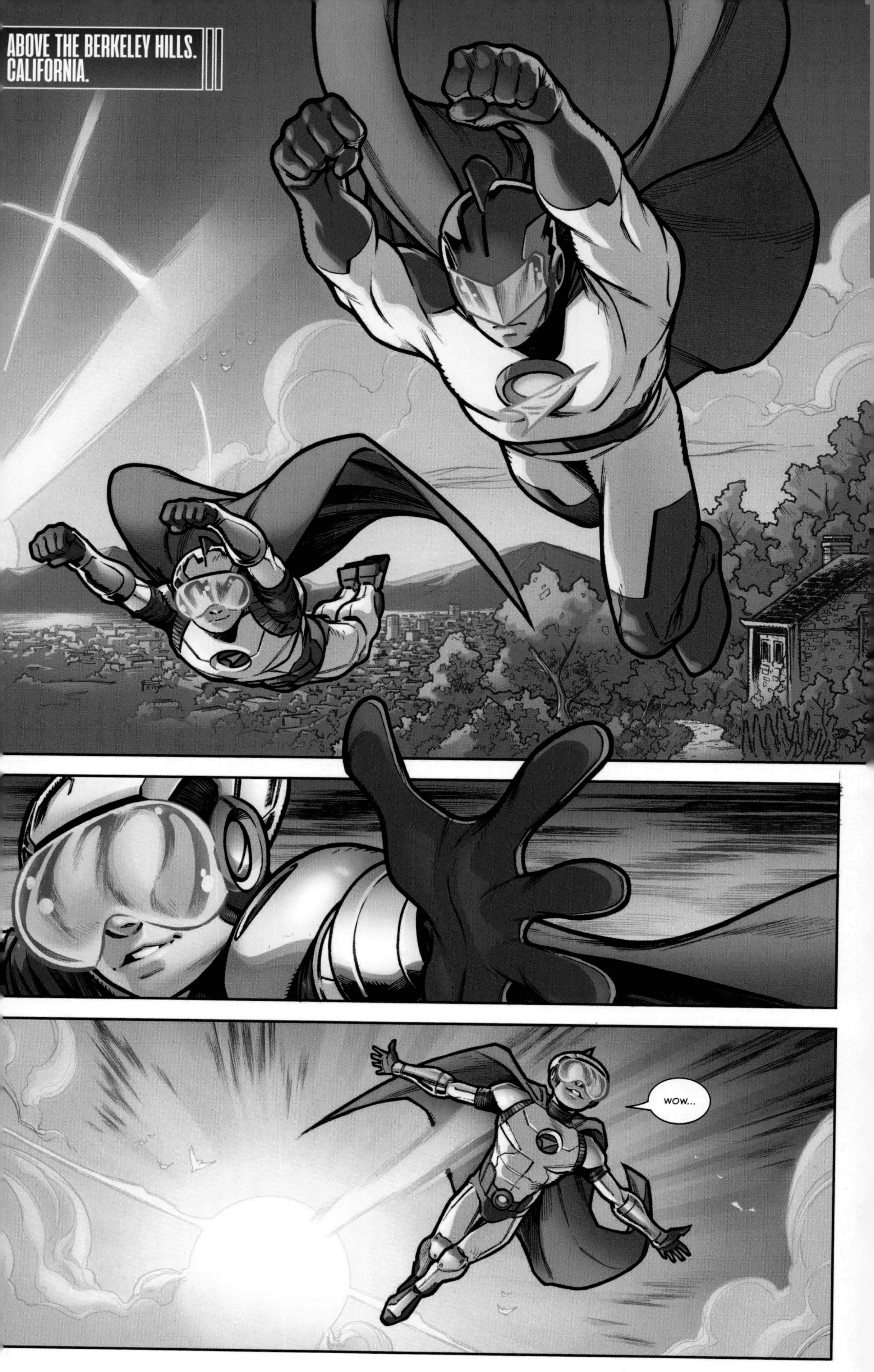
ABOVE THE BERKELEY HILLS.
CALIFORNIA.
WOW...

DOCTOR TOMORROW #2

WRITER: ALEJANDRO ARBONA
ARTIST: JIM TOWE
COLORIST: DIEGO RODRIGUEZ
LETTERER: CLAYTON COWLES
COVER ARTISTS: JIM TOWE with LEONARDO PACIAROTTI
ASSISTANT EDITOR: DREW BAUMGARTNER
SENIOR EDITORIAL DIRECTOR: ROBERT MEYERS

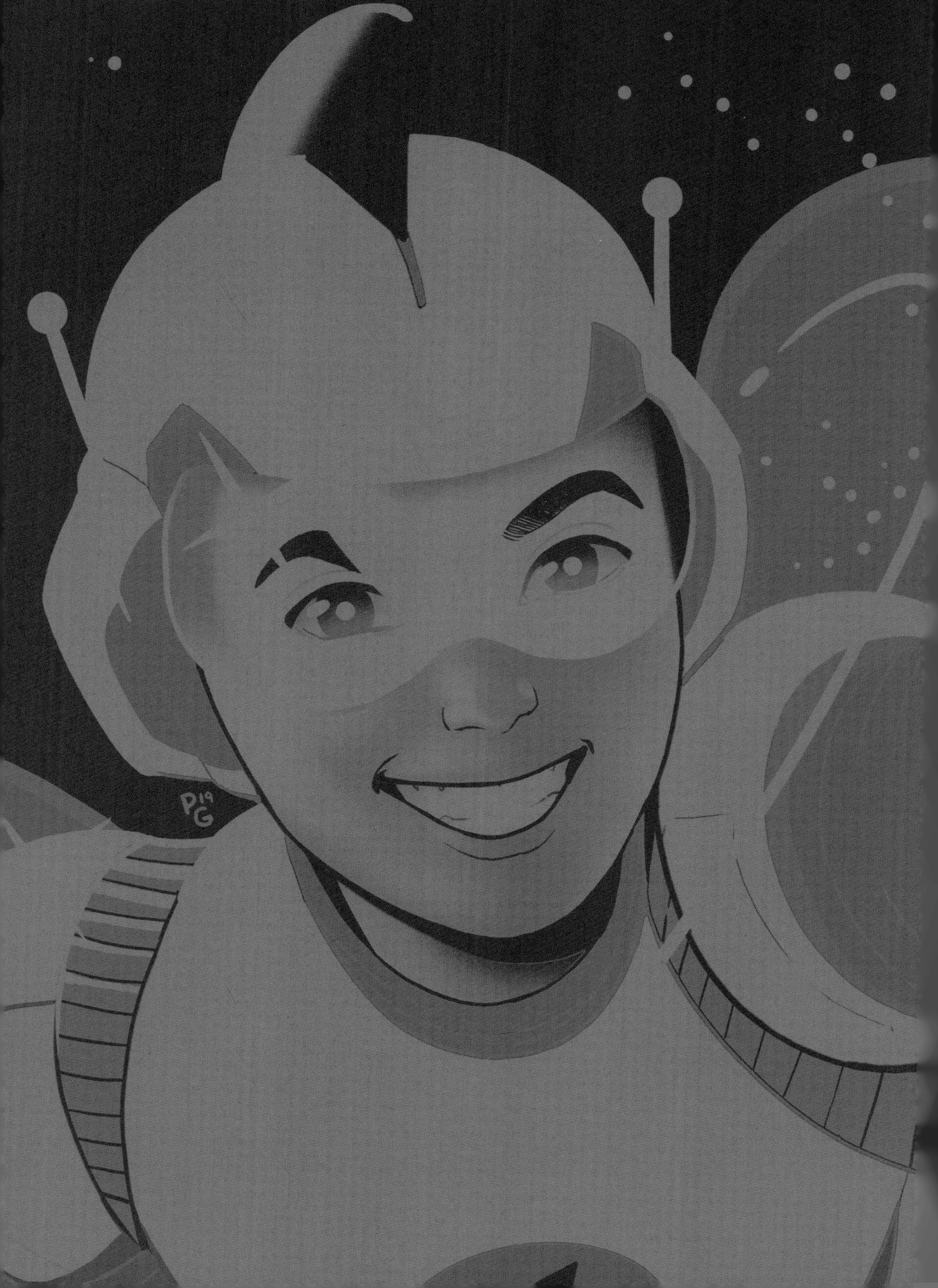

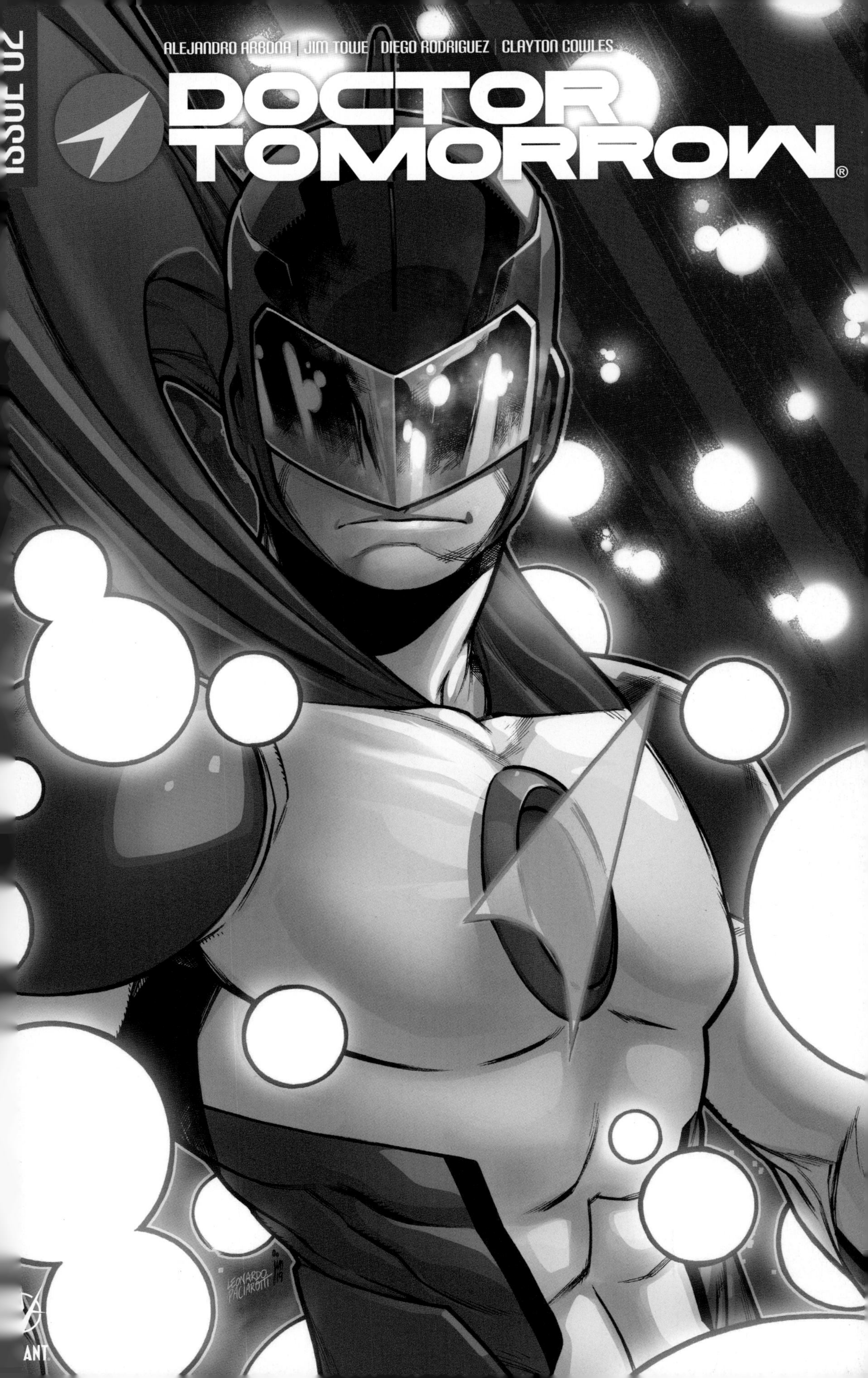
ALEJANDRO ARBONA | JIM TOWE | DIEGO RODRIGUEZ | CLAYTON COWLES
DOCTOR TOMORROW®

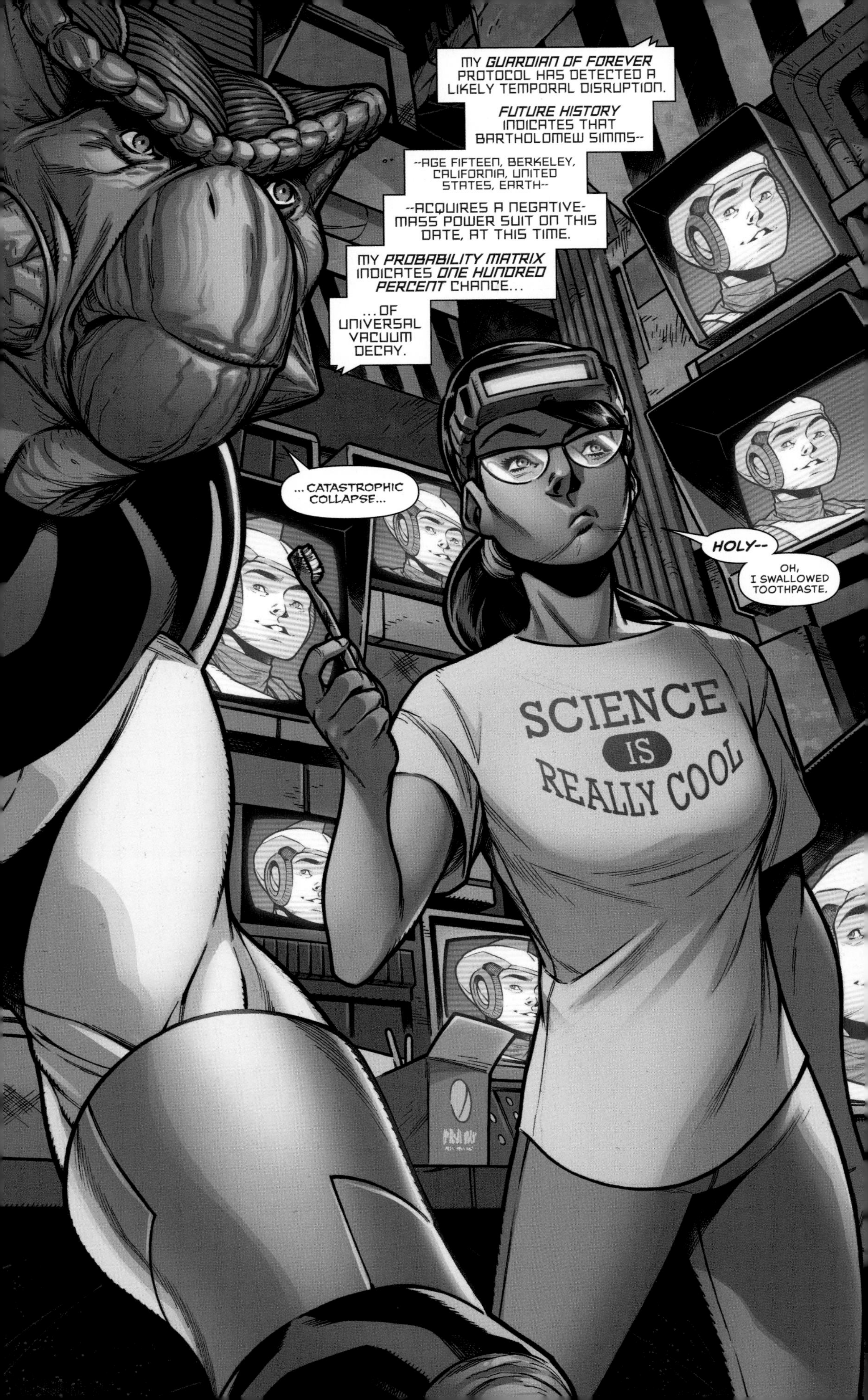
MY GUARDIAN OF FOREVER PROTOCOL HAS DETECTED A LIKELY TEMPORAL DISRUPTION.
FUTURE HISTORY INDICATES THAT BARTHOLOMEW SIMMS--
--AGE FIFTEEN, BERKELEY, CALIFORNIA, UNITED STATES, EARTH--
--ACQUIRES A NEGATIVE-MASS POWER SUIT ON THIS DATE, AT THIS TIME.
MY PROBABILITY MATRIX INDICATES ONE HUNDRED PERCENT CHANCE...
...OF UNIVERSAL VACUUM DECAY.
...CATASTROPHIC COLLAPSE...
HOLY--
OH, I SWALLOWED TOOTHPASTE.
SCIENCE IS REALLY COOL

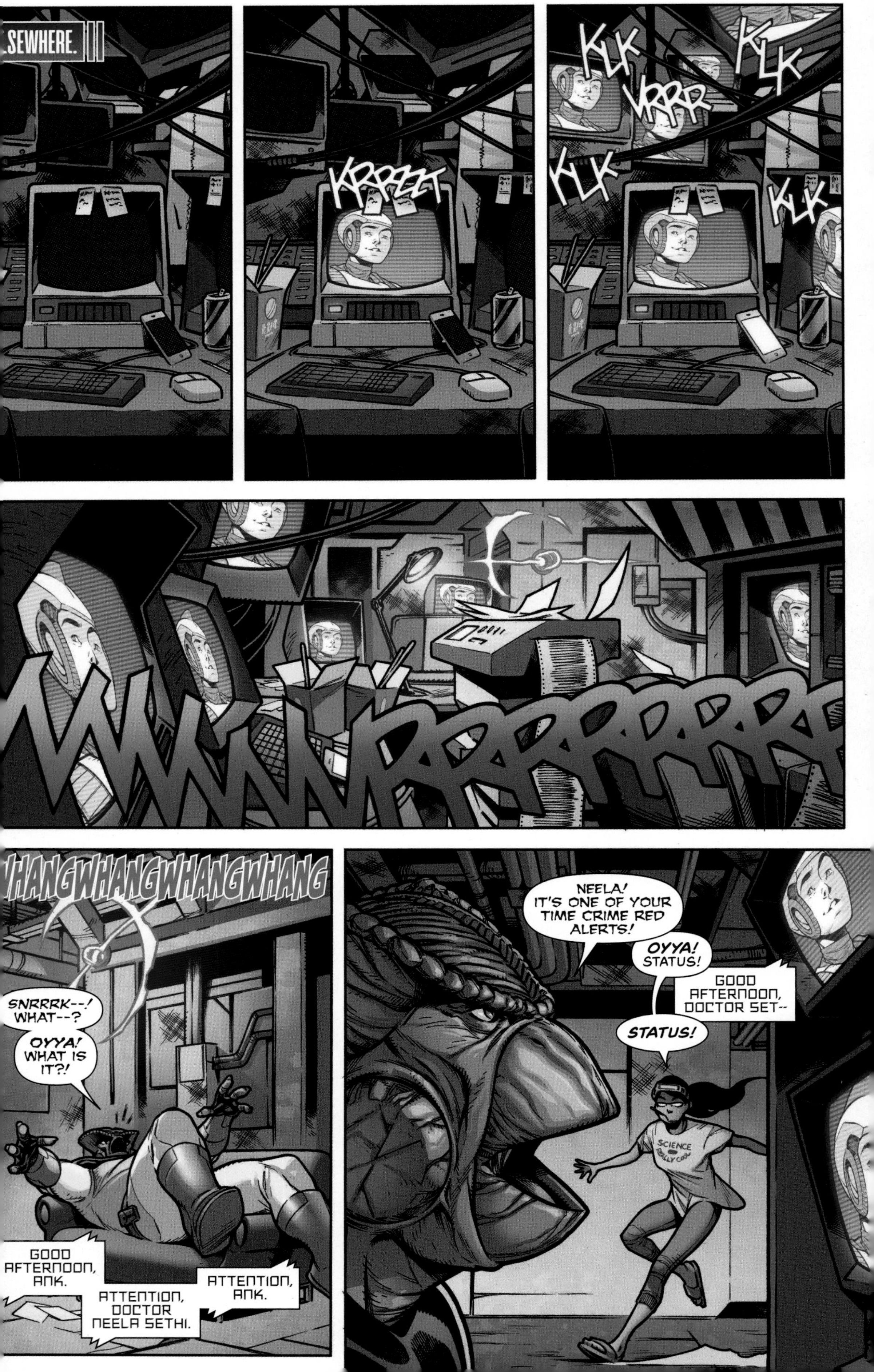
SEWHERE.
KRREEET
KLK
VRRRR
KLK
KLK
KLK
WWWWRRRRRRRRRR
WHANGWHANGWHANGWHANG
SNRRRK--! WHAT--?
OYYA! WHAT IS IT?!
GOOD AFTERNOON, ANK.
ATTENTION, DOCTOR NEELA SETHI.
ATTENTION, ANK.
NEELA! IT'S ONE OF YOUR TIME CRIME RED ALERTS!
OYYA! STATUS!
GOOD AFTERNOON, DOCTOR SET--
STATUS!

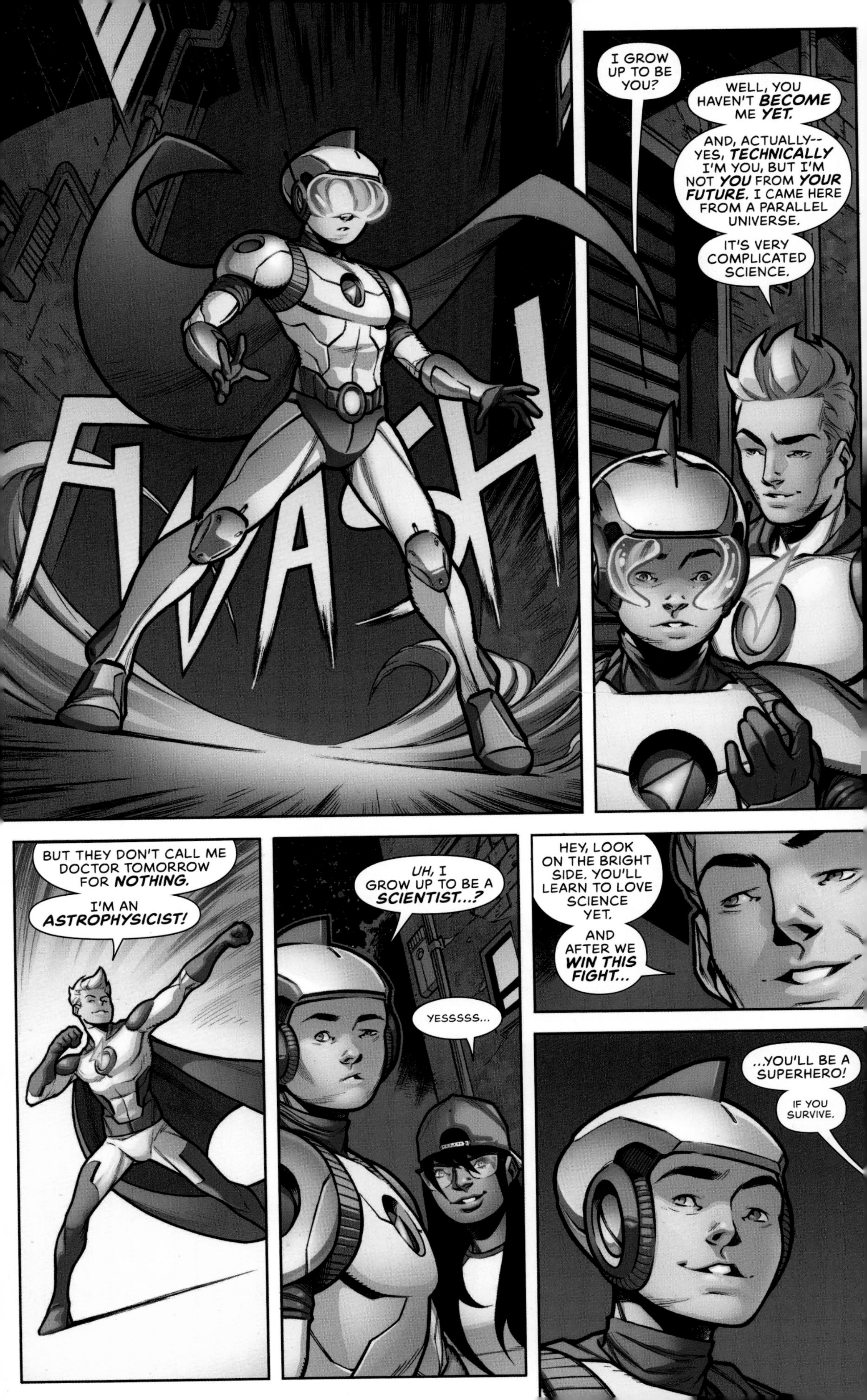
FWASH
I GROW UP TO BE YOU?
WELL, YOU HAVEN'T BECOME ME YET.
AND, ACTUALLY-- YES, TECHNICALLY I'M YOU, BUT I'M NOT YOU FROM YOUR FUTURE. I CAME HERE FROM A PARALLEL UNIVERSE.
IT'S VERY COMPLICATED SCIENCE.
BUT THEY DON'T CALL ME DOCTOR TOMORROW FOR NOTHING.
I'M AN ASTROPHYSICIST!
UH, I GROW UP TO BE A SCIENTIST...?
YESSSSS...
HEY, LOOK ON THE BRIGHT SIDE. YOU'LL LEARN TO LOVE SCIENCE YET.
AND AFTER WE WIN THIS FIGHT...
...YOU'LL BE A SUPERHERO!
IF YOU SURVIVE.

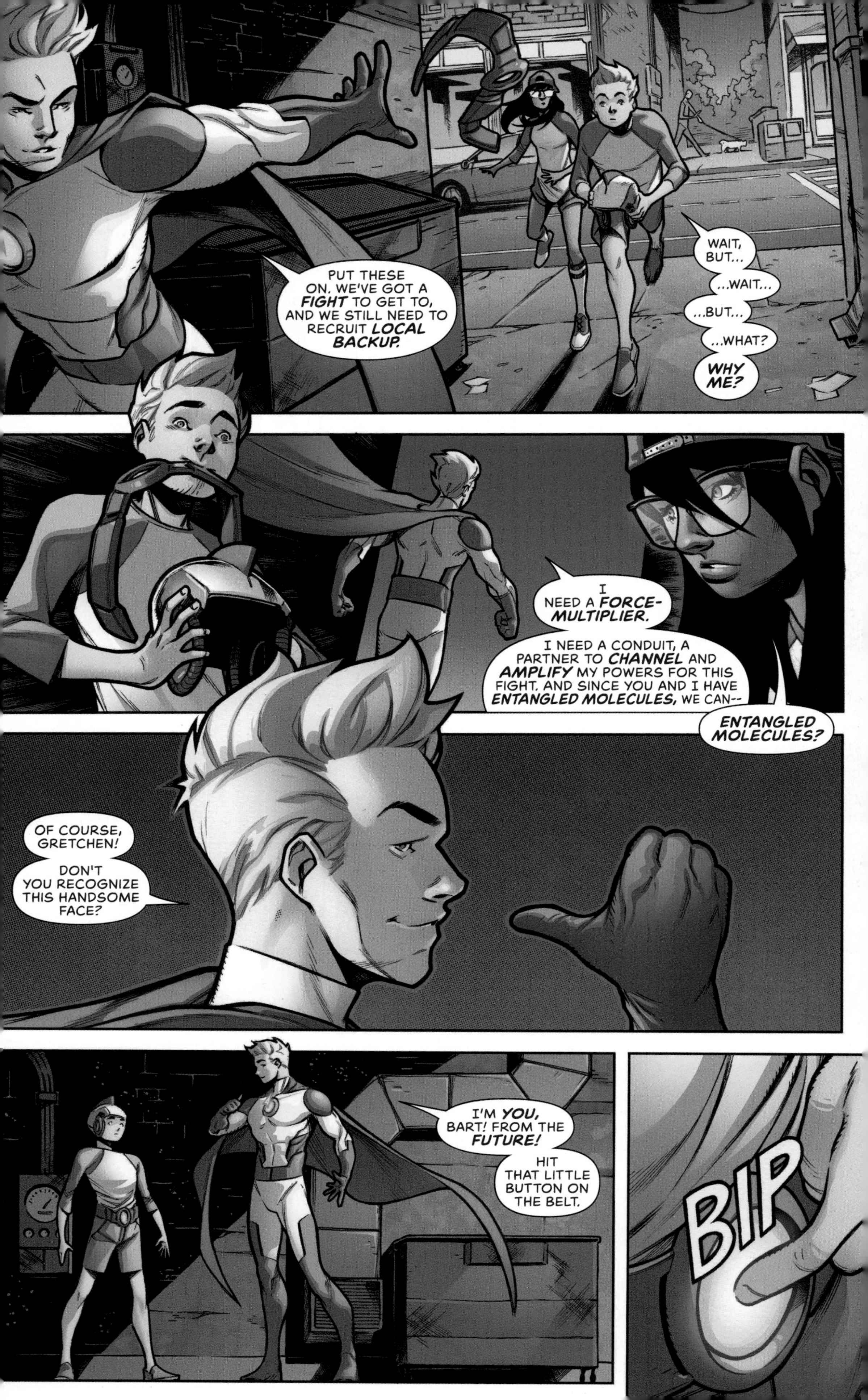
PUT THESE ON. WE'VE GOT A FIGHT TO GET TO, AND WE STILL NEED TO RECRUIT LOCAL BACKUP.
WAIT, BUT...
...WAIT...
...BUT...
...WHAT?
WHY ME?
I NEED A FORCE-MULTIPLIER.
I NEED A CONDUIT, A PARTNER TO CHANNEL AND AMPLIFY MY POWERS FOR THIS FIGHT. AND SINCE YOU AND I HAVE ENTANGLED MOLECULES, WE CAN--
ENTANGLED MOLECULES?
OF COURSE, GRETCHEN!
DON'T YOU RECOGNIZE THIS HANDSOME FACE?
I'M YOU, BART! FROM THE FUTURE!
HIT THAT LITTLE BUTTON ON THE BELT.
BIP

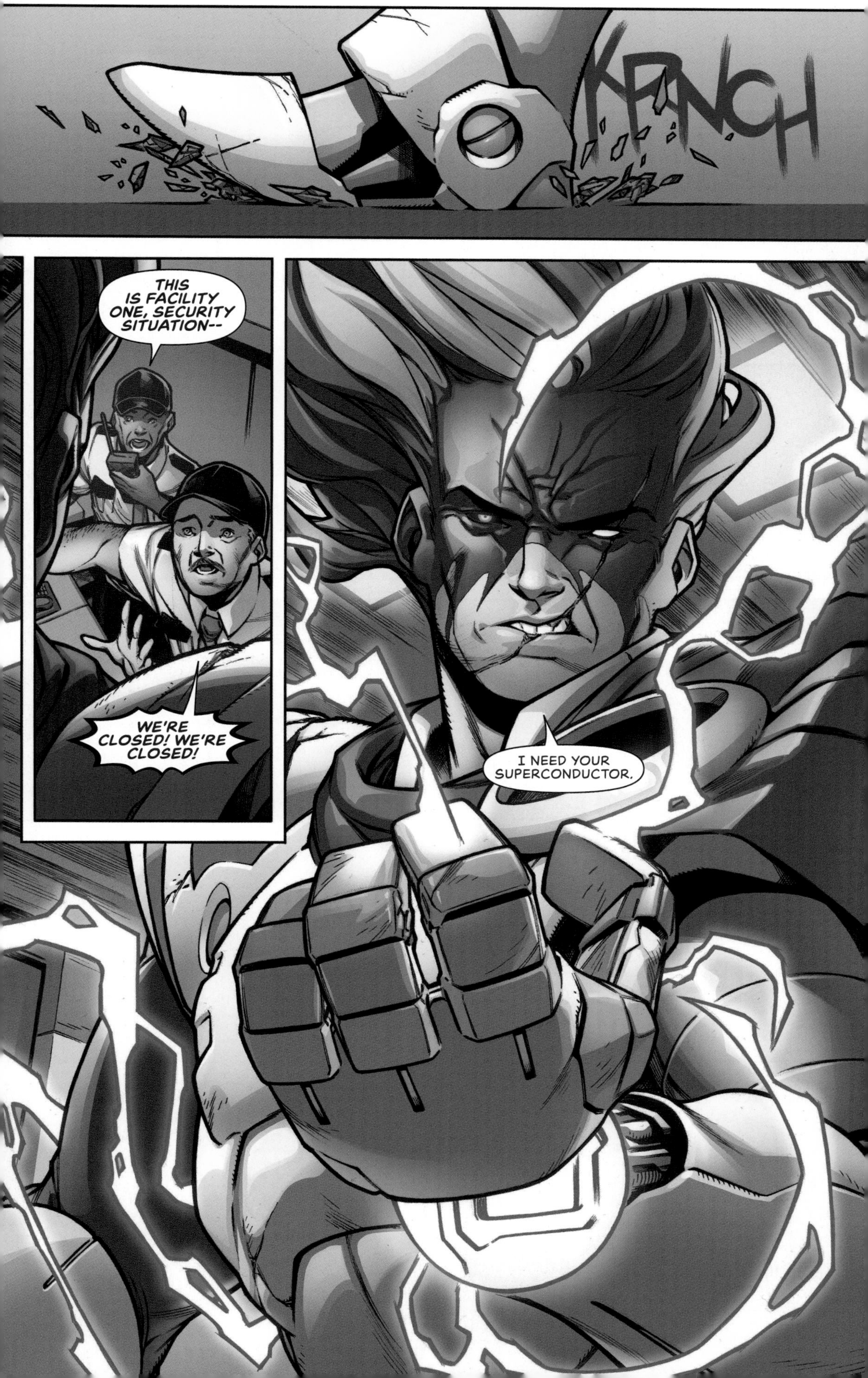
KRNCH
THIS IS FACILITY ONE, SECURITY SITUATION--
WE'RE CLOSED! WE'RE CLOSED!
I NEED YOUR SUPERCONDUCTOR.

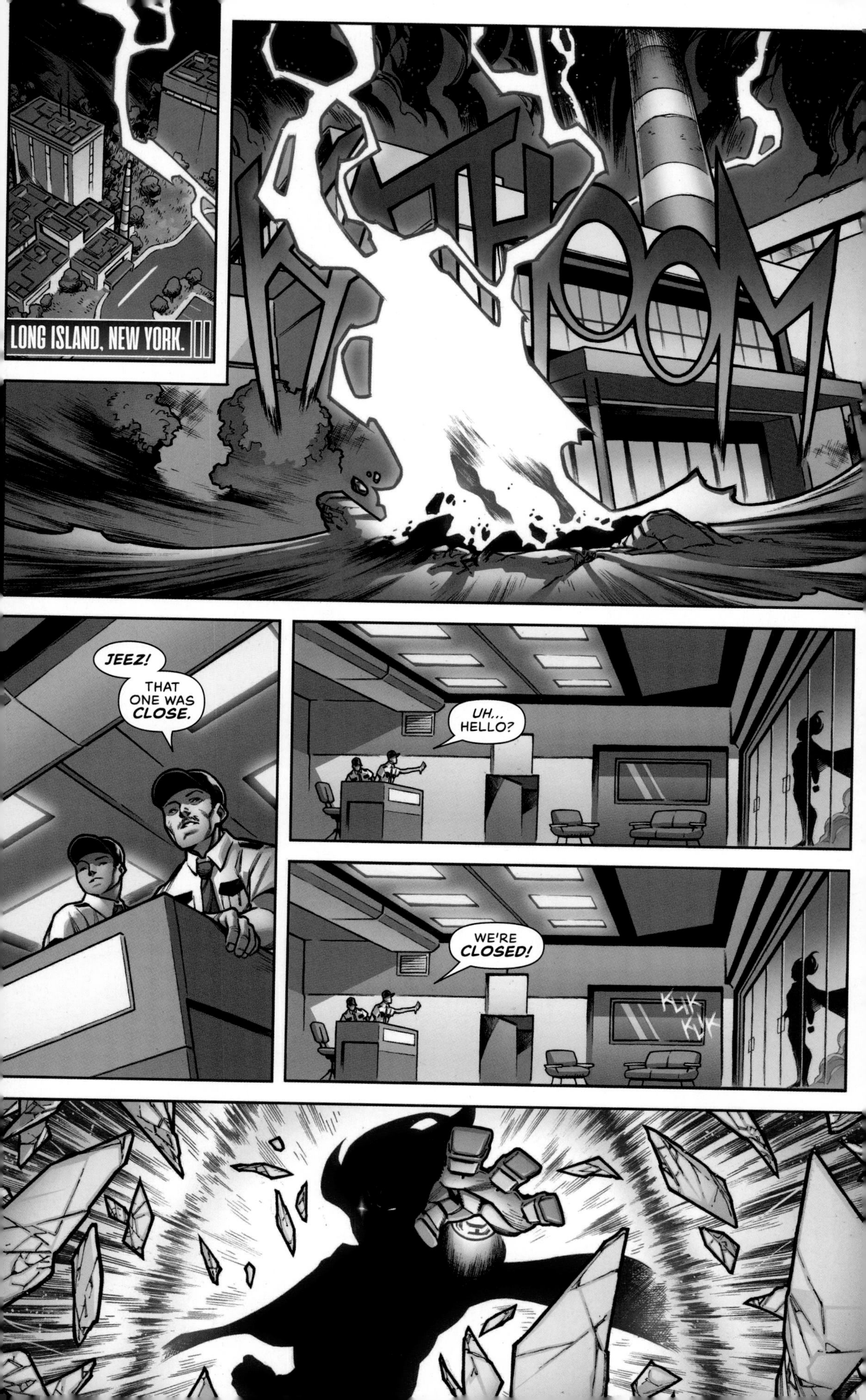
LONG ISLAND, NEW YORK.
KTHOOM
JEEZ!
THAT ONE WAS CLOSE.
UH... HELLO?
WE'RE CLOSED!
KLIK KLIK

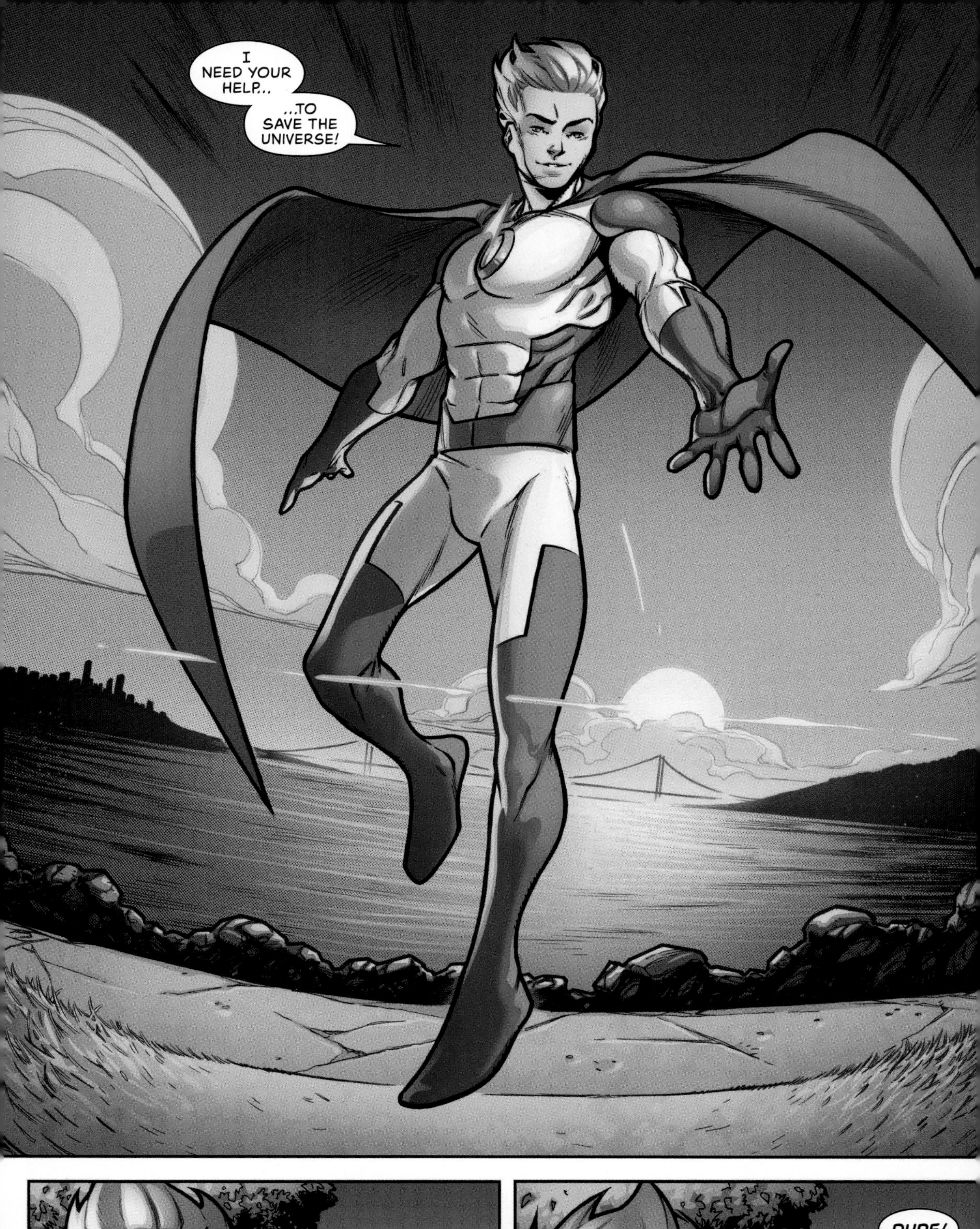
I NEED YOUR HELP...
...TO SAVE THE UNIVERSE!
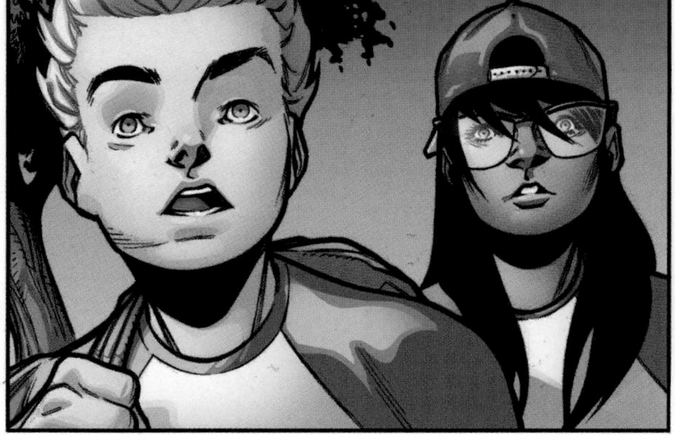
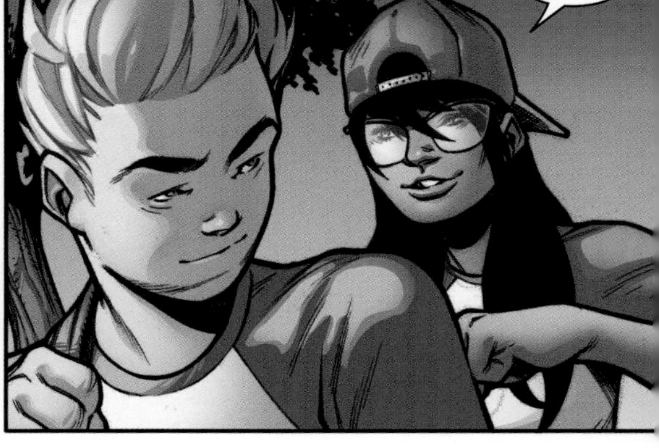
DUDE!

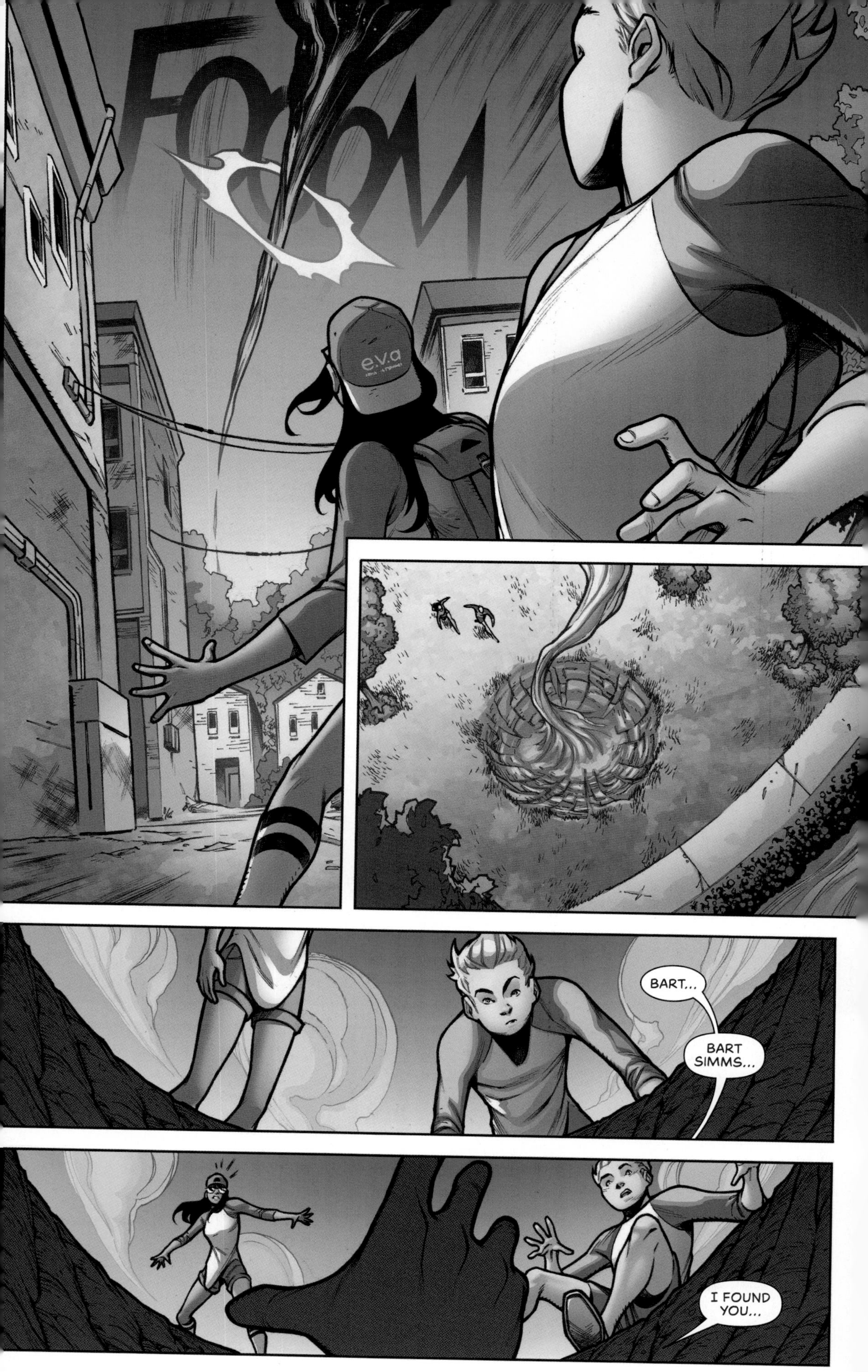
FOOOM
BART...
BART SIMMS...
I FOUND YOU...

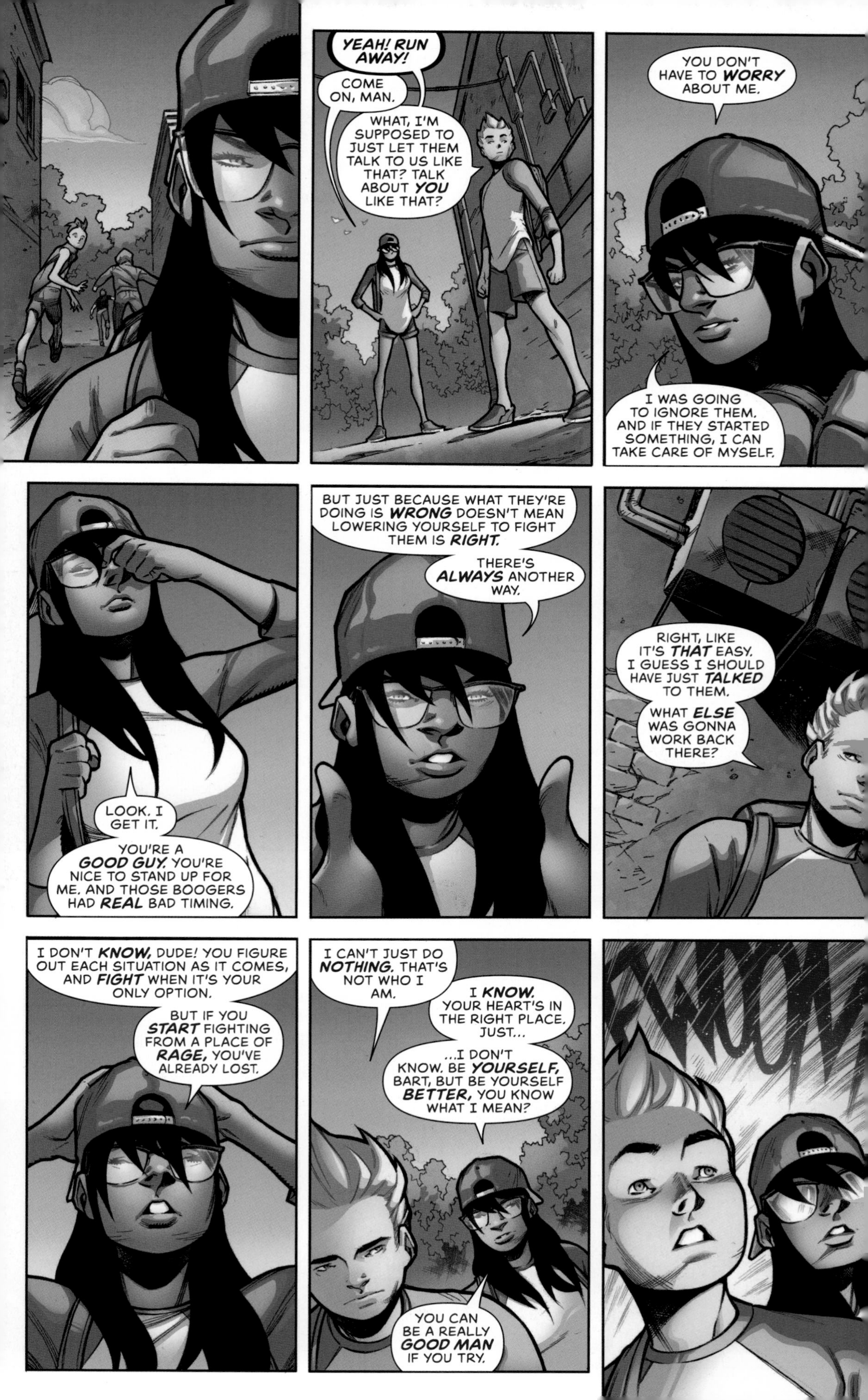
YEAH! RUN AWAY!
COME ON, MAN.
WHAT, I'M SUPPOSED TO JUST LET THEM TALK TO US LIKE THAT? TALK ABOUT YOU LIKE THAT?
YOU DON'T HAVE TO WORRY ABOUT ME.
I WAS GOING TO IGNORE THEM. AND IF THEY STARTED SOMETHING, I CAN TAKE CARE OF MYSELF.
LOOK. I GET IT.
YOU'RE A GOOD GUY. YOU'RE NICE TO STAND UP FOR ME. AND THOSE BOOGERS HAD REAL BAD TIMING.
BUT JUST BECAUSE WHAT THEY'RE DOING IS WRONG DOESN'T MEAN LOWERING YOURSELF TO FIGHT THEM IS RIGHT.
THERE'S ALWAYS ANOTHER WAY.
RIGHT, LIKE IT'S THAT EASY. I GUESS I SHOULD HAVE JUST TALKED TO THEM.
WHAT ELSE WAS GONNA WORK BACK THERE?
I DON'T KNOW, DUDE! YOU FIGURE OUT EACH SITUATION AS IT COMES, AND FIGHT WHEN IT'S YOUR ONLY OPTION.
BUT IF YOU START FIGHTING FROM A PLACE OF RAGE, YOU'VE ALREADY LOST.
I CAN'T JUST DO NOTHING. THAT'S NOT WHO I AM.
I KNOW. YOUR HEART'S IN THE RIGHT PLACE. JUST...
...I DON'T KNOW. BE YOURSELF, BART, BUT BE YOURSELF BETTER, YOU KNOW WHAT I MEAN?
YOU CAN BE A REALLY GOOD MAN IF YOU TRY.

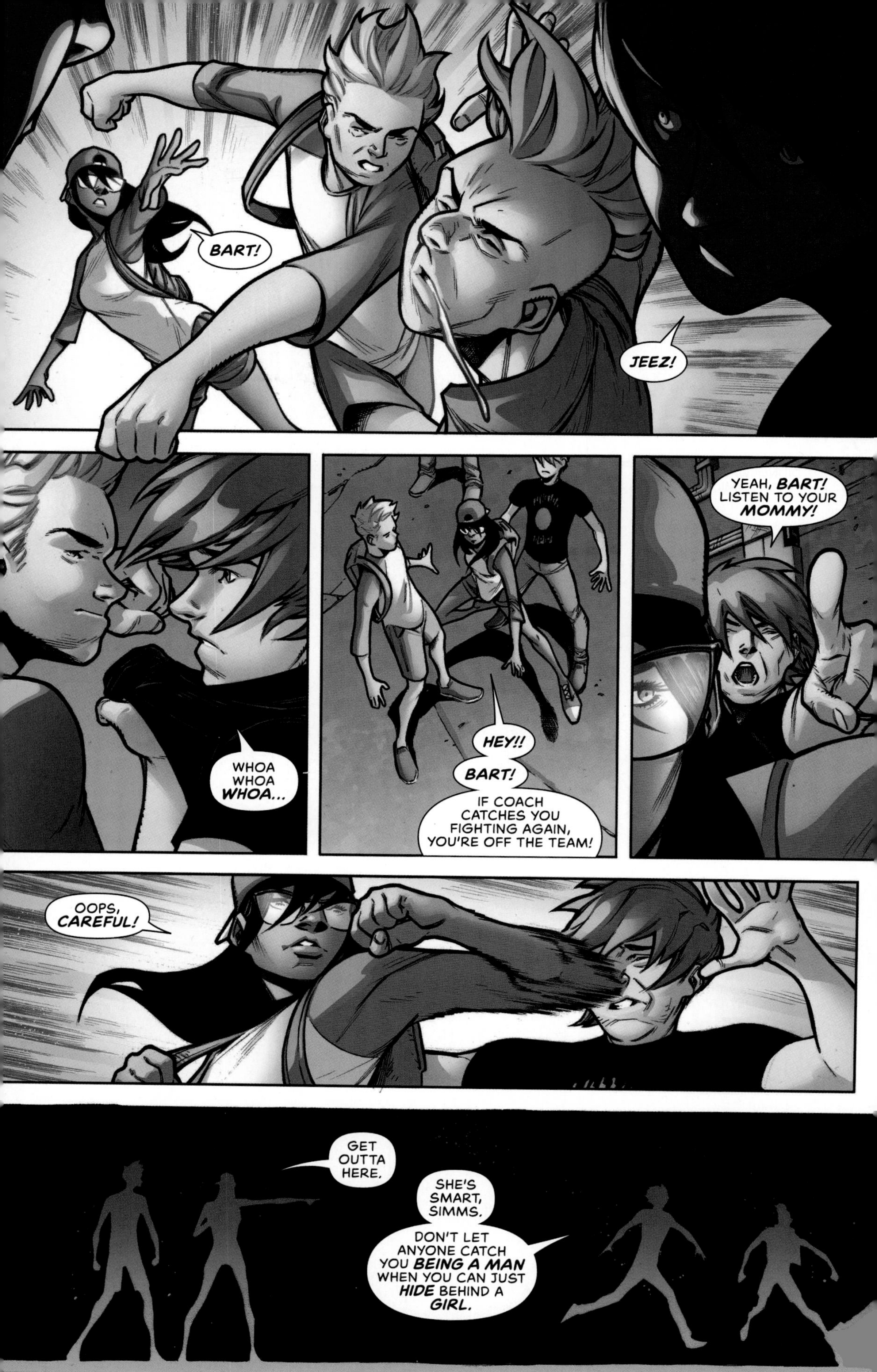
BART!
JEEZ!
WHOA WHOA WHOA...
HEY!!
BART!
IF COACH CATCHES YOU FIGHTING AGAIN, YOU'RE OFF THE TEAM!
YEAH, BART! LISTEN TO YOUR MOMMY!
OOPS, CAREFUL!
GET OUTTA HERE.
SHE'S SMART, SIMMS.
DON'T LET ANYONE CATCH YOU BEING A MAN WHEN YOU CAN JUST HIDE BEHIND A GIRL.

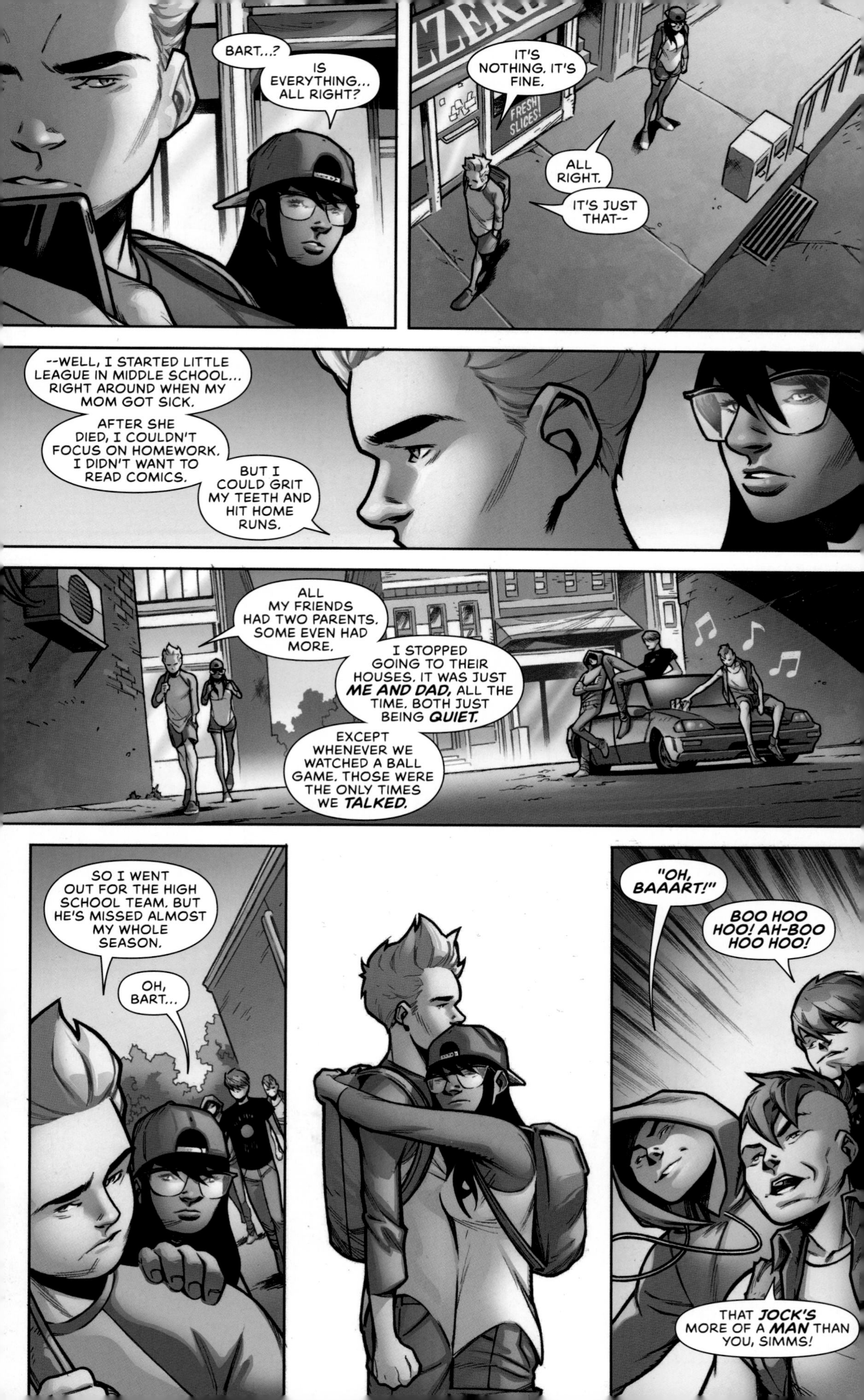
BART...?
IS EVERYTHING... ALL RIGHT?
IT'S NOTHING. IT'S FINE.
FRESH SLICES!
ALL RIGHT.
IT'S JUST THAT--
--WELL, I STARTED LITTLE LEAGUE IN MIDDLE SCHOOL... RIGHT AROUND WHEN MY MOM GOT SICK.
AFTER SHE DIED, I COULDN'T FOCUS ON HOMEWORK. I DIDN'T WANT TO READ COMICS.
BUT I COULD GRIT MY TEETH AND HIT HOME RUNS.
ALL MY FRIENDS HAD TWO PARENTS. SOME EVEN HAD MORE.
I STOPPED GOING TO THEIR HOUSES. IT WAS JUST ME AND DAD, ALL THE TIME. BOTH JUST BEING QUIET.
EXCEPT WHENEVER WE WATCHED A BALL GAME. THOSE WERE THE ONLY TIMES WE TALKED.
SO I WENT OUT FOR THE HIGH SCHOOL TEAM. BUT HE'S MISSED ALMOST MY WHOLE SEASON.
OH, BART...
"OH, BAAART!"
BOO HOO HOO! AH-BOO HOO HOO!
THAT JOCK'S MORE OF A MAN THAN YOU, SIMMS!

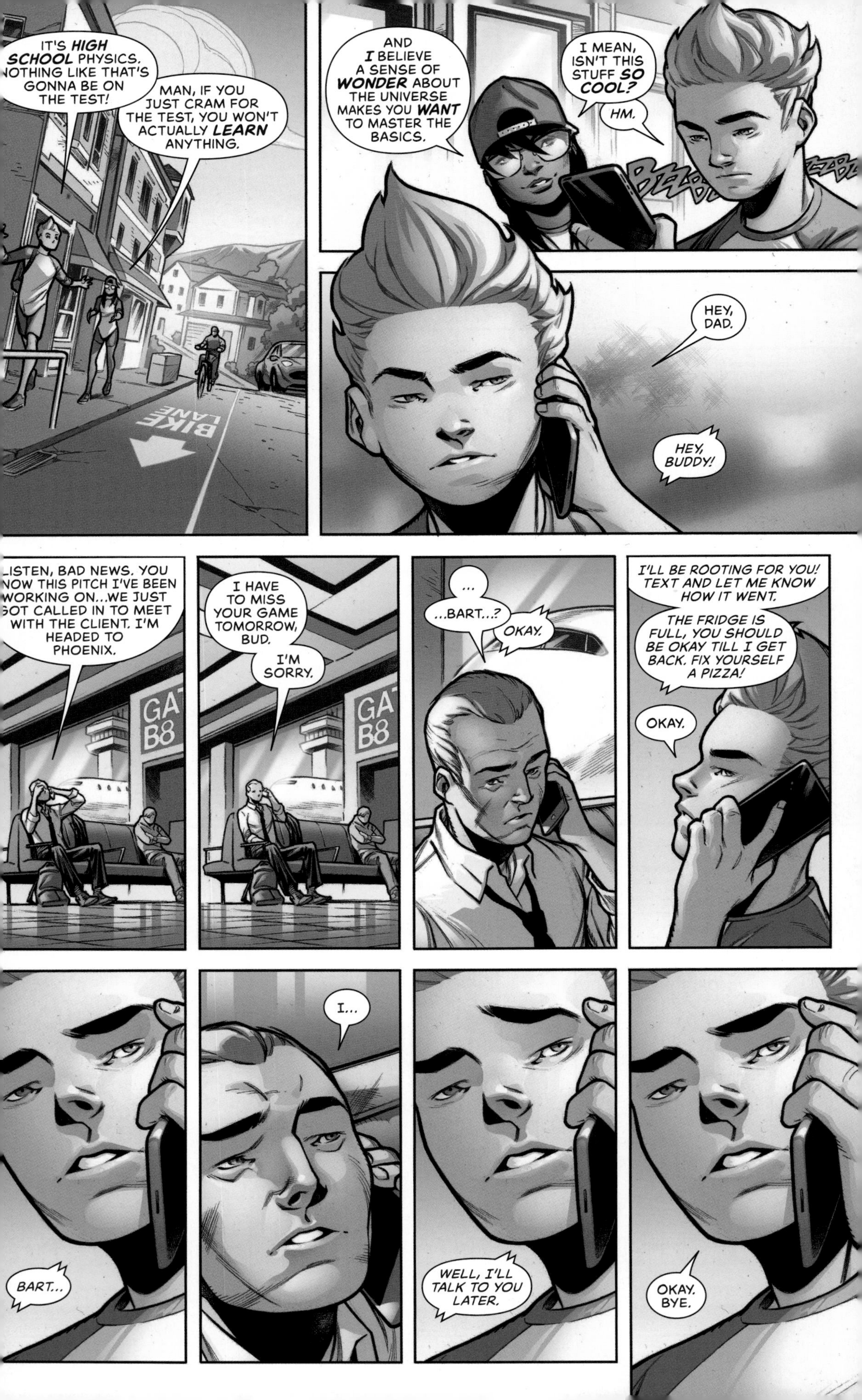

IT'S **HIGH SCHOOL** PHYSICS. NOTHING LIKE THAT'S GONNA BE ON THE TEST!
MAN, IF YOU JUST CRAM FOR THE TEST, YOU WON'T ACTUALLY **LEARN** ANYTHING.
BIKE LANE
AND **I** BELIEVE A SENSE OF **WONDER** ABOUT THE UNIVERSE MAKES YOU **WANT** TO MASTER THE BASICS.
I MEAN, ISN'T THIS STUFF **SO COOL?**
HM.
BZZZ
HEY, DAD.
HEY, BUDDY!
LISTEN, BAD NEWS. YOU NOW THIS PITCH I'VE BEEN WORKING ON... WE JUST OT CALLED IN TO MEET WITH THE CLIENT. I'M HEADED TO PHOENIX.
GAT B8
I HAVE TO MISS YOUR GAME TOMORROW, BUD.
I'M SORRY.
...
...BART...?
OKAY.
I'LL BE ROOTING FOR YOU! TEXT AND LET ME KNOW HOW IT WENT.
THE FRIDGE IS FULL, YOU SHOULD BE OKAY TILL I GET BACK. FIX YOURSELF A PIZZA!
OKAY.
BART...
I...
WELL, I'LL TALK TO YOU LATER.
OKAY. BYE.

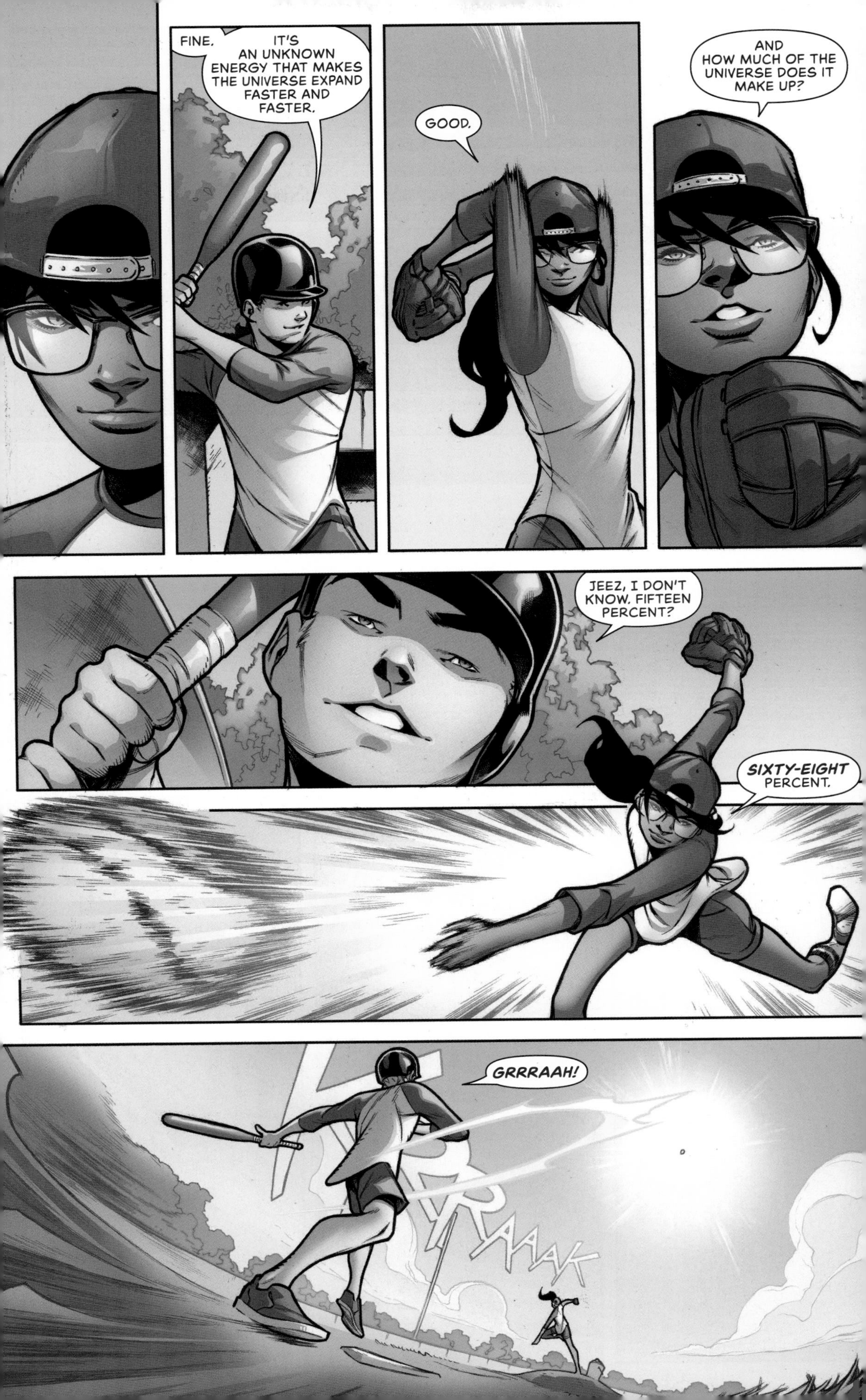
FINE.
IT'S AN UNKNOWN ENERGY THAT MAKES THE UNIVERSE EXPAND FASTER AND FASTER.
GOOD.
AND HOW MUCH OF THE UNIVERSE DOES IT MAKE UP?
JEEZ, I DON'T KNOW. FIFTEEN PERCENT?
SIXTY-EIGHT PERCENT.
GRRRAAH!
KRAAAK

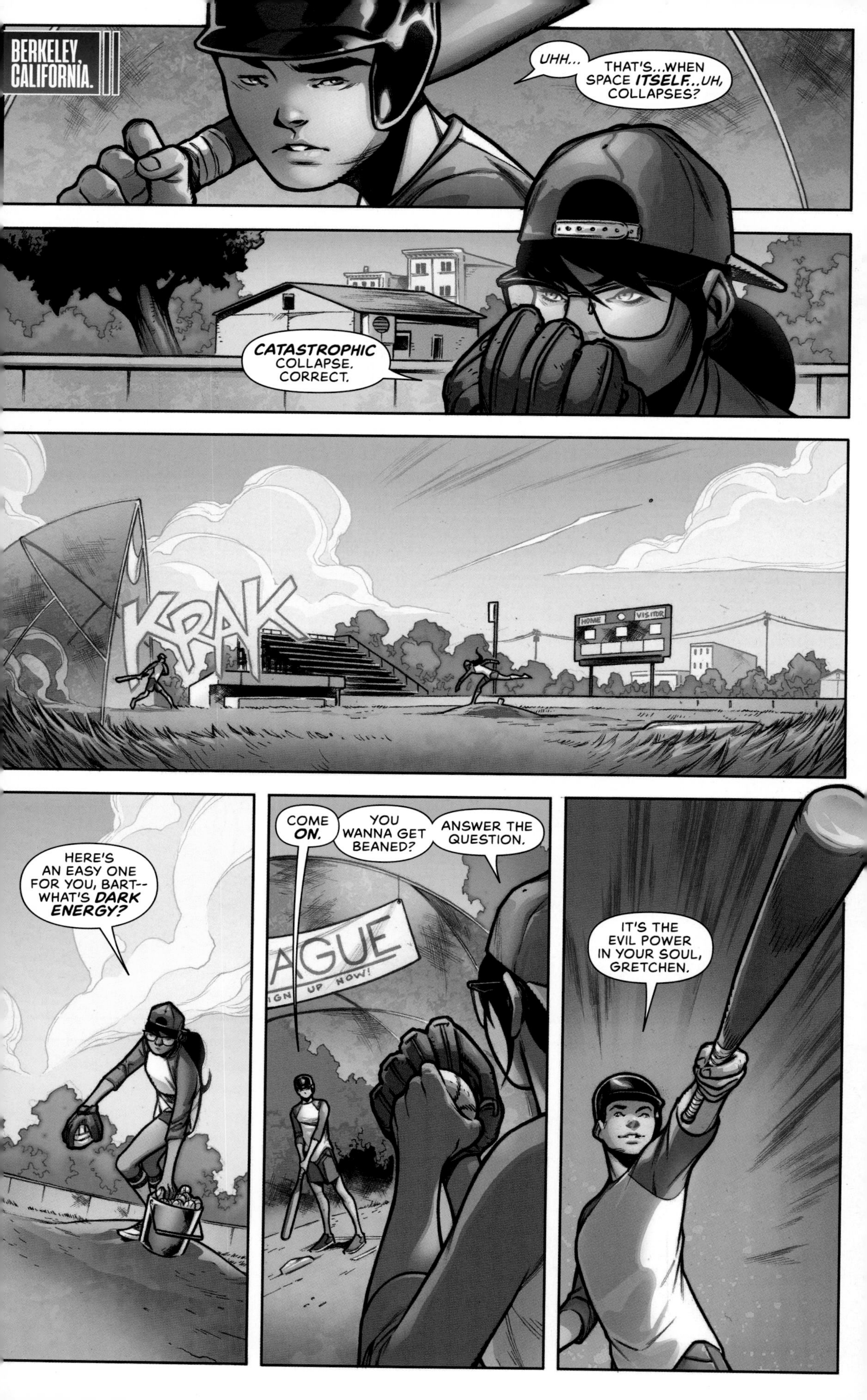
BERKELEY, CALIFORNIA.
UHH...
THAT'S...WHEN SPACE ITSELF...UH, COLLAPSES?
CATASTROPHIC COLLAPSE. CORRECT.
KRAK
HOME
VISITOR
HERE'S AN EASY ONE FOR YOU, BART--WHAT'S DARK ENERGY?
COME ON.
YOU WANNA GET BEANED?
ANSWER THE QUESTION.
AGUE
IGN UP NOW!
IT'S THE EVIL POWER IN YOUR SOUL, GRETCHEN.

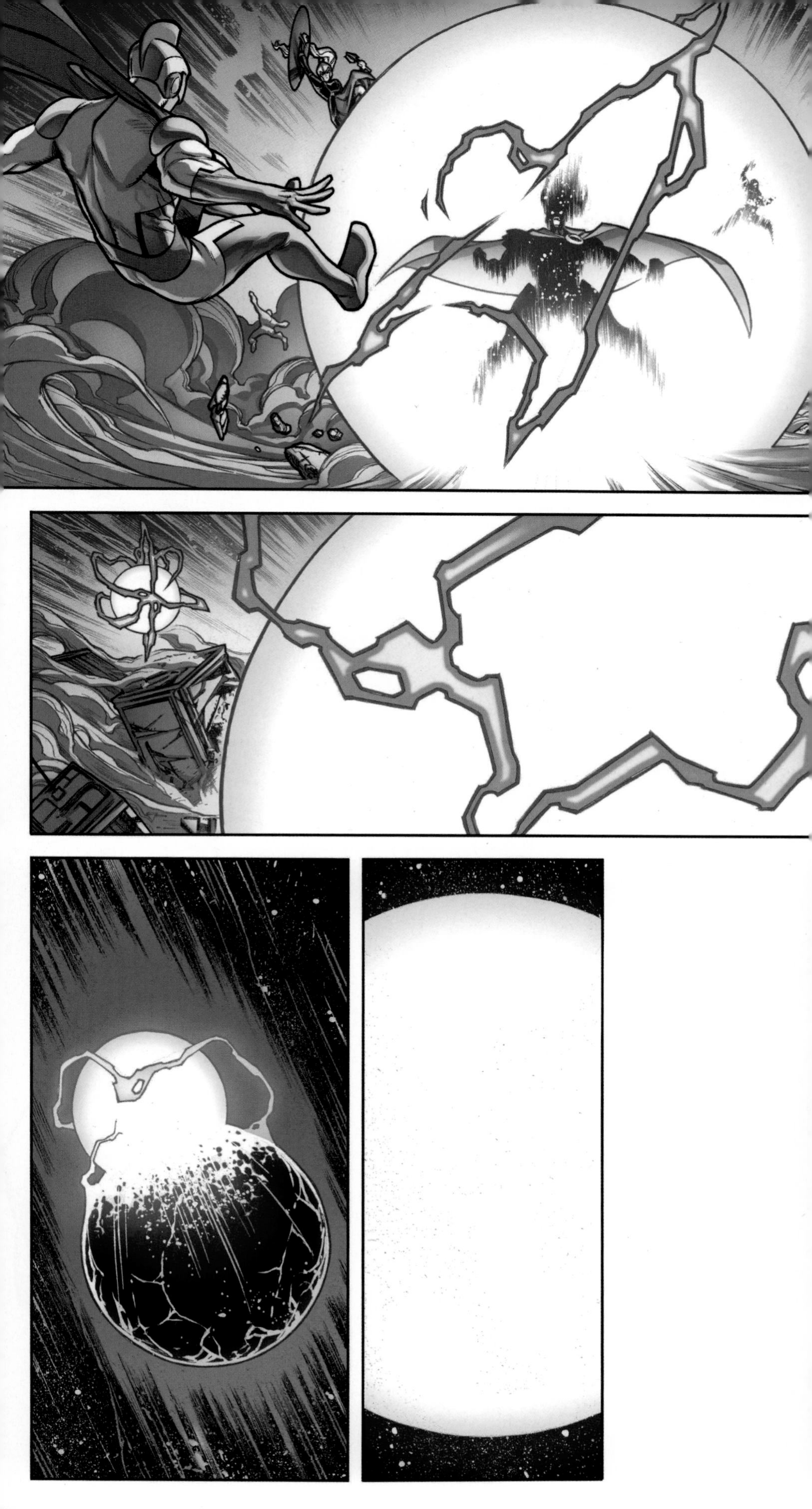

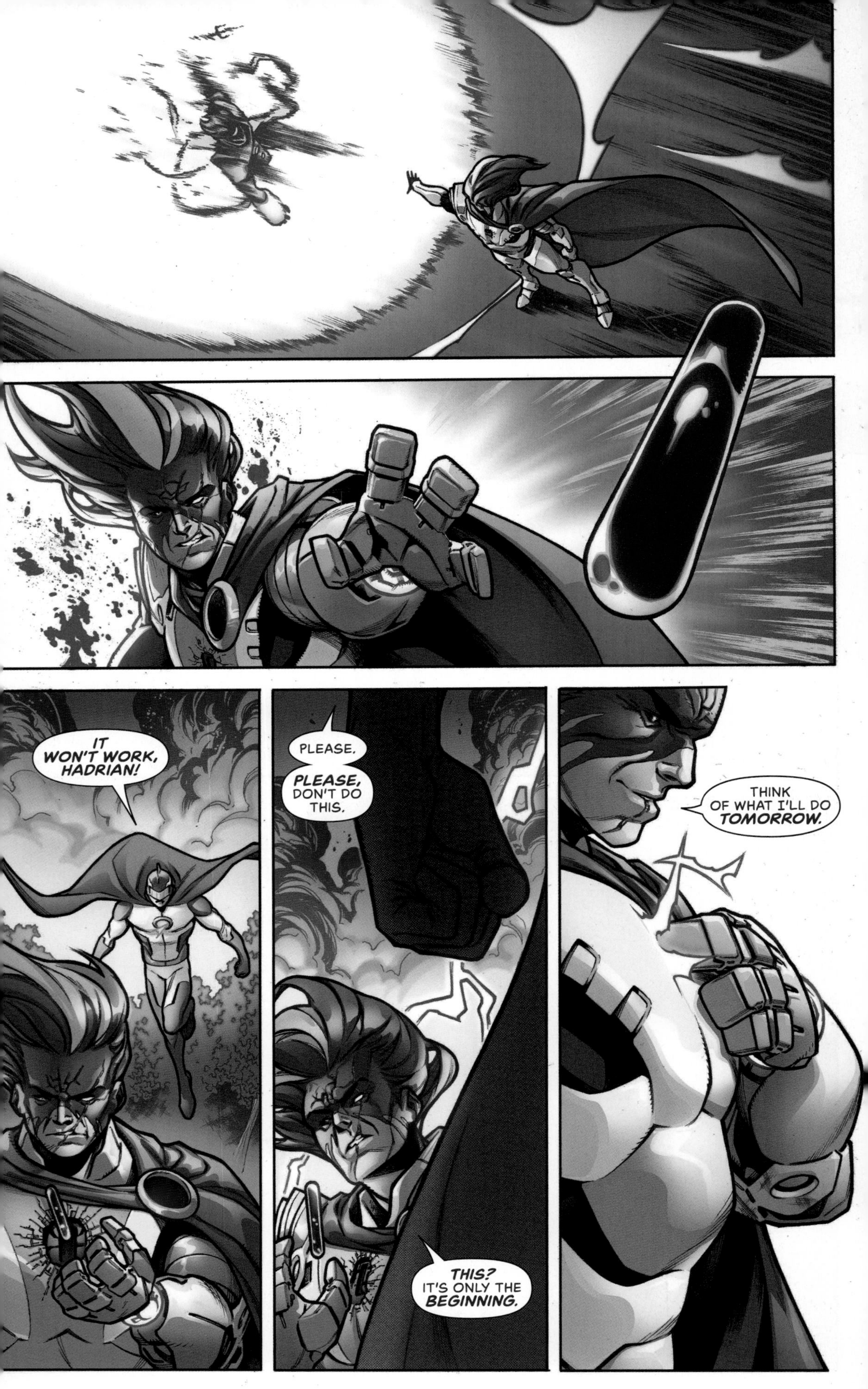
IT WON'T WORK, HADRIAN!
PLEASE.
PLEASE, DON'T DO THIS.
THIS? IT'S ONLY THE BEGINNING.
THINK OF WHAT I'LL DO TOMORROW.

HE'S GOT HWEN!!

HOW?!

STOP THIS.

LET ME WORK.

DON'T LET HIM LOAD THAT POWER SUPPLY!

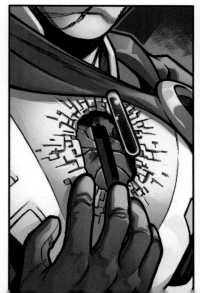

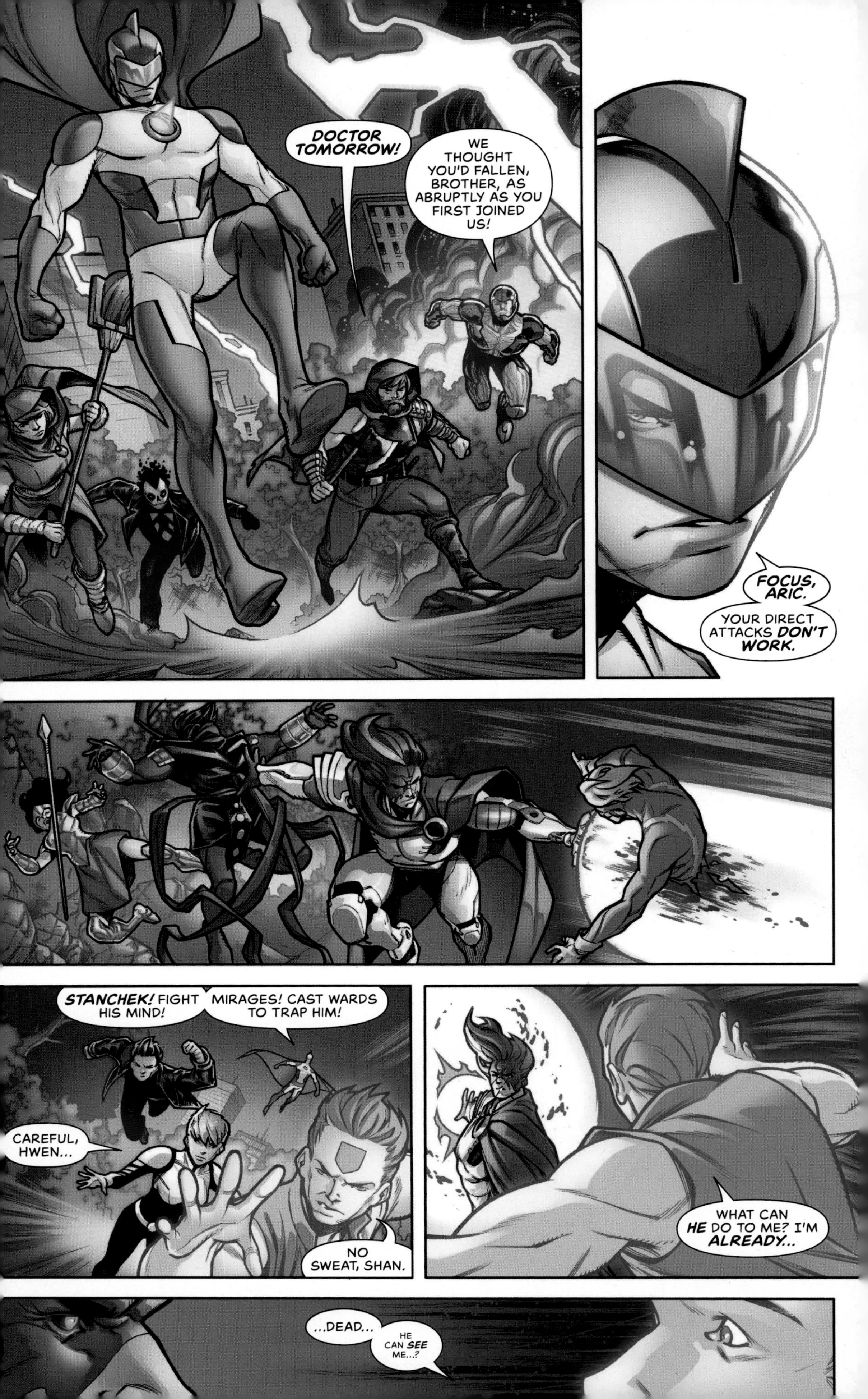
DOCTOR TOMORROW!
WE THOUGHT YOU'D FALLEN, BROTHER, AS ABRUPTLY AS YOU FIRST JOINED US!
FOCUS, ARIC.
YOUR DIRECT ATTACKS DON'T WORK.
STANCHEK! FIGHT HIS MIND!
MIRAGES! CAST WARDS TO TRAP HIM!
CAREFUL, HWEN...
NO SWEAT, SHAN.
WHAT CAN HE DO TO ME? I'M ALREADY...
...DEAD...
HE CAN SEE ME...?

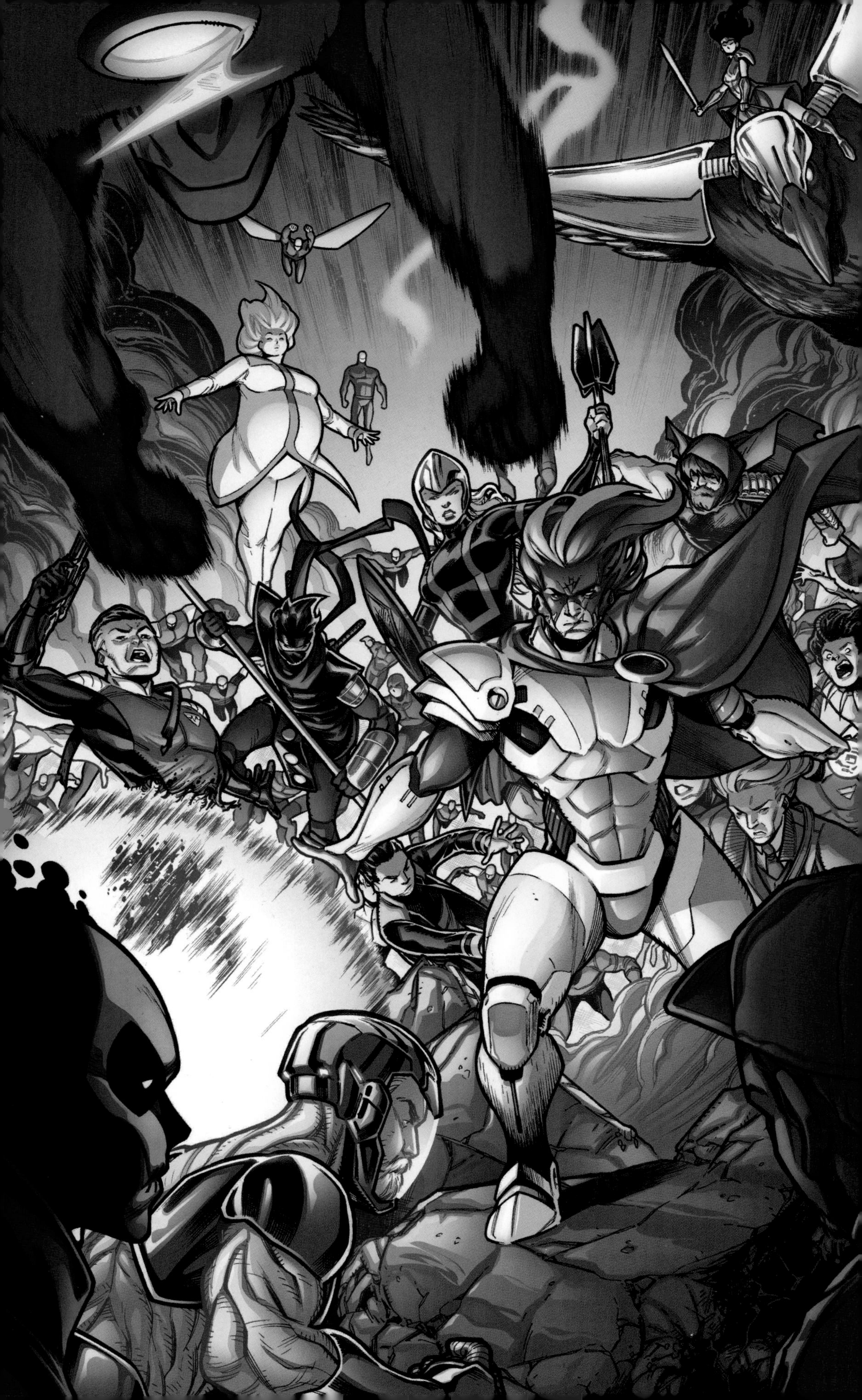

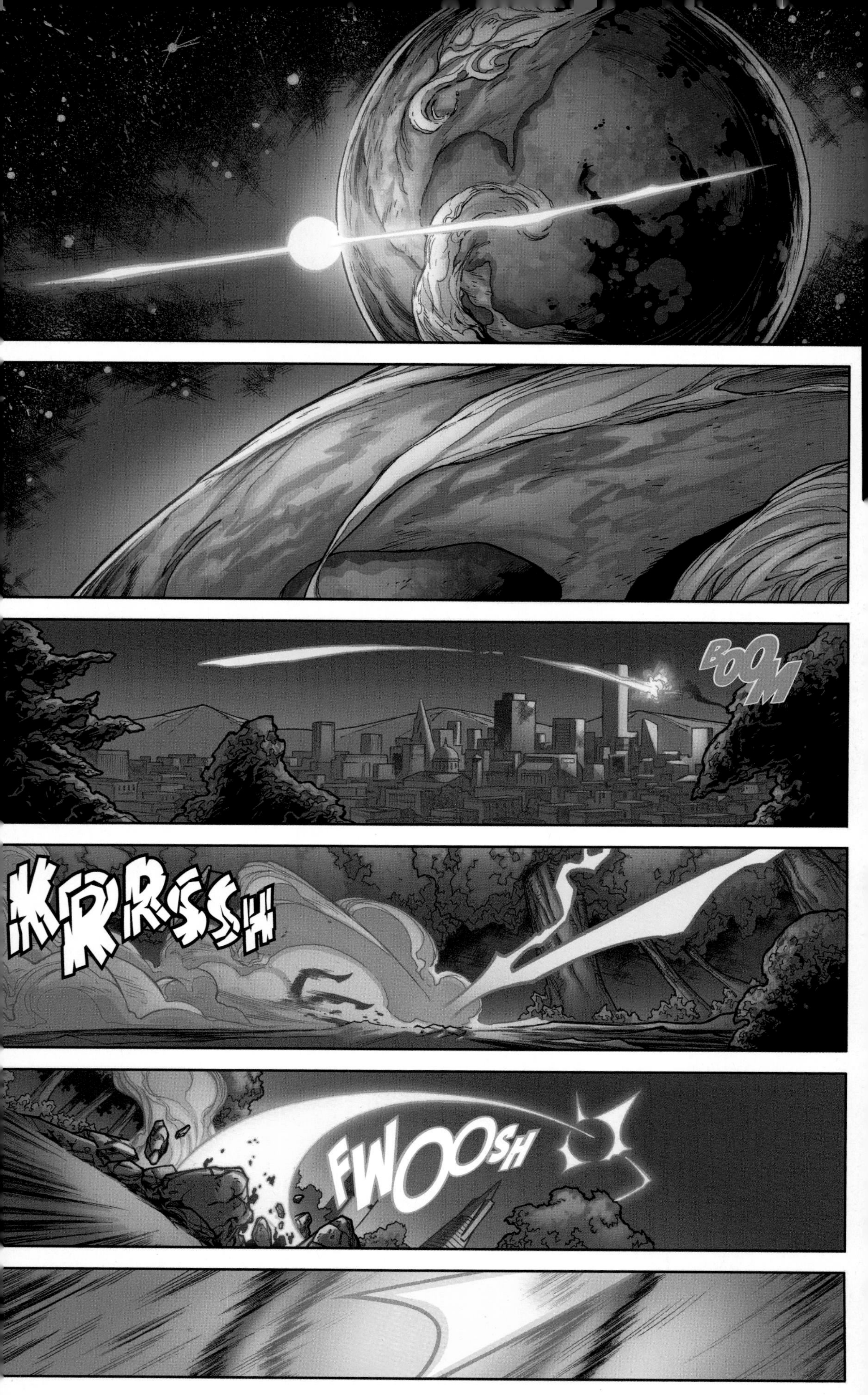
BOOM
KRRSSH
FWOOSH

DOCTOR TOMORROW #1

WRITER: ALEJANDRO ARBONA
ARTIST: JIM TOWE
COLORIST: DIEGO RODRIGUEZ
LETTERER: CLAYTON COWLES
COVER ARTISTS: DOUG BRAITHWAITE with DIEGO RODRIGUEZ
ASSISTANT EDITOR: DREW BAUMGARTNER
SENIOR EDITORIAL DIRECTOR: ROBERT MEYERS

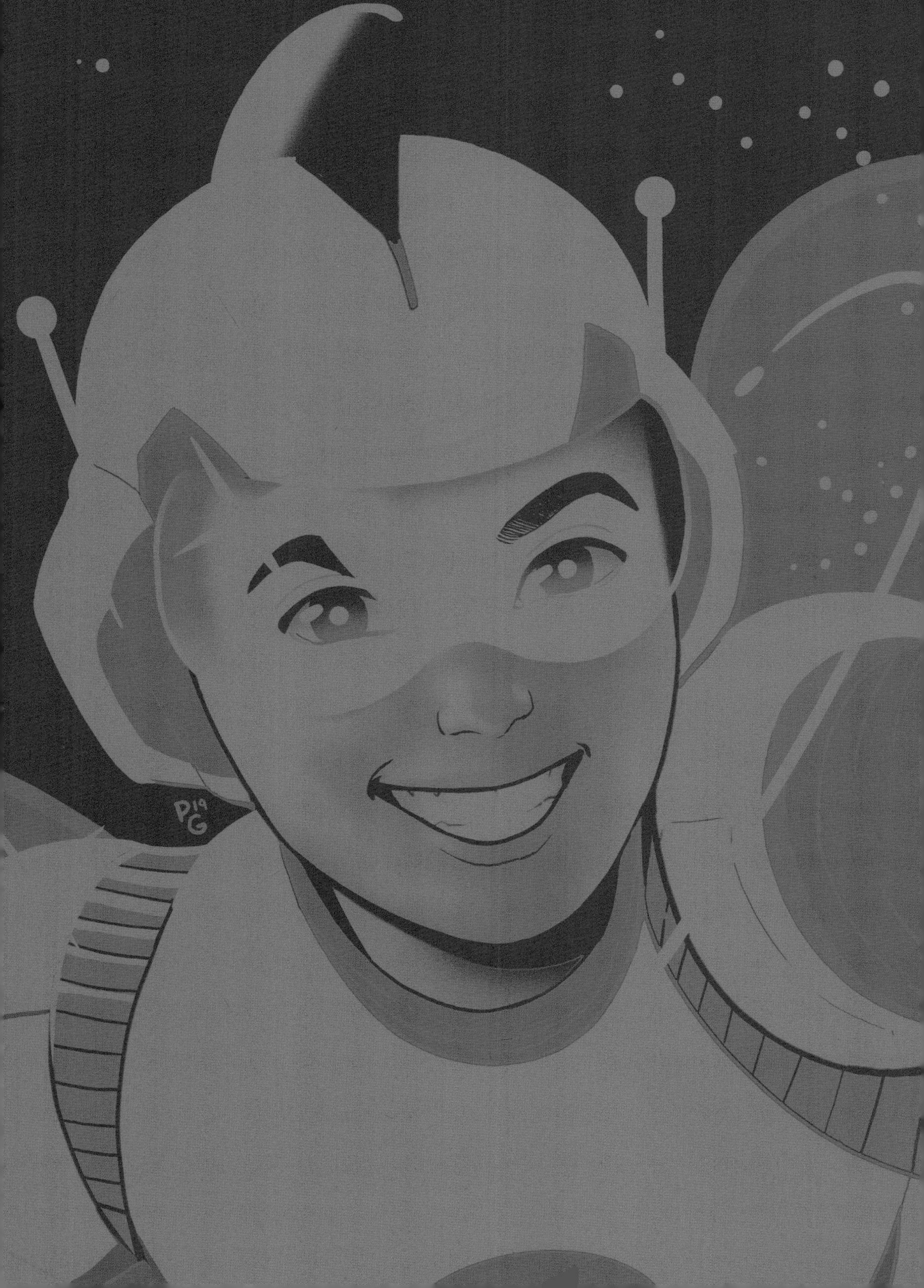

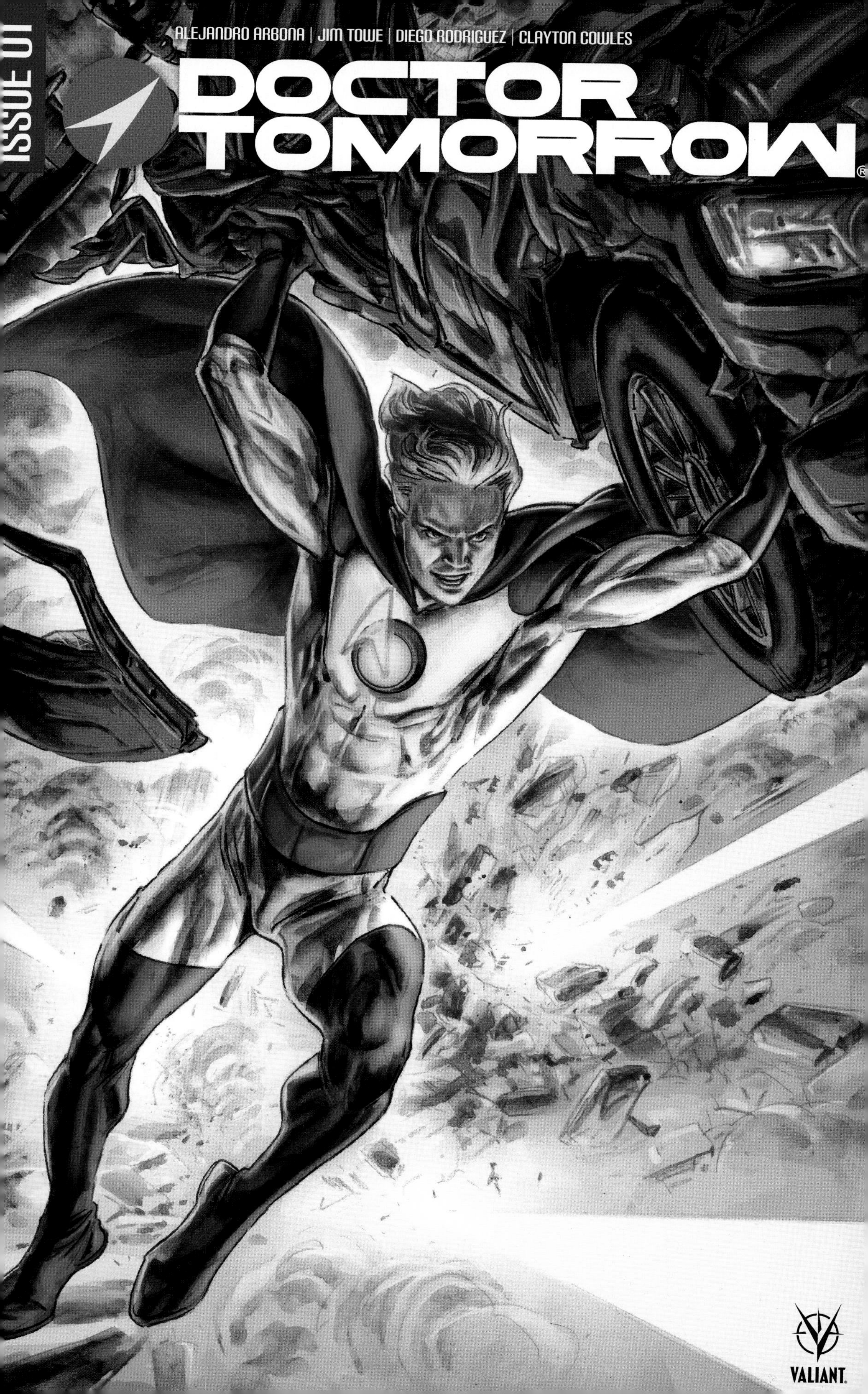
ISSUE 01
ALEJANDRO ARBONA | JIM TOWE | DIEGO RODRIGUEZ | CLAYTON COWLES
DOCTOR TOMORROW®
VALIANT.

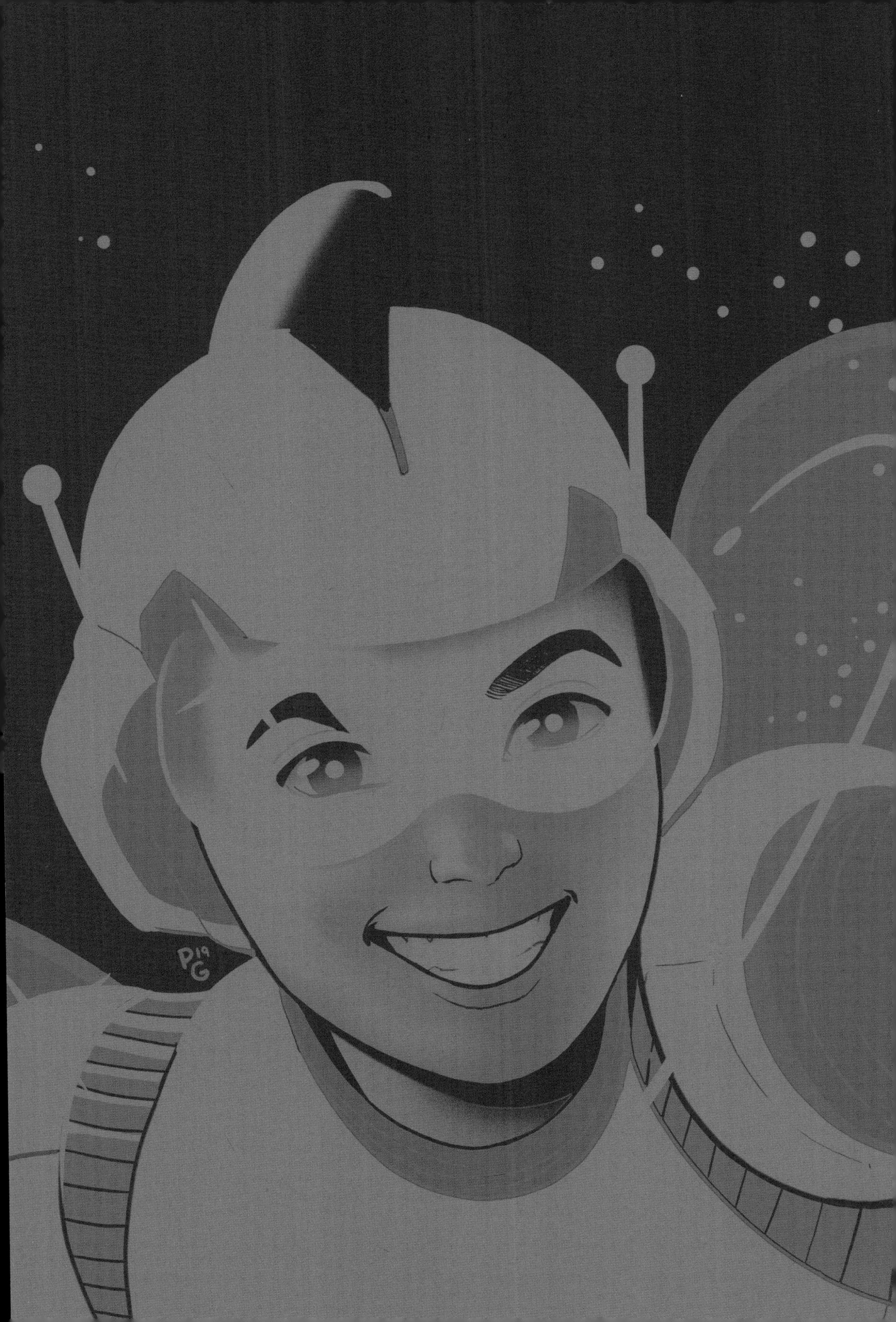

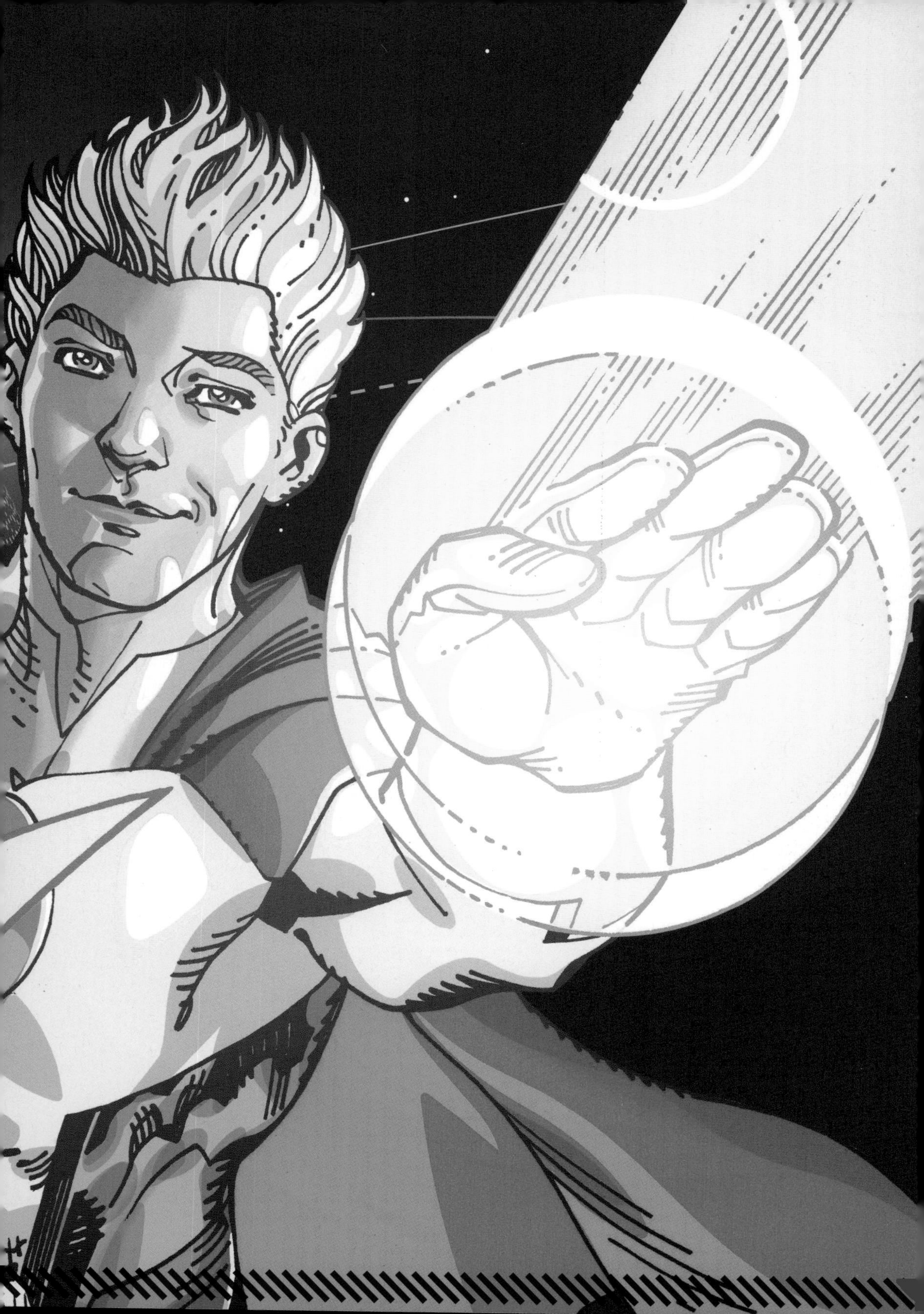

DOCTOR TOMORROW

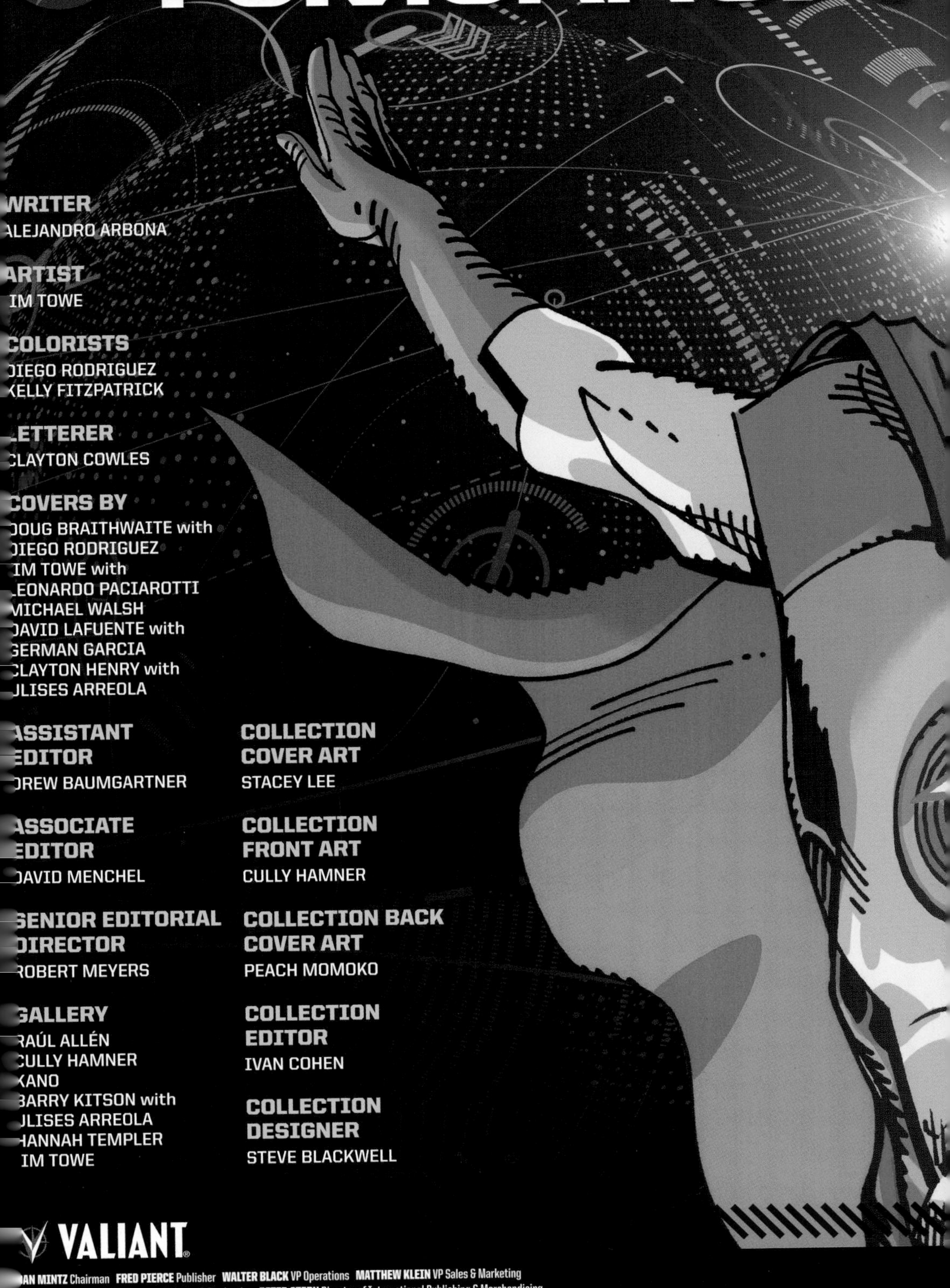

WRITER
ALEJANDRO ARBONA

ARTIST
IM TOWE

COLORISTS
DIEGO RODRIGUEZ
KELLY FITZPATRICK

LETTERER
CLAYTON COWLES

COVERS BY
DOUG BRAITHWAITE with
DIEGO RODRIGUEZ
IM TOWE with
LEONARDO PACIAROTTI
MICHAEL WALSH
DAVID LAFUENTE with
GERMAN GARCIA
CLAYTON HENRY with
ULISES ARREOLA

ASSISTANT EDITOR
DREW BAUMGARTNER

ASSOCIATE EDITOR
DAVID MENCHEL

SENIOR EDITORIAL DIRECTOR
ROBERT MEYERS

GALLERY
RAÚL ALLÉN
CULLY HAMNER
KANO
BARRY KITSON with
ULISES ARREOLA
HANNAH TEMPLER
IM TOWE

COLLECTION COVER ART
STACEY LEE

COLLECTION FRONT ART
CULLY HAMNER

COLLECTION BACK COVER ART
PEACH MOMOKO

COLLECTION EDITOR
IVAN COHEN

COLLECTION DESIGNER
STEVE BLACKWELL

VALIANT®

AN MINTZ Chairman FRED PIERCE Publisher WALTER BLACK VP Operations MATTHEW KLEIN VP Sales & Marketing
RAVIS ESCARFULLERY Director of Design & Production PETER STERN Director of International Publishing & Merchandising
YSA HAWKINS, HEATHER ANTOS & DAVID WOHL Senior Editors JEFF WALKER Production & Design Manager
OHN PETRIE Senior Manager - Sales & Merchandising DANIELLE WARD Sales Manager GREGG KATZMAN Marketing & Publicity Manager

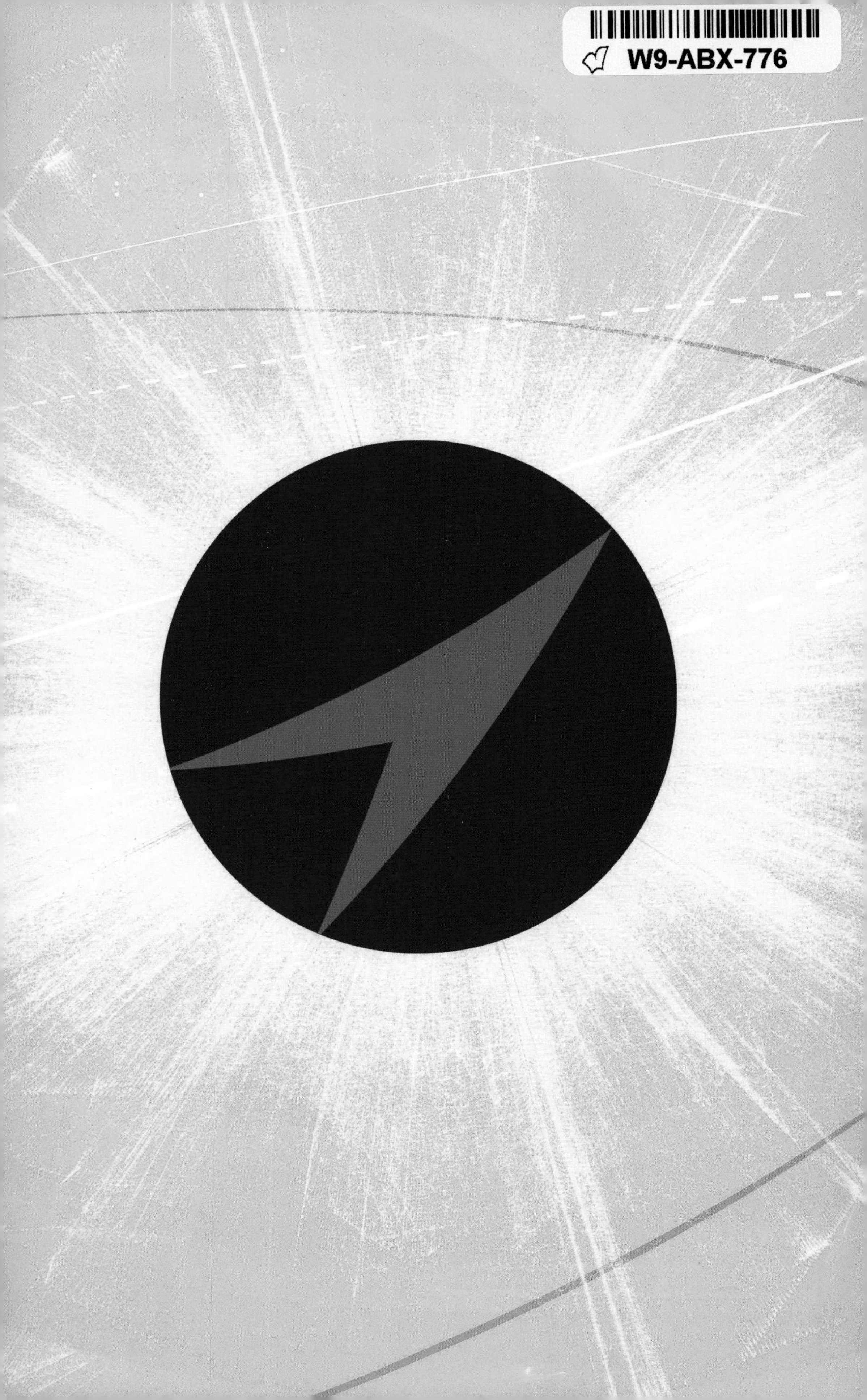